AF568129

WOMEN IN DEVELOPMENT
CHALLENGES AND ACHIEVEMENT

WOMEN IN DEVELOPMENT
CHALLENGES AND ACHIEVEMENT

Edited by
Dr. Ram Krishna Mandal
Head & Associate Professor of Economics
Dera Natung Government College
Itanagar - 791 113
Arunachal Pradesh
(INDIA)
E-mail: rkm_1966@yahoo.co.in

DISCOVERY PUBLISHING HOUSE PVT. LTD.
NEW DELHI-110 002

Published by:
Namit Wasan

DISCOVERY PUBLISHING HOUSE PVT. LTD.
4383/4B, Ansari Road, Darya Ganj
New Delhi-110 002 (India)
Phone : +91-11-23279245; 23253475; 43596065
E-mail : discoverybooksindia@gmail.com
discoverypublishinghouse@gmail.com
namitwasan9@gmail.com
web : w.ww.discoverypublishinggroup.com

Reprinted: **2019**

First Edition: **2015**

ISBN: 978-93-5056-698-5

Women in Development: *Challenges and Achievement*

Printed at:
Infinity Imaging Systems
Delhi

Dedicated
to
Miss Anusree Krishna Mandal

Acknowledgement

The present study is an attempt at a comprehensive and critical analysis for the role of women in socio-economic development with special reference to educational levels, entrepreneurship, attitude of the society towards women, social and religious taboos, women's own awareness and political attainments in society.

The present volume is a collection of twenty papers contributed by eminent scholars, academicians, policy-makers, bureaucrats and thinkers from different parts of India. The publication of this book is not possible without their contributions. Their work is based on diverse source materials which consist of official reports, published journals, books and findings of field work. Most of their writings are based either on the social structural aspects or on the social dynamism and rapid regional socio-economic transformation or on the empowerment of women. I have felt the need to put some of their writings together so as to enable the readers to get an overall idea about the same aspect. Some of their writings have been updated, revised and edited for the purpose. I hope that the readers will find it relevant for understanding the features of women in a better way. I hope, this book will benefit immensely the students, teachers, young scholars, planners and administrators in the area of women study in particular and society of our country in general. I am conscious of the bulk of the work which becomes largely inevitable on account of the intrinsic sweep of the subject. I acknowledge my heartiest gratitude to all paper contributors, whose works are consulted in the preparation of this volume.

I would be falling in my duty if I do not extend my gratitude to our Principal, Shri Tomar Ete, Dera Natung Government College, Itanagar, Arunachal Pradesh, India for generating in me an interest to edit this book.

I also acknowledge the inspiration received from my beloved teacher and guide, Prof. Chandan Kumar Mukhopadyaya, Department of Economics, University of North Bengal, West Bengal. I express my deep sense of gratitude to him.

I have received supports and cooperation from my colleagues Dr. Madhuparna Bhattacharjee Dr. A. I. Singh, Dr. Suparna Bhattacharya and Miss Anjali Biswas, my Research Assistant, I express a deep sense of gratitude to them.

I am also taking the opportunity to thank profusely to Shri Tilak Wasan, Managing Director, Discovery Publishing House Pvt. Ltd., New Delhi, for publication this book. Needless to say, I beg apology for any error which may remain in this volume during the course of editing work.

Lastly, I am grateful to the members of my family: Mrs. Archana Mandal (wife) and Miss Anusree Krishna Mandal, KVPY Fellow (Daughter) and Master Avinandan Krishna Mandal (son) for their untiring support and patience during the work of this volume.

Dr. Ram Krishna Mandal

Introduction

The status of women in society is directly linked with social and cultural traditions, stages of economic development achieved, educational levels, attitude of the society towards women, social and religious taboos, women's own awareness and political attainments for women in society. Such factors affect the national and also regional characteristics of the status of women. The economic status of women is determined by the role played by them in carrying on economic and non-economic activities in society. The nature and type of economic and non-economic role played by women have undergone continued transformation in accordance with the changes in socio-economic factors, education levels and technological developments and with the changing concepts regarding the extent to which women's contribution is desirable and necessary. In the world over it is now recognised that the status of women in society, both in the developed and under developed countries, continues to be inferior to men. Although women's role is crucial in the family and household economy, women have not been given equal rights in social, political as well as economic fields. The necessity of improvement of status of women has been recognised all over the world as an important aspect of national progress and development. It is also felt that the problem of poverty cannot be tackled without providing opportunities of productive employment to women. Productive employment to women would provide necessary economic base and improve their social status. But it is still a fact that women in many countries of the world are facing discriminatory attitude in varying degrees on ground of sex in employment and working conditions (Mandal and Minto, 2007).

President A. P. J. Abdul Kalam, said empowering women was a prerequisite for creating a good nation, "when women are empowered, society with stability is assured. Empowerment of women is essential as their thoughts and their value systems lead the development of a good family, good society and ultimately a good nation".

Women now make up 20 per cent of the U. S. Senate. A woman is the leader of the House Democrats. The number of women governors declined slightly in the last election, but more women is active in state politics at other levels. Three women sit on the U. S. Supreme Court. Women occupy all of New Hampshire's top state and federal legislative offices. The two most popular members of the recent presidential campaign were Michelle Obama and Ann Romney. For the first time, a woman has been appointed as Head of the Secret Service. The new Director of the Securities and Exchange Commission (one of our most important regulatory agencies) is a woman. More than half of the medical and law students in America are women (*www.leanin.org/discussions/welcome-to-the-century-of-wome*).

According to last year's National family health survey, 51 per cent of Indian men and 54 per cent of Indian women find it's justifiable for a man to beat his wife and around 40 per cent of women have experienced some form of abuse from their husbands – pushing, slapping and hair pulling, punching, kicking, choking or burning. Yes, it's worst! Well, not really worst for a nation where women are often tagged as self-sacrificing immortals, who must be ready to offer her for the self-righteous, holier-than-though attitude of her men?

The report says that there is a deep-rooted mindset that women are inferior and must be kept inside and away from decision-making. It also highlights the tendency of dangerous acceptance of discrimination and violence against women in the society. It too lists the fact that 52 per cent women think it's justifiable for a man to beat his wife (UNICEF, 2012).

During the era of the 21st Century woman, there has also been an acute increase in child delinquency. The moral of the 21st Century woman's children is weaker as compared to those of the 19th and 20th Century. Despite the increase in technology and security crime rate have become sophisticated and 'unreasonable'. Most children now enter into internet scam make addition money for 'boisterous' things and research also shows that most of them are from families with a few foundations and also from homes where parents prefer money to anything else.

Beauty of a woman has the last of all priorities during match-making. However, it becomes a potential determinant if a man is highly-educated and earns extremely well. Then, no matter his own looks and age he is considered deserving to get a beautiful, well-earning, and highly educated girl belonging to a well-settled family. This gender bias is prevalent in workplaces as well. A talented and intelligent woman faces mental abuse from her male seniors who consider her as to be a potential threat to their designation. Physical abuse and exploitation is present to some extent in glamour industries (www.*groundreport.com/status-of-women-in-the-21st-century-india).*

A significant growth in women's movement took place in the south in the 1980's. In India the first meeting of Development with women for a New Era (DAWN) took place in 1984. A group of women researchers from both the north and the south had joined forces to criticize neo-liberal development paradigm. They stressed the idea of transformation of patriarchal societies at large as well as feminist idea of development (Shamkaranarayana and Sreedhara, 2005).

In his article 'Young India' and 'Harijan', Bapuji said that men and women are different in physical but in many matters especially those of tolerance and Sacrifices, the Indian women are superior to male. He did not see women as object of reforms, as helpless creature deserving charitable concern; instead he was concerned with about radical social construction. The message of Gandhi in all the Women Conference 1936, 'when women, whom we call Abala become Sabala, all those who are helpless will become powerful' reflects that Gandhi gave crucial importance to the issue of women's freedom and strength in the struggle to built a human and exploitation-free society. In autobiography of Gandhi you will find that he admitted that the technique of non-violence, passive resistance and following the path of truth, he learned it from women especially from his wife Kasturba and mother Putli Bai.

Social change is possible only by empowering and educating women. Jawaharlal Nehru once said, "To awaken the people, it is women who is meant to be awakened, once she is on the move, the family moves, village moves and the nation moves". Swami Vivekananda also once said, "There is no chance for the welfare of the world unless the condition of women is improved. It is not possible for a bird to fly on one wing". Like-wise no nation can flourish keeping half of its population in negligence and ignorance, as women constitute half of its human capital. A modern society cannot bring all round development without utilising the talent of its women.

Definitely, the volume will give the socio-economic scenario of women of different parts of the country. It consists of twenty papers collected from different scholars from different corners of the country.

Content

Contributors

1. ***Prof. A. Sree Ram***, Professor, Hyderabad Business School, Gitam University.
2. ***Dr. R. Radhika***, Assistant Professor, Hyderabad Business School, Gitam University.
3. ***Dr. R. Prabhakar Rao***, Associate Professor, Department of Economics, Sri Sathya Sai Institute of Higher Learning, Prasanthi Nilayam 515134, A. P., India.
4. ***Dr. M. R. Geetha Bala***, Assistant Professor, Ananthapur Campus, Sri Sathya Sai Institute of Higher Learning (SSSIHL), A. P., India.
5. ***Dr. K. A. Rasure***, Associate, Professor of Economics, Nrupatung P. G. Centre, Sedam 585222, Gulbarga, Karnataka), India.
6. ***Dr. Ira Das,*** Assistant Professor, Department of Economics, Pragjyotish College, Guwahati 09, Assam, India.
7. ***Dr. M. Dhanabhakyam***, Assistant Professor, School of Commerce, Bharathiar University, Coimbatore, Tamil Nadu, India.
8. ***Nisamudheen T.***, Ph.D Research Scholar (JRF), School of Commerce, Bharathiar University, Coimbatore, Tamil Nadu, India.
9. ***R. Sathyakumar***, M.Phil Scholar, Bharathiar University, Coimbatore 641046, Tamil Nadu, India.

10. ***Mr. K. P. Bholane***, Assistant Professor, V. P. College, Vaijapur, Dist. – Aurangabad 423701, India.
11. ***Anu Priya. M***, M. Phil Scholar, Department of Commerce, Bharathiar University, Coimbatore 641046.
12. ***Mr. Anjan Kumar Bordoloi***, Asst. Professor, Department of Management, Margherita College, Margherita 786181, Tinsukia, Assam, India.
13. ***Mr. Bishnu Prasad Chetry***, Asst. Professor, Department of Economics, Margherita College, Margherita 786181, Tinsukia, Assam, India.
14. ***Dr. Pankaj Kumar***, Assistant Professor in Sociology, Haldia Law College, West Bengal, India.
15. ***Dr. Philip Mody***, Sr. Assistant Professor, Department of Commerce, Rajiv Gandhi University, Rono Hills, Doimukh, Itanagar, Arunachal Pradesh, India.
16. ***Dr. Surajit Kumar Bhagowati***, Assistant Professor, Department of Commerce, Nowgong College, Nagaon 782001, Assam, India.
17. ***Miss Rupali (Goswami) Sarma***, Research Scholar, NEHU and Documentation and Information Officer Indian Institute of Bank Management, Guwahati 22, Assam, India.
18. ***Arundhati Bhattacharyya***, Assistant Professor, Department of Political Science, Bhairab Ganguly College, Kolkata 56, West Bengal, India.
19. ***Soma Dhar***, Guest Lecturer, Department of Political Science, Bhairab Ganguly College, Kolkata 700052, West Bengal.
20. ***Mrs. M. Jahnavi***, Asst. Prof, MBA, KIMS, Bangalore, Karnataka, India.
21. ***Shanthi V.***, Asst. Prof, MBA, KIMS, Bangalore, Karnataka, India.
22. ***Mary Princess Lavanya***, Asst. Professor, Dept. of Social Work, Plot No. 3062, New No. 54, 14th Main Road, Anna Nagar, Chennai 34, Tamil Nadu, India.
23. ***Dr. Sadhna Gupta*** (LL.B, LL.M, PGDHR, Ph.D), Assistant Professor, Department of Law, Hooghly Mohsin Government College, West Bengal, India.

24. ***Dr. Sarita Agrawal***, M. S. University of Baroda, Baroda 390008, India.
25. ***Miss Tejaswini Ranjan***, 3rd Semester B.A. LLB Student, Chanakya National Law University, Girls Hostel, Room No. 221, Mithapur, Patna 800001, Bihar, India.
26. ***Mrs. Archana Mandal***, PGT, Balupara Colony Nibedita Balika Vidyalaya, P.O.: Gopalganj, Dist: Dakshin Dinajpur, West Bengal, India.
27. ***Dr. Swapnali Baruah***, Researcher, R. C. S. Main Road, Door No: 132/128, Nattrampalli (Post), Thirupattur (T. K.), Vellore (Distt.), Tamil Nadu 635852, India.

1

Women Entrepreneurship in Informal Sector

Prof. A. Sree Ram
Dr. R. Radhika

Abstract

Women have plunged into the field of entrepreneurship and they have been found effective in emerging social economical role. Women had been managers since long from the time the concept of living in a family emerged. She had been an entrepreneur within the four walls where she was innovative in terms of budgeting with the limited income resources. With the changing role that women accepted over the past decade the role of entrepreneurship amongst women has gained considerable importance. This article deals with sociological and demographic factors influencing women entrepreneurship. The article has also identified certain special action strategies for the development of women entrepreneurship in urban informal sector.

INTRODUCTION

There is widespread belief that economic strength is the basis of social, political and psychological power in society. Women's low status is seen to stem from their low economic status and consequent dependence and lack of decision-making power. And if women gain economic strength they gain both visibility and a voice in the homes, workplace and community.

Women have been involved in economic activities both in rural as well as urban sectors both in the formal and informal setting. Women's work participation rate according to the 1981 census showed that it was 13.99 per cent and men's work participation rate was 51.62 per cent.

Throughout the world women earn anywhere from 50 to 92 paisa for every rupee earned by men.

In developing countries women hold 8 per cent of the administrative and managerial position compared to 24 per cent in developed world. Agriculture employs about 70 per cent of the working population of the country and almost 84 per cent of all economically active women.

Informal Sector

The ILO has been the pioneering agency which has initiated extensive studies on Informal Sector (IS) in Africa, Latin America and the Asian countries. These studies have reaffirmed that the existence of the IS is not a transitory phenomenon, and that its presence and contribution are acknowledged at all levels of development. The studies have identified the different sub-sectors of IS, namely, trade, service, production, construction, transport, etc. Of the above mentioned sub-sectors, production occupies a place next only to trade and services in terms providing gainful employment opportunities, higher income, and growth potential in different vocations.

The Urban Informal Sector

The concept of Informal Sector has developed in the historical context of urbanisation, migration and dualism. Industrialisation of peasant economies led to the process of urbanisation and large-scale migration from the countryside towards cities. But due to the slow pace of industrialisation, all the migrated labour force could not be absorbed in the industrial sector. This surplus labour managed to find avenues of self-employment and wage-employment in Informal ways. This situation has been created within the urban economic system, as a subsistence segment, that has come to be called Urban Informal Sector.

The concept of Urban Informal Sector was first used by Keith Hart (1973) in his study of Urban 'Ghana'. He identified a number of Income and employment generating activities in the unenumerated sector of urban areas, which constitute this sector. This sector has been associated with poverty, under-employment and unemployment.

The Urban Informal Sector assumes significance in the context of economic reforms relating to the industrial sector, which offers opportunities for further expansion of the Informal sector. In India, over the last two decades, the share of the Informal Sector in the total non-farm employment has remained as high as 92 per cent.

Need and Scope for the Study

The growth of entrepreneurial community in the informal sector will contribute much to the socio-economic development of the country. The share of informal sector is significant to the total employment and to the growth of urban incomes. The factors that have contributed to the growth of informal sector are urbanisation, migration and slow growth of industrialisation. In the process of urbanisation and migration, the role of women entrepreneurial community in the informal sector is a crucial factor. Hence, women entrepreneurial supply also became important for the growth of the informal sector. Women entrepreneurship in informal sector depends upon the social, cultural and ethical base of the society. But these conditions vary from one region to another hence the regional studies would contribute enormously to understand the process of entrepreneurial growth in general and women entrepreneurship in particular. Though some scholars have made studies on these aspects, these studies are confined to specific regions and specific contexts. There are very few studies on women entrepreneurship in urban informal sector. In view of this it is proposed to study the impact of socio-cultural and psychological factors on the growth of women entrepreneurship in the urban informal sector with the following objectives in Vijayawada City.

Objectives

1. To study the sociological and demographic factors influencing women entrepreneurship.
2. To know the impact of psychological factors on women entrepreneurship.
3. To formulate action strategy for the development of women entrepreneurship in urban informal sector.

Methodology

The World Employment Commission under ILO has given a set of characteristics to identify IS production activities like units employing less than 10 workers, not having fixed hours of work, operating from semi-permanent premises and sale of output directly to consumers, etc. According to it a manufacturing unit may be included in IS if it satisfies one or more above characteristics. In this study the manufacturing units are selected if they satisfy at least two characteristics.

Since each activity is confined to a specific area in all towns, the list of different activities located in different areas is collected from Municipal Corporation Authorities. In order to identify the entrepreneurs under different activities a census survey covering all the manufacturing units engaged in IS activities in specified areas are conducted in the Vijayawada city. Among all the IS manufacturing activities, sandal making, Toys, Kalamkari, Rolled Gold, Basket making, Body Building, making steel furniture, tyre retreading and few others are found to be major IS activities in Vijayawada city. Among the above activities, it is proposed to select the activity Basket making because the more number of women entrepreneur are engaged in this activity. This activity is concentrated in the areas: Auto Nagar, Chappala market, Kothapet, Yanamalakuduru, Poranki, Rama Nagar-Sarada College, Chappala Market-Ganapathi Rao Road, New Giripuram of Vijayawada city.

A sample of 45 production units were selected from the above areas using stratified random sampling with probability proportion.

Profile of the Study Area

33.2 per cent of the total population Vijayawada city the total work force in Urban areas. The corresponding figures for Urban

India and Urban Andhra Pradesh are 32.2 and 32.2 per cent respectively. Data also shows that the distribution of main workers in Urban population comes to 29.3, 29.1 and 30.7 per cent respectively for India, Andhra Pradesh and Vijayawada. The distribution of marginal workers is 2.9, 3.1 and 2.6 per cent respectively for India, Andhra Pradesh and Vijayawada.

Informal house-hold and other industry (including agro based industries construction and transport constitute) 15.7 per cent in Vijayawada of the total Informal Enterprises operating. In terms of work force participating in Informal Sector in Urban Krishna district, it may be observed that trade and commerce, manufacturing/processing/servicing appear to be taking almost the same share (34.6% and 32.5% respectively). Household industry workers account for 20.7 per cent and other industries for 12.2 per cent; together they constitute 32.9 per cent. Given the data gaps and other enumeration problems, it may be safely stated that these reflect the size of the informal sector in Urban Vijayawada, in terms of number of enterprises.

Sociological and Demographic Factors Influencing Women Entrepreneurship

An individual is a product of his social, economic, political and cultural environment. Out of these, social imperative, interaction with his immediate human environment like family member's, peers, caste members, religious groups etc., especially family members and close relatives plays a dominant role in the socialisation process of an individual. The quality and content of socialisation exerts decisive influence on person's behavioural patterns.

Domiciliary Character of Women Entrepreneurs

Migrating from one place to another for better economic opportunities reflects the spirit of adventure, the capacity to face uncertainties and start an enterprise in a new environment, the capacity to adjust to self-confidence, and risk taking ability.

Nearly 35.6 per cent of the selected women entrepreneurs are from the same town, this shows that the study area is source of rich supply of entrepreneurs, and it further shows that the locals are quick to seize the opportunities. The majority of the sample entrepreneurs (64.4%) have migrated from other districts and from other states (40% from other districts 15.6% from other parts of the same district and 8.8% from other states). This shows that opportunities for innovative entrepreneurs do exist in the local market, and they can flourish without any encumbrance. This also indicates the openness of the local people as well as scope for the economic development.

Age of Women Entrepreneurs

The highest percentage (55.5%) of sample women entrepreneurs belong to the age group of (31-50) years at the time of conducting the survey (44.4%) of them in 31-40 years, and 11 per cent in 41-50 years and 20 per cent of women entrepreneurs are below 30 years age. Above 50 years age group, there are only 22.3 per cent of persons.

The modal age group at the time of starting the enterprise is said to be below 20 years of age *i.e.* 95.6 per cent of the women entrepreneurs started their activity at the age of below 20 and only 4.4 per cent of the responding entrepreneurs fall in age group of 26-30 years. This shows that the activity is of hereditary in nature. Thus sizeable number of women entrepreneurs start new ventures at the age below 20; this shows that the skill learnt by entrepreneur as a child in rendering help to the family enabled them to start the activity as a source of livelihood at the early age *i.e.*, below 20.

Educational Level of Women Entrepreneurs

On an average 93.3 per cent of the respondents are uneducated, where as 4.5 per cent of the selected entrepreneurs have primary education and only 2.2 per cent of them have plus two education. From this we can deduce that as majority of the respondents are uneducated and they have chosen the family profession in which they have acquired skill.

Religion and Social Group of Women Entrepreneurs

Caste influences entrepreneurship. Socio-cultural factors like the norms and values of the immediate social circle contribute substantially to entrepreneurship development. Of the sample entrepreneurs majority (64.4%) belong to Hindu religion, (35.6%) are from Christian community *i.e.,* converted Christians caste-wise distribution shows that 100 per cent of the sample entrepreneurs are from backward communities.

Marital Status of Women Entrepreneurs

On an average 100 per cent of the sample respondents are married at the time of conducting of the survey. Hence marriage is an influencing factor to facilitate entrepreneurship.

Rural-Urban Background of Women Entrepreneurs

Nearly 82.2 per cent of women entrepreneurs have urban background, and 17.8 per cent are from rural background. This may be because an urbanite had better resources and exposure to opportunities and variety of experiences better employment, better contacts and better access to information.

Impact of The Family on Women Entrepreneurship

Three aspects have been studied to analyse the influence of the family on the entrepreneurial career:

1. Structure of the family.
2. Order of birth among female children.
3. Occupation of the father and husband and previous background of the entrepreneur.

A majority of sample entrepreneurs 55.6 per cent come from nuclear families or single family system, because of its advantages when compared to the joint family or extended family. Order of birth of female children reveals that entrepreneurs are, generally, either the second female child or at best, the elder female child (37.8% and 33.3% respectively). Regarding younger children other than the first two children the need for affiliation is strong for them, and hence a lower drive towards becoming an entrepreneur.

The influence of Father's occupation is found to a greater extent on the respondent women entrepreneurs. All the respondent entrepreneurs father's occupation is Basket making which is a family profession.

Analysis of the husband's background reveals that 100 per cent of sample entrepreneurs husbands profession is basket making.

Previous background of the women entrepreneur reveals that all selected respondent women entrepreneurs are involved in Basket making. It shows that women entrepreneurs have taken up the same family profession which is hereditary.

Age of Enterprises of the Women Entrepreneurs

Majority of the respondents started their enterprises (31-20) years back *i.e.* (80%), [28.9% of them started 31 years back, and 15.6 per cent of them started 21-25 years back, and 15.6 per cent of them started 26-30 years back] and only 20 per cent of the enterprises were started 15 years back. (11.1%) have started (11-15) years 6.7 per cent have started (6-10) years back and 2.2 per cent have started (1-5) years back. It shows that very few number of enterprises were started in the recent past. It means that present generation is not showing interest to start the enterprises, which is a serious threat for the existence of the handicraft activity like Basket making.

Location of the Business of the Women

Entrepreneurs

Majority of the women entrepreneurs have the locations of the business on pavements *i.e.* (82.2%) 13.3 per cent of the women entrepreneurs had their location of business in own house and only 4.5 per cent of the women entrepreneurs had their business in own shop. It means that the respondents are not financially sound to have own shops or may be the due to pavement is the good marketing place.

Products Manufactured by the Women Entrepreneurs at the Time of Field Survey

Majority of the respondents are manufacturing all items *i.e.* 60 per cent. 26.7 per cent of the women entrepreneurs are involved in manufacturing of only rolling mats and 13.3 per cent of the women entrepreneurs are involved in making baskets. All the selected Women Entrepreneurs are involved in manufacturing the products and selling the products.

Type of Ownerships of the Women Entrepreneurs

On an average 93.3 per cent of selected women entrepreneurs are involved in sole proprietaryship and only 6.7 per cent of them are under partnership. This shows the impact of fragmentation of joint families into nuclear families.

Types of Business of Women Entrepreneurs

100 per cent of the selected women entrepreneurs are having seasonal business because raw material of the business, bamboo is available only few months.

Psychological Factors Influencing Women Entrepreneurship

The significance of human behaviour in economic development is well recognised by all social scientists. Modern psychologists believe that economic development can undergo a change through human motivation. Hence, researchers on entrepreneurship have given much importance to achievement motivation. The critical motive in entrepreneurship has been identified as n-ach. Some studies revealed that people with high need for achievement (n-ach) could emerge as entrepreneurs and exploit economic opportunities. A successful entrepreneur takes moderate risks, and stretches himself to achieve goals which are not impossible but are achievable through improved efficiency and perseverance. For this reason, entrepreneurial development programmes have been started and organized in both developed and developing countries to develop motivational characteristics.

Need for Achievement

The way in which need for achievement is perceived by entrepreneurs is to be understood. The n-ach can be opertionalised, either directly or indirectly. A large percentage (82.2) of entrepreneurs feels that financial status as their achievement. 13.3 per cent feel product credibility as their achievement and 4.5 per cent feel establishment of unit as their achievement.

Perceptions Regarding Strengths and Weaknesses on Women Entrepreneurs

One has to find out one's own strengths to become a successful entrepreneur. Nearly 84.4 per cent of the sample women entrepreneurs have felt that their strength is hard work and will power. 6.7 per cent of the sample entrepreneurs felt that technical knowledge is their strength and 8.9 per cent of them felt frustration tolerance as their strength.

If the entrepreneur is not in a position to perceive the weakness in her, she is called a less effective entrepreneur. The majority of the sample entrepreneurs feel that lack of finance is their weakness (84.4%). This followed by factors such as straight forwardness (4.5%) Laziness (2.2%).

Entrepreneurial Traits or Characteristics

In order to be a successful entrepreneur, one must possess attributes such as perseverance, self-confidence, dynamism, etc. The majority of sample entrepreneurs felt that hard work, financial background related job experience and strong will power (51.1%, 31.1%, 11.1% and 6.7% of respondents respectively) are positive traits that are found to be responsible for entrepreneurial success.

Factors Responsible for Choosing the Entrepreneurial Career

Entrepreneurs emerge from the society. They have an urge to build their own empire. The factors which are external as well as inherent are responsible for choosing the entrepreneurial career. The selected women entrepreneurs have considered the inherent factors like hereditary (93.3% of respondents) and desire to be independent (6.7%) responsible for their entrepreneurial career.

Causes for Delay in the Progress of Implementation of Projects

It is usual for an individual to attribute success to himself and failure to the environment. A large number of respondents attributed reasons such as shortage of raw material (44.5%) marketing problems (31.1%) and lack of finance (22.2%) for the delay in the progress of implementation of projects.

Impact of Discouraging Experience

When faced with problems or failures the majority of sample entrepreneurs stated that they had learnt how to adjust to the hazards (68.9%), resorting to job (8.9%) and development of tolerance (6.7%).

Long-Term, Short-Term Goals of Women Entrepreneurs and Career Goals of Children

The majority of sample entrepreneurs have felt that re-investment is their long term goal and 51.1 per cent of them felt expansion of unit as their short-term goal, and academic pursuit is their children's career goal (57.8%).

Conclusions

In the light of the findings of the above study, the following conclusions are drawn about the informal sector women entrepreneur who is involved in basket making activity.

An entrepreneur in the informal sector is a person belonging to a family occupation with the skill acquired from family occupation which is of hereditary in nature.

Age of the entrepreneur for promoting an enterprise can be below 20 years age. Preparatory to starting of an enterprise the entrepreneur has to acquire the skills needed for entrepreneurship through apprenticeship in a family enterprise.

Entrepreneurs have a high level of motivations, self-confidence, perseverance and dynamism, willing to put in hard work, what they need is necessary stimulus as catalytic factors for creating a conducive environment for growth of the enterprise.

REFERENCES

Acharya, B. T. (1992), *Rural Industrialisation – Experience of Block Adoption Programme of IDBI/SIDBI,* Bombay, Himalaya Publishing House.

Carland, J. W., Hoy, F. and Carland, J. A. (1988), Who is an Entrpereneur? Is a Question Worth asking? *American Journal of Small Business*, Vol. 12 No. 10.

Drucker. Peter, F. (1985), *Innovation and Entrepreneurship*, London, William Heinemann Ltd.

Gupta. M. C. (1987), *Entrepreneurship in Small-Scale Industries*, New Delhi, Anmol Publications.

Rao. TV. (1975), Development of An Entrepreneur – A Behaviouristic Model. *SEDME* Vol. 1 No. 4, December.

Surjit Singh (1994), *Urban Informal Sector*, Jaipur, Rawat Publications.

J. S. Saini and S. K. Dhameja, *Entrepreneurship and Small Business*, Rawat Publications.

Joshi, (1980), The Informal Urban Economy and Its Boundaries, *Economic and Political Weekly,* Vol. 15 No. 13, pp. 638-644.

Davla, Sarath (ed.) (1994), *Unprotected Labour in India – Issues and Concerns,* New Delhi, Friedrich Ebert Stiftung.

Vasant Desai (1996), *Entrepreneurship Development (in 3 Volumes),* Bombay, Himalaya Publishing House.

Leibenstein, Harvey (1968), Entrepreneurship and Development, *American Economic Review*, Vol. 58 No. 2.

2

Some Problems and Prospects of Indian Women

Education and Health

R. Prabhakar Rao
M. R. Geetha Bala

Abstract

About fifty per cent of population around the world as well as in India is women. But since ancient times they have not been enjoying their rightful share in the society. For the development of woman and hence the nation the two key areas are education and health of women. After the independence of India the government has taken several steps to improve the educational and health facilities in India. However, not many analytical studies were conducted in India to measure the progress. Here, in this paper we analysed the data on education and health with emphasis on women. The analysis shows that there is considerable improvement over the years. But still lot more has to be done in this regard to achieve equal status with men.

INTRODUCTION

Women in India have always been topics of concern since ancient times.. In Indian society, on one hand they were revered and worshipped in the form of Saraswati, Lakshmi, Parvati, Gayatri, Kali etc.,

Womanhood has been reverenced in the ancient Indian culture as a manifestation of divine qualities. Womanhood is a symbol of eternal virtues of humanity expressed in compassion, selfless love and caring for others. Seeds of divinity grow and blossom in a truly cultured society where women are given due respect and dignity. In Vedas, Women was extolled in many virtues such as Ida, Jyotha, Kamya, Kshma, Mahi, Ratna, Shubda etc. On the other hand the society also abuses the women in the form of several evils like child-marriage, female infanticide, Sati, dowry system etc. From an unknown period in Medieval India to the modern times the condition of women is still the same with hardly any change.

Throughout the history, women have generally been restricted to the role of home maker, that of a mother and wife. Women were never given any rights of liberty and equality. Women were not only abstained from being educated but also were not permitted to step out of the house. Despite major changes that have occurred in recent decades, the traditional, cultural and economic factors restrict the majority of women to the home in India.

India is one of the few countries where women enjoy comparatively better status than many women in other parts of the world. Undoubtedly, women today in India enjoy a better status and freedom than women in the past. After independence the constitution of India provided equal rights to men and women in all spheres of life. But even today we cannot say that all women enjoy equal rights with men in all matters. However, one could see that condition of women has improved a lot. Modernity has resulted in a growing flexibility and securing a place in public life. The revolution in science and technology has removed the disparities considerably between men and women. Now there are adequate educational facilities for girls and women. Special incentives and reservations are provided for encouraging them to study and serve in public and private institutions.

Over the past decade, gender equality and women's empowerment have been explicitly recognised as key not only to the health of nations, but also to social and economic development. India's National Population Policy 2000 has empowering women for health and nutrition's one of its crosscutting strategic themes. In India, examples of health and population indicators that are driven by gender differences in the perceived worth of males and females include sex ratios at birth, infant and child mortality by sex, and low ages at marriage for women. Further, at the household level, disempowerment of women results in their lowered access to resources such as education, employment, and income, and limits their power over decision-making and freedom of movement.

Sustainable economic development cannot be sustained without a dependable supply of highly educated and skilled human capital for which a high level of educational attainment of both women and men is necessary. However, ensuring a continued supply of skilled human capital to sustain economic growth is only one objective of reducing gender inequalities in educational attainment. The other is that education, particularly higher education of women, is a key enabler of demographic change, family welfare, and better health and nutrition of women and their families. Higher education has the potential to empower women with knowledge and ways of understanding and manipulating the world around them. Several studies have shown that education of women is associated with lower fertility, infant mortality, and better child health and nutrition.

By keeping in the view of the role of education and health of women in growth of economic and social well-being, in this paper, we are making an attempt to analyse the status of women education and health in India. We discuss the educational issues and health issues in chapter 2 and chapter 3 respectively. The summary of this paper is given in chapter 4.

Women's Education in India

Women constitute almost half of the population in the world. But the hegemonic masculine ideology made them suffer a lot as they were denied equal opportunities in different parts of the world. The rise of feminist ideas has, however, led to the tremendous improvement of women's condition throughout the world in recent times. Access to education has been one of the most pressing demands of theses women's rights movements. Women's education in India has also been a major preoccupation of both the government and civil society as educated women can play a very important role in the development of the country. It not only helps in the development of half of the human resources, but in improving the quality of life at home and outside. Educated women not only tend to promote education of their girl children, but also can provide better guidance to all their children. Moreover educated women can also help in the reduction of infant mortality rate and growth of the population.

History of Women's Education in India

Although in the Vedic period women had access to education in India, they had gradually lost this right. However, in the British period there was revival of interest in women's education in India. During this period, various socio-religious movements led by eminent persons like Raja Ram Mohan Roy, Iswar Chandra Vidyasagar emphasised on women's education in India. Mahatma Jyotiba Phule, Periyar and Baba Saheb Ambedkar were leaders of the lower castes in India who took various initiatives to make education available to the women of India. However women's education got a fillip after the country got independence in 1947 and the government has taken various measures to provide education to all Indian women. As a result women's literacy rate has grown over the three decades and the growth of female literacy has in fact been higher than that of male literacy rate. While in 1971 only 22 per cent of Indian women were literate, by the end of 2001 54.16 per cent female were literate. The growth of female literacy rate is 14.87 per cent as compared to 11.72 per cent of that of male literacy rate.

Literacy in India has made remarkable strides since Independence. This has been further confirmed by the results of the Census 2001. The literacy rate has increased from 18.33 per cent in 1951 to 64.84 per cent in 2001. This is despite the fact that during the major part of the last five decades there has been exponential growth of the population at nearly 2 per cent per annum.

Gender discrimination still persists in India and lot more needs to be done in the field of women's education in India. The gap in the male-female literacy rate is just a simple indicator. While the male literary rate is 75.26 per cent according to the 2001 census, the female literacy rate is 54.16 per cent. Prevailing prejudices, low enrollment of girl child in the schools, engagements of girl children in domestic works and high dropout rate are major obstacles in the path of making all Indian women educated.

Literacy Levels

The crude literacy rates in Indian census shows that there was phenomenal growth after 1961. However the percentage change in 1971 was less than that of 1961. In almost all the decades percentage growth in males is higher but in 2001 the female percentage was (13.6) higher than that of males (11.4). The figure 2.1 shows that male female literacy rates over a period of 1901 to 2001 and we can see the wide gap but is reducing in more recent years. Also we can observe the steady increase in the literacy rates thought the Centaury. The literacy status among the adults (15+years) in India is poor when compared to the most populous countries in the world. Except Pakistan and Bangladesh Indian literacy rates are lower. When compared to world average of 86 per cent total literacy, India is far away 61 per cent. However, except in Brazil all other countries have male literacy level higher than female. There exists the literacy gap we can see between rural and urban areas in both male and female literacy levels. However, the difference in males decreasing over the decades, but in female literacy levels the still considerable difference is there. The gender difference is exists in the rural areas in percentage of boys and girls attending school in all the age groups in but not much difference is there in urban areas in 2005-06 (IIPS Survey NFHS-3).

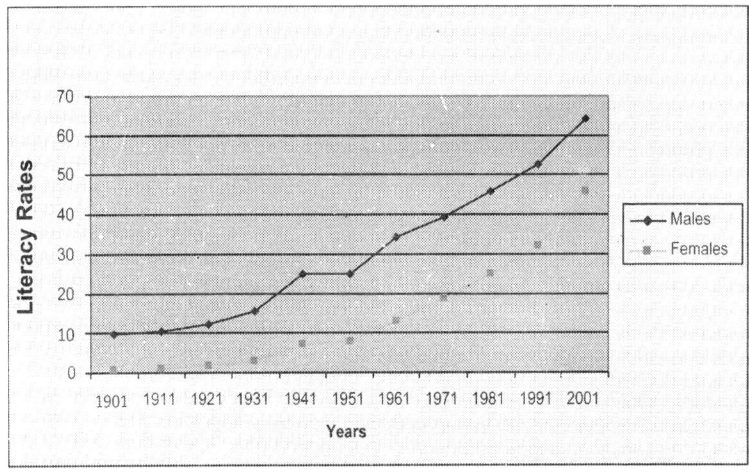

Fig. 2.1: Literacy Rates over the Census Period in India

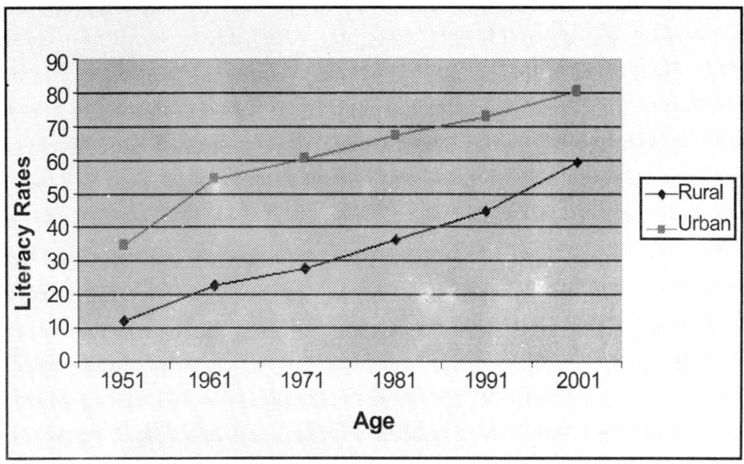

Fig. 2.2: Trends in Female Literacy Rates by Regions: 1951-2001

From the figure 2.2, we can observe that there in a steady growth of female literacy rates in both rural and urban regions in India. In the year 1951, the rural female literacy was 12 per cent and urban female literacy was 34.59 per cent. This situation had remarkably improved with in fifty years and reached to higher levels of 59 and 80 per cent in rural and urban regions respectively (see fig. 2.2). Though there has been a steady upward trend in both the rural and urban female literacy rates, it is observed that the rural female literacy is increasing much faster than that of urban. This fact is clearly evident from the index numbers, revealing that the disparity between rural and urban literacy rates is narrowing down in recent years.

Expenditure on Education

It is customary to express the total allocation to education as a percentage of GDP/GNP and take it as an indicator of the importance accorded by the government to the educational development of the country. The trends in this respect for India show that the expenditure on education increased two-fold over the period 1966-86 (from 1.8% of GNP in 1965-66 to 3.7% in 1985-86). The highest that it could reach in later years was 4.4 per cent in 2000-01. Until the 1990s it was commonly believed that shortage of financial resources was one of the major reasons for India's poor educational achievements.

No more India's economic trajectory in the last 15 years has made advocates of education raise the issue of allocation of existing resources as a problem area. It is all to do with political will. When the Eighth Five-year Plan was announced, it was announced that 4.9 per cent of the GDP would be invested in education. Ironically, the percentage share of education to GDP has declined.

Women's Health in India

Experts generally believe that the level of health status of persons in a nation is a robust reflection of the state of development of the nation. Based on experience and logical thought process, it can be concluded with a fair amount of certainty that a nation with good health tends to be productive and that productivity tends to uplift economic and societal developments. Economic and societal developments, in turn, tend to improve the indicators of health status and quality of life. A generally important factor in the consideration of status of health in relation to the overall developmental process is the health among women and children in the total population .The merit of this doctrine is easily understood in terms of biological norms of growth potential, and growth succession in children and reproductive energy utilisation in women. Under the above-mentioned norms and based on consideration of available indicators of health, it appears that the present state of health in India is poor.

Examination of available data for Indian women reveals very disturbing facts. It has been pointed out that women and men in India have nearly same life expectancy at birth (~64 years), while life expectancy at birth should be typically higher in females; it is indicative of systemic problems with women's health in India. There is a deficit of at least 35 million girls and women in this country, and it largely stems from higher mortality in females than males for every age group up to age 30.

Some Demographic Indicators in India

Initially policy-makers thought that economic growth would automatically reduce poverty and slow down the growth of population. Later the notion of development has changed considerably. Over time, the focus shifted from economic growth to 'social development', with the latter calling for economic growth to be supplemented with direct action in fields such as public health, elementary education and social security. The emphasis on social development gained acceptance as a growing body of empirical research substantiated the view that public action in these fields had much to contribute both to better living conditions and to reducing population growth.

India is in the midst of a significant demographic transition. India is not a model of social development by any means, but it is making reasonable progress with fertility decline through non-authoritarian methods. This progress owes a great deal to the improvement of female literacy and the decline of child mortality, and much more can be achieved in that direction. From figures 2.3, 2.4 and 2.5 we can see that there is steady decline in all the demographic indicators such as: CBR/CDR, IMR and TFR. The crude birth rate 36.9 per 1000 persons in 1971 and it was continuously declined to 21.76 in 2009. The crude death rate was 14.9 per 1000 persons in 1971 and increased during 1970's but after 1977 again it decreased significantly to 6.23. The infant mortality rates were also shown some increase in 1970's but after 1980's it declined continuously. Another important indicator is total fertility rate was shown continuously declined from 5.2 births per women in 1971 to 2.72 in 2009.

The total fertility rate (TFR) is a more direct measure of the level of fertility than the crude birth rate, since it refers to births per woman. This indicator shows the potential for population change in the country. A rate of two children per woman is considered the replacement rate for a population, resulting in relative stability in terms of total numbers. Rates above two children indicate populations growing in size and whose median age is declining. Higher rates may also indicate difficulties for families, in some situations, to feed and educate their children and for women to enter the labour force.

If we look at the life expectancy, in almost all regions of the world female life expectancy was more that of males. Though the life expectancy was improved in India over the years, still it is the group of less developed regions only. The life expectancy of males and females in India were respectively 62.7 and 66.1 in 2006.

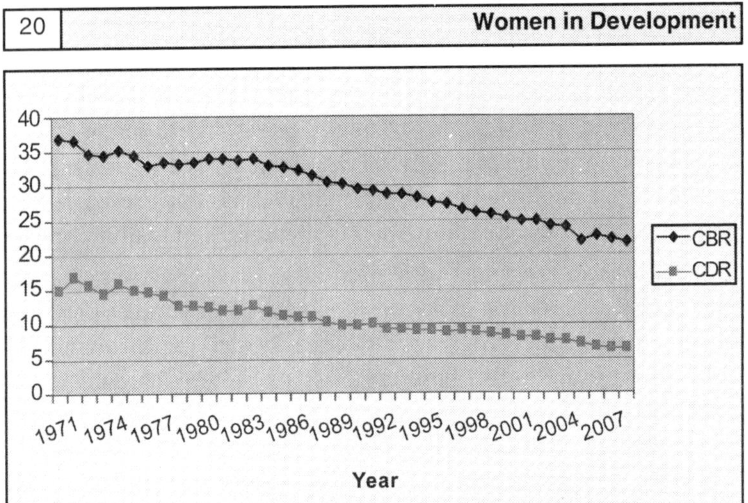

Fig 2.3: Trends in Birth and Death Rates: 1971-2009

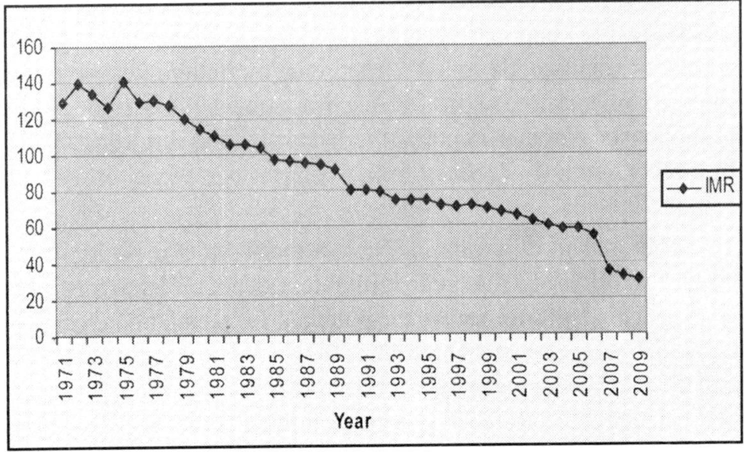

Fig 2.4: Total Fertility Rates in India: 1971-2009

Women Health and Family Welfare

The holistic perspective not only takes into account existing technologies and their organization, it also underlines the importance of social determinants that contribute to people's well-being such as food availability and nutritional status of populations, drinking water supply, housing, transport, education, employment and, last but not least, the status of women. People's health can then be defined as an

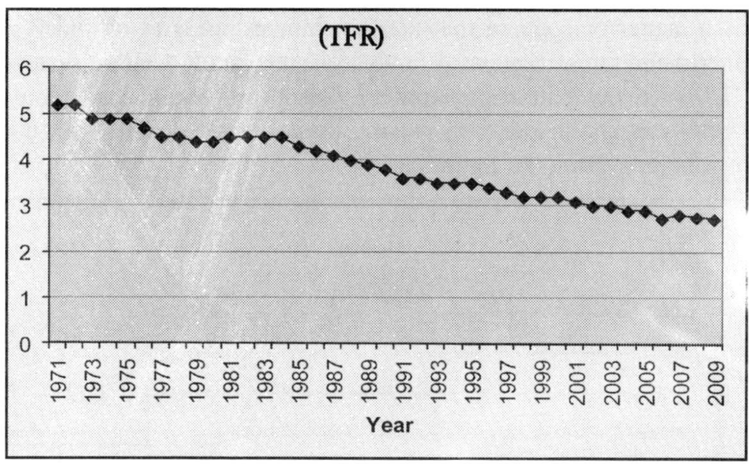

Fig 2.5: Infant Mortality Rates in India: 1971-2009

outcome of the interplay of socio-economic, cultural, political, and technological forces. This outcome varies, depending on gender and caste, class stratification, regional and ethnic factors. The fact is that the typical female advantage in life expectancy is not seen in India. This suggests that there are systematic problems with women's health. Indian women have high mortality rates, particularly during childhood and in their reproductive years. The health of Indian women is intrinsically linked to their status in society. Poor health has repercussions not only for women but also their families. Women in poor health are more likely to give birth to low weight infants. They also are less likely to be able to provide food and adequate care for their children. Finally, a woman's health affects the household economic well-being, as a woman in poor health will be less productive in the labour force.

Expenditure on Health and Family Welfare

Public expenditure on health care today is a dismal 0.9 per cent of GDP; the overwhelming majority of health costs are paid by patients out of pocket. Health sector in India suffers from gross inadequacy of public finance and therefore an immediate and significant scaling-up of resources is an imperative. The government spends on health and family welfare over the five-year plans are varying and percentage health to total is decreasing from third plan to ninth plan period. This is a matter of concern that the government needs to do much in increasing the allocation of funds to health family welfare sectors. However, the central government spending on health and family welfare is continuously increasing from 1992-93 to 2009-10, this can be seen from the figure 2.6.

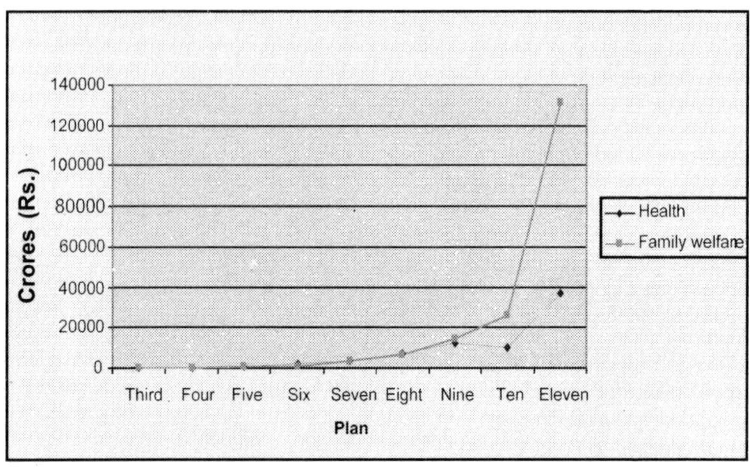

Fig. 2.6: Plan Expenditure on Health and Family Welfare

On the face of it, there is only 3.3 per cent of total plan investment allocated for the health sector in India. A nation without comprehensive outlook, plan and proper investment for improving the health of her citizens cannot afford to stand developing. It is now imperative that due importance is given in this respect without further delay. Yet despite the celebrations of 9 per cent growth, in the 'Other India' millions of poorer Indians remain excluded from the most basic rights and subject to the tyranny of mass hunger, illiteracy, and ill-health.

Summary

The role of women is very crucial in social and economic development. In many countries including Indian the women have not got their significant place in society due to various traditional and cultural practices prevailed in the society since ancient times. However, in recent scientific, technological and economic progress in modern society has brought a lot of change in the status of women. In particular in the areas of education and health of women there is a considerable improvement in India over the last few decades the literacy levels of women have improved. The good sign is the rural female literacy rate is increasing much faster than that of urban. Another positive indication is that the demographic indicators such as CBR, CDR, TFR and IMR showing a steady decline during the last few decades. In spite of these indicators showing an impressive growth, still India is in a league of developing nations. Hence, much more has to be done in this direction to achieve the status of developed nation.

REFERENCES

Mahendra K. Premi, India's Literarcy Panorama, Seminar on Progress of Literacy In India: What the Census 2001 Reveals NIEPA, New Delhi, 2002.

N. Sharmila, Dhas, A. C., Development of Women Education in India, MPRA Archive, Paper No. 20680, 2010.

Rural Urban Literacy Rates of India, Census Report, 2001.

Sample Registration System, Registrar General, Vol. 45, No. 1, Jan. 2011, India.

www.planningcommission.com

www.rbi.org

www.nfhsindia.org

3

Generation of Income for the Poor through Micro-Enterprises

Dr. K. A. Rasure

Abstract

The present study examines the role of micro-enterprises set-up through SHG mode towards enhancing the income level of rural poor women. The study was conducted in two selected districts of Pune in Maharashtra and Morigaon in Assam. The major analysis of this study was based on micro-enterprises set-up set-up by 71 entrepreneurs randomly drawn from 26 SHGs promoted by two NGOs. Among other findings the most important revelation of this study is that the SHG programme in fact helped to revive the traditionally performed household activities which other-wise discontinued due to lack of house hold income. The study also showed that micro-enterprises set-up through micro-finance also provided some sorts of economic support whatever little it may be but really helping them to fall back on during economic crises.

INTRODUCTION

Through various self-employment programme, the Government has been making several attempts to enhance the economic status of rural people living below poverty line. The major important Self-employment programme implemented by the government include, Integrated Rural Development Programme, Development of Women and Children in Rural Areas, Self-employment for Educated Unemployed Youth, Sworna Jayanthi Gram Sworajgar Yojana etc. These programme have been under implementation for the past few decades, and definitely helped to create material asset and employment among the poor. Nevertheless, these programme could not enhance the economic status of poor beyond certain threshold due to the faulty implementation particularly associated with the selection of the beneficiaries or problem associated with delivery of credit.

Although there are several formal financial institutions operating in the country to meet the credit needs of weaker Sections, particularly the poor, our past experiences showed that the smooth delivery of credit to the poor was adversely affected due to the formalized procedure and apathy of concerned officers. Of late, amongst other measures to tackle poverty, self-employment through Micro-finance programme has evolved as a major approach to benefit low-income groups of society. The emergence of Self-Help Groups of the poor came handy for the effective delivery of micro-finance to the poor. Studies have shown that SHGs are acting as an alternative mechanism for the smooth delivery of credit to the poor (Srinivasan: 1996; Kumaran: 1997).

Under the SHG mode, poor particularly the women are mobilised and organised in to informal groups. Of late, several agencies are coming forward to form SHGs among the poor through the process of mobilisation. The size of the group varies in the range of 10 to 20. Apart from other collective actions, the major focus is on thrift and credit. After six months of its formation, the group starts rotating their saving in the form of small loan for undertaking micro-enterprises and meeting important consumptions need.

Apart from serving as a viable organization for the delivery of credit to the poor, studies have also shown that these organisations particularly managed by women, successfully demonstrated how to mobilise and manage thrift activities, appraise credit needs, enforce financial discipline, maintain credit linkage with banks and effectively undertake income-generation activities. These studies also have shown that the poor as a group are quite credit worthy and repayment of loan is quite satisfactory. (Rao: 1992; Kumaran: 2002).

In a comparative study between the micro-enterprises set-up under DWCRA and through the SHGs promoted by NGO and Banks it is found that the enterprises set-up by the later are more viable and sustainable as compared to those formed by the former. The reason being that the DWCRA is a loose knit organisation where it lacks saving and the micro-enterprise set-up were without any proper logistic support. (Kumaran: 2002). The present study tries to examine the role of micro-enterprises set-up through SHG mode towards enhancing the income level of the rural poor particularly the poor women.

Methodology

The study was conducted in the state of Maharashtra and Assam. From these two states, one developed and one underdeveloped district were selected on the basis of certain development indicators. Thus from Maharashtra Pune (developed) and from Assam Morigaon (relatively under developed) were selected for the study. In this study, only those SHGs promoted by NGOs were examined. The NGOs selected for the study were BAIF and Chaitanya from Pune and Morigaon Mahila Mehfil and Morigaon Zilla Gramya Puthibharel from Morigoan. From the SHGs promoted by the first two NGOs, 15 groups on a random basis were selected which are five and above years old. Similarly, following the same procedure from the SHGs promoted by the other two NGOs 11 groups were selected. Among them, five groups were more than five years old and the rest around three years old. Further, from the selected SHGs, again following the same procedure 22 and 49 entrepreneurs were selected respectively from Pune and Morigoan for detailed study about the type of enterprise set-up by them and the financial benefits accrued to them from these activities. Information about SHGs were collected by interviewing group leaders and micro-enterprises by interviewing entrepreneurs with the help of an interview schedule. Information from available secondary sources was also collected, to support the primary data.

Profile of SHG

As mentioned earlier, from Pune 11 and from Morigoan 15 SHGs were studied. As per the information furnished by the SHG leaders in Pune, 38 per cent of the SHG members belong to APL and 62 per cent BPL. It was informed in the course of survey that when the SHGs were initially formed most of them belonged to the category of BPL and in the course of time by accruing benefits some of them graduated in to the category of APL. While in the case of Morigaon, 84 per cent belong to the category of BPL and rest APL. As per the latest BPL survey undertaken by the department of Rural Development, in Assam 70 per cent of the house holds in the district fall in the BPL group. Examination of managing committee showed that in each SHG there were two leaders and generally they are called President and Secretary who look after the affairs of SHG. In few cases, Treasurer was also appointed to take care of financial management. In Pune, in most of the cases, the Presidents post is filled up by forward castes and most of them are educated and agricultural labour by profession. While in the case of Morigaon, the Presidents post is mostly held by members belonging to OBCs. Most of them are educated to the level of primary and above and working as agricultural labour. Rotation of office bearers is rarely found in both districts, as a result, the same person continued in the same post for years.

Thrift and credit form the major activities of SHG. In the district of pune, initially the entire group started the saving at a rate of Rs. 10/- per month. Currently, the amount varies from Rs. 20/- to 100/-. While in the case of Morigaon, the monthly saving varies from Rs. 10/- to 50/-. Saving is regular in all the SHGs in both the districts and loans are disbursed to the members with certain interest as per the collective decision made by the SHG members. The saving capacity of SHG members in Pune is better than those in morigaon. In the district of pune, the major sources of loan were from group fund, bank and revolving fund. While in Morigaon the main source is from group fund and bank. In both the districts, repayment of group loan is cent per cent and that of bank loan above 95 per cent.

Profile of Entrepreneurs

In the following section socio-economic profile of the 71 entrepreneurs selected for the study is given. In the district of Pune, nearly half of them fall in the age group of 30 to 50 years .Those who are above 50 constitute 13 per cent and the rest below 30 years. While in Morigaon nearly half of them fall in the age group below 30 years and the rest above this. The age distribution in these two districts showed that the members are relatively younger in Morigaon as compared to Pune. Information about marital status showed that in Pune all are married and one of them remained widow. While in the case of Morigaon 61 per cent of them married and 33 per cent unmarried. Widows constitute 6 per cent. Caste-wise information showed that most of them belonged to other castes and OBCs. While in Morigoan, most of them belong to OBCs. Educational qualifications of the entrepreneurs showed that in Pune exactly half of them educated above primary level. Illiterates constitutes more than one fourth of them. While in morigoan, it is found that majority of them (69%) educated between middle and higher secondary. Two of them had college education. Only two cases of illiterates were reported. This showed that the level of education among the entrepreneurs is on the higher side in morigoan as compared to Pune. Occupational status of the entrepreneurs in both the districts showed that they are predominantly agricultural labors followed by non-agricultural labors. Distribution of yearly House hold income from all sources showed that in Pune 41 per cent of them have income 24000/- and above. Those who earned income between Rs. 15,000-24,000 constituted 32 per cent of the sample and the rest had an income up to Rs. 15,000/- while in Morigoan, whose income below 15000/- constituted 49 per cent and between 15,000/- to 24,000/- constituted 26 per cent and the rest 25 per per cent had income above Rs. 24000/.

Training of Entrepreneurs

Information about training undergone by the entrepreneurs after joining the SHG has been collected. In Pune, several agencies were involved in training The training on basic information about SHG, accounting and book keeping etc., done by the promotion agency, while entreprenurship development programme (EDP) was conducted by agencies like Maharashtra Centre for Entrepreneurship (MCED), Maharashtra Industrial and consultancy Organisation (MITCON, Central Khadi and Village industries, and Banks. While in Morigoan, the training on the above subjects was imparted by the promotion agency in consultation with NABARD, SIRD and Banking Institutions. In Pune, all the entrepreneurs and in Morigoan 68 per cent of them underwent training programme related to income-generation.

Micro-credit and Micro-enterprises

In this study we have analysed 71 micro-enterprises set up by 22 entrepreneurs from Pune and 49 from Morigoan. Information about various activities related to micro-enterprises was collected for the year 2002-03. While undertaking the survey it was found that only one unit in pune was incurring loss and the rest of the units were showing profits with varying degree.

Type of Micro-enterprises

In the district of Pune, the most common enterprises set-up by the entrepreneurs is tailoring (26%) followed by dairy and petty business set-up by 27 per cent each of the entrepreneurs. The rest of the entrepreneurs pursued activities such as poultry and goat rearing. While in Morigaon the most important common activity was weaving pursued by nearly one fourth of the entrepreneurs. The next important activity was tailoring pursued by nearly 18 per cent of the entrepreneurs. Duckery was pursued by 4 per cent of them. The other activities include dairy, fishery, and land based agricultural activities pursued by the rest of the entrepreneurs. In Pune, most of the units were set-up under the non-farm sector while in Morigaon basically traditionally pursued income-generation activities at household level were undertaken.

Cost of Micro-enterprises

In Pune the cost of micro-enterprises set-up by the entrepreneurs varied from Rs. 600/- to 25000/-. Those who have invested up to Rs. 5000/- constituted 41 per cent. The next highest investment was in the range of Rs. 5, 000 to 10,000/- was made 23 per cent of the entrepreneurs. Those who have invested between Rs. 10, 000 to 20,000/- constituted 27 per cent. The remaining 9 per cent of them invested Rs. 20, 000 and above.

While in the case of Morigaon the maximum and minimum limit of amount invested was Rs. 600/- to 5,000/. What is notable in the case of Morigaon is that the investment made by lion's share of

(85%) the entrepreneur's do not exceed Rs. 5,000/-. Those entrepreneurs invested between Rs. 5000/- to 10,000/- accounted for 6 per cent of them. Similarly, only 7 per cent of them invested in micro-enterprises that cost above Rs. 10, 000/-. This shows that investment made in enterprises is relatively less in the case of Morigaon as compared with Pune. More than three fourth of the entrepreneurs invested below Rs. 5,000/-. While in the case of Pune, the same amount of investment was made by 41 per cent of the entrepreneurs.

In the district of Pune, all the 22 entrepreneurs cumulatively invested an amount of Rs. 2, 10,300/- indicating an average investment of Rs. 9, 560/- per entrepreneur. While in the case of Morigaon, the total amount invested by the 49 entrepreneurs amounted to Rs. 2, 81,400/- thus indicating that the per capita investment made by each entrepreneurs amounted to Rs. 5740/-. This showed that average investment in Pune is relatively on the higher side as compared to Morigaon.

Source of Finance

In the district of Pune 56 per cent of the total amount (Rs. 1, 77,700/-) invested in the enterprises was received from the SHG group loan. Another 33 per cent (Rs. 69, 400) was mobilised as bank loan. The total individual contribution made by each member for undertaking the economic activity amounted to 11 per cent (Rs. 23, 150/-) of the total invested amount. Where as in the case of Morigaon 56 per cent of the total finance (Rs. 1, 85,730/-) was mobilised collectively through SHG group loan and bank loan. The own contribution made by entrepreneurs constituted the remaining portion of 34 per cent of the investment (Rs. 95, 670/-).

Information collected from the entrepreneurs showed that in pune 5 per cent of them and in morigaon 2 per cent of them experienced problems in repaying the loan taken for setting up of micro-enterprises. In such cases it was reported that the members either depended on moneylender or fall back on their friends or relatives to cope up with the situation.

As far as raw material required for undertaking income-generating activities is concerned, most of the entrepreneurs admitted that they got the materials required for various activities within the village and the rest got it from outside village. In response to another question related to market, only 2 per cent of them in each district faced the problem of marketing of their products.

Cost of Production and Return

In the district of Pune, the total turnover in a month during the year 2002-03 from all the 22 enterprises amounted to Rs. 81305/- indicating an average turnover of Rs. 3, 695/- per unit. The total cost of production for all the units stood at Rs. 37, 310/- showing an average cost of production of Rs. 1, 696/- per unit. Thus, the total net profit per month for all the 22 units stood at Rs. 43, 995/- indicating an average net profit of Rs. 2000/- per unit. The maximum and minimum net profit earned by the entrepreneurs varies from Rs. 150/- to 12,000/-. From the above analysis it is also found that 60 per cent of the units are earning a profit margin above Rs. 2000/-.

While in the case of Morigaon, the total monthly turn over from all the enterprises for the same year under reference amounted to Rs. 78, 000/- with an average per capita turnover of Rs. 1, 592/- per unit. The total cost of production was Rs. 36, 400/- indicating per capita cost of production at Rs. 743/-. Thus the net profit at aggregate level is Rs. 41, 600/- and the per unit is Rs. 849/- which is very low the net profit among the units varies from Rs. 100 to 2500/-. The profit earned by three fourth of the units is less than Rs. 1000/-. Only 10 per cent of the units could earn profit margin of Rs. 2000 and above.

Pattern of Expenditure

Information is also obtained on the pattern of utilisation of profit derived from the enterprises. In Pune, 25 per cent of the profit derived from the enterprises was used for repaying loan, 40 per cent towards meeting household expenditure and the rest 35 per cent meeting general and emergency expenses. While in the case of Morigoan, major share of the profit (73%) was used for meeting household expenses. Around 19 per cent of the profit utilised for repaying the SHG and Bank loan and the rest used for meeting emergency needs. While in Pune, the major portion of the surplus has been reinvested for the purchase of assets like land, cattle, ornaments, etc.

Summary and Conclusion

In this study an attempt is made to examine the role of micro-enterprises set-up through SHG mode towards enhancing the income level of the rural poor particularly the women. As part of the study we have analysed 71 micro-enterprises set up by entrepreneurs drawn from 26 SHGs.. Out of this 22 units were set-up in Pune and the rest 49 in Morigoan. Most of the finance required for undertaking the enterprises was channalised through SHGs withers for group loan or external loan from banks. We have seen that in the district of Pune the most important micro-enterprises set-up included tailoring, petty business, darying, and vegetable vending. While in the case of morigaon the most important activity was weaving followed by tailoring, petty business, poultry, dairy and duckers. Investment in terms of money made in setting up of micro-enterprises was relatively less in morigaon where more than three fourth of the entrepreneurs invested less than Rs. 5000/- per unit. While the investment made in Pune was relatively on the higher side. In both the districts the major source of finance was received from SHG group loan and bank loans. What is noticeable in the case of Morigaon is that nearly one third of the finance for setting up enterprises is contributed through own source, which is very low in Pune. The average net profit earned by each of the unit in Pune was Rs. 2000/-, while in Morigaon the same distribution is only 849/- which was very low. In Pune 60 per cent of the units earned a profit margin of Rs. 200/- in Morigoan more than three fourth of them earned less than Rs. 1000/- and only 10 per cent of the units could earn a profit above Rs. 20000. The relatively low profit from the units set-up in Morigaon is mainly due to the fact that many of the units were set-up recently while those in Pune were matured by more than five years. The pattern of utilisation of profit accrued from the SHG showed that in Morigaon nearly three fourth of the profit was used for meeting household expenses and 19 per cent used for repaying SHG loan. The study showed that after becoming member of SHG and particularly after setting up micro-enterprises the income of the entrepreneurs in Pune has increased considerably, while the increase in Morigaon was marginal. In Pune the entrepreneurs invested the surplus mostly to acquire fixed assets like land, cattle, ornaments. While in Morigaon, the same was used for procuring household items and facilities. But the important revelation of the study is that people of Morigaon could revive their traditionally performed house hold activities with the help of micro-finance mobilised through SHGs which was other-wise discontinued due lack of house hold income. The study also showed that micro-enterprises set-up through micro-finance also provided some sorts of economic support, whatever little it may be, but really helping them to fall back on during economic crisis.

REFERENCES

Dinakar, Rao K. 1992, Women's Savings and Credit Schemes, Three Case Studies, NIBM, Pune.

Kumaran, K. P. 1997, Self-Help Groups: An Alternative to Institutional Credit to the Poor, A Case Study in AP *Journal of Rural Development*, Vol. 16 (3).

Kumaran, K. P. 2002, Role of Self-Help Groups in Promoting Micro-Enterprises through Micro-Credit *Journal of Rural Development* Vol. (21) No. 2.

Srinivasan and Rao 1996, Financing of SHG by Banks-Some Issues BIRD, Lucknow.

4

Status of Women in the North Eastern Region of India

Where do they Stand?

Dr. Ira Das

Abstract

Although men and women share the same space, everywhere in the world, women are accorded a lower status than men. The North Eastern Region of India has been considered as a backward region in terms of growth in per capita income. However, there is a perception that the status of women is higher in the North Eastern Region of the country in comparison with the status of women in all India average. In this study, an attempt has been made to examine the status of women in the North Eastern Region in comparison with all India average. It is found from the analysis that the status of women in the region is comparatively better than the rest of the country only in some selected indicators. The indicators reveal that women have a very low degree of freedom of movement and low level of control over themselves in North Eastern Region.

Keywords: *Men, Women, North Eastern Region, India, Status.*

INTRODUCTION

Men and women are not treated equally in the world, although they share the same space. The fact that 'Women hold up half the sky' – does not give women an equal position of dignity and equality in comparison with men (Swayam, 2001). Women have come a long way in trying to establish a respectable position in the society. However, for a long time, women have been treated as the weak gender. But what is the status of women in 21st century? In today's ultramodern society, does the situation remain same as it was centuries ago?

'Status of Women' refers to the position of women in society in relation to men. The status of women has two dimensions: *(a)* The extent of control enjoyed by women over their lives, and *(b)* The extent to which they have access to the decision-making process and are effectively in position of power and authority (Zehol, 2010). A scholar Talcott Parsons identifies six attributes of status of women, which are both ascribed and achieved:

(i) Membership in a kinship unit.
(ii) Personal qualities.
(iii) Achievements.
(iv) Possession.
(v) Authority.
(vi) Power (Zehol, 2010).

A precise and complete assessment of the status of women require both quantitative as well as qualitative factors.

Everywhere in the world, women are accorded a lower status than men. There exists inequality in women's access to education, healthcare, physical and financial resources and opportunities in the political, economic, social and cultural field. According to Mohiuddin (1995), women's lower status is manifested in women's low wage rates than men in all occupational fields and industries, in their limited upward mobility, and in their greater family responsibilities due to divorce, abandonment, etc., in the developed countries. In the developing countries, women's lower status is reflected not only in their work being underpaid, unrecognised, but also in their limited access to productive resources and support services such as health and education. It has been advocated by Amartya Sen (1990) that independent earning opportunities reduce the economic dependence of woman on men and increase her bargaining power in the family.

The status of women can be judged by some indicators. To measure the status of women a composite index is constructed by the Population

Crisis Committee (PCC) and used by the World Bank and the United Nations which focuses on indicators measuring health, education, employment, marriage and childbearing and social equality. Mohiuddin (1995) argues that these indicators have a poverty-bias and measure women's status in terms of structural change rather than in terms of their welfare vis-a-vis men. Therefore, he formulated an Alternative Composite Index (ACI) of the status of women, based on many more indicators reflecting women's issues in both developed and developing countries. The ACI is based on several indicators in eight sectors: *(i)* health, *(ii)* schooling, *(iii)* adult education, *(iv)* labour force participation, *(v)* conditions of employment, *(vi)* domestic life, *(vii)* political representation and *(viii)* legal rights. Rustogi (2004) tried to measure women's status with the help of a diverse set of indicators. She selected some broad indicators across Indian states namely: education, health, survival, participation in private/public decision-making and safety/security to measure the status of women in the society.

The region located on the north east part of India are regarded as the North Eastern Region (NER) and it consists of Arunachal Pradesh, Assam, Manipur, Meghalaya, Mizoram, Nagaland, Tripura, and Sikkim. The NER of India has been considered as a backward region in terms of growth in per capita income. In 2012-13, the per capita Net State Domestic Product (NSDP) of the state at constant prices (2004-05) was Rs. 24, 198 against the per capita Net National Product (NNP) for the country of Rs. 39,143 (Government of Assam, 2012-13). Generally, it is thought that the status of women is comparatively better in tribal society (Handsdak, 2012; Burman, 2012). The tribal people are more in numbers in the NER. The scheduled tribe are 94.75 per cent in Mizoram, 87.70 per cent in Nagaland, 85.53 per cent in Meghalaya, 63.66 per cent in Arunachal Pradesh, 34.41 per cent in Manipur, 30.95 per cent in Tripura, and 12.82 per cent in Assam (Zehol, 2010). Moreover, there is matrilineal system[1] in Meghalaya.

There is a perception that the status of women is better in the states of the North Eastern Region of the country in comparison with the status of women in rest of India. The status of women is much better in the North east and they use to enjoy greater mobility and visibility compared to other regions of the country (Phukon, 2009).

---

1. The Matrilineal Societies are those Societies where Property is Transmitted from Mother to Daughter.

The woman's role in the domestic as well as social sphere has been determined by her capacity to control or participate in the production process in the tribal societies of North East. However, there appear some changes due to the commercialisation of agriculture and the play of market forces. Now, the subsistence economy is being transformed leading to the emergence of class interests and appropriation of resources belonging to the community. These forces have greatly undermined the position of women depriving them from participation in the process and control of the production, which they used to control till recently (Parwez, 2012). In fact, the nature and type of economic and non-economic role of women have now undergone continued change in accordance with the changes in time and related development in the society (Mandal and Ete, 2010).

In this study, an attempt has been made to examine the status of women in North Eastern Region in comparison with the all India average. This paper is organised in four parts. The introductory part introduces the study problem and presents the objectives of the study. The second part describes the data source and methodology of the study. While results and discussion are presented in the third part, conclusion is presented in the final part.

Data Source and Methodology

The study is based on secondary data. The data are mainly collected from the Census reports of the government, National Sample Survey Organisation (NSSO), Registrar General of India etc.

The status of women in North Eastern Region in comparison with the rest of India is examined on the basis of different indicators, namely: Female Literacy (FL), Female Workforce Participation Rate (FWPR), Gross Enrolment Ratio, Dropout Rates, Sex Ratio, Female Infant Mortality, Age at Marriage, Women's Participation in Decision-making/ Women Empowerment and Violence against Women. Mostly, status is examined with the help of the method of ranking of states in different indicators. Rankings are assigned from the best to worst performing states. However, in case of the negative indicators like dropout rates, infant mortality, violence etc., (where high values are unfavourable for the society), rankings are given from worst to best performing states.

Results and Discussion

The status of women in NER is examined on the basis of the following indicators.

Female Literacy and Gender Gap

The female literacy and the gender gap of NER along with the other states of the country are presented in Table 4.1. Ranking of the states in the Table 4.1 depicts the picture that the states with high women literacy rates are the states of NER (except Arunachal Pradesh), and Kerala. These are also the states where the gap in literacy rates between men and women is low. Both non-economic and economic factors are discussed in the literature to explain the prevalence of the gender gap in literacy rates.

Table 4.1: Female Literacy and Gender Gap in Literacy Rates (GLR)

State	Rank in Female Literacy	Rank in GLR
Kerala	1	2
Mizoram	2	3
Lakshadweep	3	5
Tripura	4	7
A and N Islands	5	6
Goa	6	8
Nagaland	7	4
Maharashtra	8	12
Meghalaya	9	1
Manipur	10	10
Uttarakhand	11	16
Gujarat	12	14
Assam	13	9
India	14	15
Orissa	15	17
Chhattisgarh	16	22
Madhya Pradesh	17	20
Andhra Pradesh	18	13
Arunachal Pradesh	19	11
Uttar Pradesh	20	18
Jammu and Kashmir	21	19
Jharkhand	22	23
Bihar	23	24

Source: Census of India (Provisional Data), 2011.

Female Work Participation Rate

The female workforce participation rate of the states of NER in comparison with the rest of India is presented in Table 4.2. Table 4.2 reveals the fact that female work participation rates (FWPR) are higher in most of the NER states with hilly regions and those inhabited by tribals than other states of rest of India, even in Kerala. Except Assam, Manipur and Tripura, the FWPR are higher than all India average for many NER states. These are also the states where there are low gender disparities in terms of work participation. Higher FWPR can be partially explained by the fact that community-based organisation of subsistence production requires a high level of women's labour participation. Some scholars have linked higher participation of women with rice cultivation. Another factor associated with better work participation levels is educational attainment.

Table 4.2: Female Work Participation Rate (FWPR)

States/Uts	Rank	FWPR
1	2	3
Chhattisgarh	1	62.7
Himachal Pradesh	2	58.8
Nagaland	3	56.5
Andhra Pradesh	4	52.7
Meghalaya	5	51.4
Rajasthan	6	46.2
Mizoram	7	45.4
Arunachal Pradesh	8	45.1
Karnataka	9	43.0
Maharashtra	10	42.9
Sikkim	11	41.2
Tamil Nadu	12	41.1
Madhya Pradesh	13	41.1
Jharkhand	14	39.8
Jammu and Kashmir	15	38.4

Contd...

1	2	3
Gujarat	16	37.9
Orissa	17	37.8
Uttarkhand	18	36.6
India		35.6
Manipur	19	31.5
Kerala	20	27.3
Punjab	21	26.3
Assam	22	20.8
Tripura	23	15.6

Source: Based on Calculations from NSSO (2010).

Gross Enrolment Ratio

The gross enrolment ratio of the states of NER with the other states of India is presented in Table 4.3. When the enrolment rates of Class I-VIII of Schools for General Education in different states of India are compared, it is seen that the enrolment rates are comparatively higher in NER than some states of the rest of India like Bihar, Goa, UP and Chandigarh.

Table 4.3: Gross Enrolment Ratio in Class I-VIII of Schools for General Education

States/UTs	Classes I-VIII (6-13 years)		
	Girls	Boys	Total
1	2	3	4
Andhra Pradesh	90.11	90.18	90.15
Arunachal Pradesh	138.1	146.31	142.26
Assam	84.9	82.21	83.54
Bihar	86.03	100.79	93.72
Goa	86.13	88.75	87.5
Gujarat	106.04	108.88	107.56
Haryana	87.58	84.31	85.79
Himachal Pradesh	109.38	110.37	109.9

Contd...

1	2	3	4
Jammu and Kashmir	104.27	104.67	104.48
Karnataka	97.66	99.81	98.76
Kerala	97.11	98.58	97.86
Madhya Pradesh	130.18	133.32	131.81
Maharashtra	96.4	99.82	98.18
Manipur	147.73	155.44	151.64
Meghalaya	141.86	135.15	138.49
Mizoram	133.58	142.98	138.33
Nagaland	83.45	83.2	83.32
Orissa	104.68	105.62	105.16
Punjab	100.6	102.84	101.83
Rajasthan	98.71	109.97	104.63
Sikkim	123.37	118.82	121.08
Tamil Nadu	114.07	114.32	114.2
Tripura	121.74	123.56	122.66
Uttar Pradesh	96.27	94.65	95.42
West Bengal	110.74	107.16	108.92
A and N Islands	73.04	75.62	74.34
Chandigarh	64.71	62.62	63.55
D and N Haveli	101.98	105.24	103.69
Daman and Diu	83.48	72.35	77.1
Delhi	116.35	116.31	116.33
Lakshadweep	75.68	73.99	74.83
Puducherry	100.39	95.6	97.87
India	101.09	103.75	102.47

Source: Government of India (2012), *Data for use of Deputy Chairman*, Planning Commission, 10 April.

Dropout Rates

The disgusting point revealed by Rustogi (2004) on the basis of the Government of India (2001) data is that the dropout rates are very high in the states of NER than many states of rest of India. Rustogi (2004) opined that the use of girls in sibling care, as additional hands for helping mothers in the household, farm and off-farm work and so on operate to reduce the availability of formal education for them. Given low retention at the primary level, very few girls reach middle and secondary school or higher levels of education. Lower literacy also impacts upon women's awareness levels regarding their own health needs, thereby foreclosing the possibility of improving their access to the available services for their well-being. Here, the dropout rate of the states of the NER is compared with the dropout rates of the other states of the country and accordingly ranking is assigned in Table 4.4. Table 4.4 shows that the dropout rates of the states of the North East are higher than the all India average for 2010 data. These findings are in line with the findings of Rustogi (2004) for the 2001 data.

Table 4.4: State-wise Dropout Rates in Classes I-X (6-16 years) in India

States and UTs	Total	Girls	Rank
1	2	3	4
Sikkim	80.73	79.36	1
Assam	77.6	77.82	2
Meghalaya	77.89	76.46	3
Bihar	77.56	76.06	4
Nagaland	74.86	73.97	5
Rajasthan	71.64	73.42	6
Madhya Pradesh	65.71	71.32	7
West Bengal	71.83	70.7	8
Orissa	68.19	65.91	9
Gujarat	62.14	64.41	10
Arunachal Pradesh	64.86	64.7	11
D and N Haveli	58.83	63.48	12
Tripura	62.9	62.34	13

Contd...

1	2	3	4
Mizoram	62.87	60.72	14
Manipur	56.79	55.71	15
Andhra Pradesh	53.36	54.02	16
India	52.76	51.97	
Karnataka	46.62	46.33	17
Jammu and Kashmir	44.3	40.63	18
Punjab	40.42	39.45	19
Goa	34.3	32.63	20
Tamil Nadu	34.06	30.28	21
Daman and Diu	35.93	29.75	22
A and N Islands	30.06	27.07	23
Lakshadweep	25.13	22.67	24
Haryana	19.84	19.46	25
Himachal Pradesh	20.65	18.93	26
Uttar Pradesh	23.83	15.09	27
Delhi	1.97	9.15	28
Chandigarh	3.78	7.86	29
Puducherry	7.34	1.39	30
Kerala	-4.06	-5.2	31

Source: Government of India (2012), *Data for use of Deputy Chairman*, Planning Commission, 10 April.

Sex Ratios

A decline in the proportion of women in the populations of many countries in the world has been witnessed over the years. Researchers have linked many factors like son preference to gender bias against girls in healthcare, nutrition, food allocation etc., to explain the declining sex ratio. The Census, 2011 (provisional) data reveals the low proportion of girls in the states of Haryana, Punjab, Gujarat, Rajasthan and Uttar Pradesh and comparatively higher proportion of girls in the states of NER (refer Table 4.5).

Table 4.5: Child Sex Ratio among the States of India

States	2011	Rank
Andhra Pradesh	992	3
Arunachal Pradesh	920	19
Assam	954	14
Bihar	916	21
Chhattisgarh	991	4
Goa	968	10
Gujarat	918	20
Haryana	877	26
Himachal Pradesh	974	9
Jammu and Kashmir	883	25
Jharkhand	947	15
Karnataka	968	11
Kerala	1084	1
Madhya Pradesh	930	17
Maharashtra	925	18
Manipur	987	6
Meghalaya	986	5
Mizoram	975	8
Nagaland	931	16
Orissa	978	7
Punjab	893	23
Rajasthan	926	17
Sikkim	889	24
Tamil Nadu	995	2
Tripura	961	13
Uttar Pradesh	908	22
Uttarakhand	963	12
West Bengal	947	15

Source: Census of India, 2011 (Provisional Data).

Age at Marriage among Females

The age of marriage among female of the states of the country is compared and ranking is done in Table 4.6. Despite the legally stipulated minimum age of 18 years at marriage, girls still get married before attaining this age in the states of Madhya Pradesh, Rajasthan, Andhra Pradesh, Bihar, and Uttar Pradesh which is not the case with the states of NER.

Table 4.6: Mean Age at Marriage among Females (MAMF)

States	Rank	MAMF
Rajasthan	20	16.6
Madhya Pradesh	19	17.0
Bihar	18	17.2
Andhra Pradesh	17	17.5
Uttar Pradesh	17	17.5
Haryana	16	18.0
India		18.3
West Bengal	15	18.4
Maharashtra	14	18.8
Karnataka	13	18.9
Orissa	13	18.9
Gujarat	12	19.2
Tripura	11	19.3
Arunachal Pradesh	10	19.6
Assam	9	19.7
Tamil Nadu	8	19.9
Sikkim	7	20.2
Meghalaya	6	20.5
Punjab	6	20.5
Kerala	5	20.8
Manipur	4	21.5
Nagaland	3	21.6
Mizoram	2	21.8
Goa	1	22.2

Source: Census of India, 2001.

Anaemia among Women

Anaemia among women in different states of India is presented in Table 4.7. The majority of women in India are anaemic. Iron deficiency is particularly pronounced among women inhabiting in the eastern and almost all of the NER states (except Manipur).

Table 4.7: Women Suffering from Anaemia in India

States	Pregnant Women age 15-49 who are Anaemic (%)	Rank
1	2	3
Assam	72.0	1
Haryana	69.7	2
Jharkhand	68.4	3
Jammu and Kashmir	68.3	4
Orissa	68.1	5
Chhattisgarh	63.1	6
West Bengal	62.6	7
Sikkim	62.1	8
Rajasthan	61.7	9
Gujarat	60.8	10
Karnataka	60.4	11
Bihar	60.2	12
Meghalaya	60.2	12
Andhra Pradesh	58.2	13
India	57.9	
Madhya Pradesh	57.9	14
Maharashtra	57.8	15
Tripura	57.6	16
Tamil Nadu	54.6	17
Arunachal Pradesh	51.8	18
Mizoram	51.7	19

Contd...

1	2	3
Uttar Pradesh	51.6	20
Uttaranchal	50.8	21
Punjab	41.6	22
Nagaland	n.a	
Himachal Pradesh	39.2	23
Goa	36.9	24
Manipur	36.4	25
Kerala	33.8	26
Delhi	29.9	27

Source: NFHS-3.

The Female Infant Mortality Rate

Generally, male infants are known to be more susceptible to death than females due to biological and genetic reasons. However, in India, the female infant mortality rate surpasses that of males, which reflects socio-cultural influences on mortality (Rustogi, 2004). The female infant mortality rate of the states of India is presented and ranking is done in Table 4.8. Although the position of NER regarding IMRF is improving for some states of NER, the IMR of female is still high in Assam and Meghalaya and is significantly higher than all India average. *(table 4.8 on next page)*

Women's Participation in Decision-making/ Women Empowerment

As reported by Rustogi (2004) in the last eight general elections from 1977 to 1999, 51 to 59 per cent of women have participated as voters in India. Of the few contestants among women, the winning rate is higher than that of men. Therefore, women's participation in public decision-making is gradually improving. The percentage of currently married women who usually participate in household decisions is more in the states of the NER than the national average. However, the percentage of women who are allowed to go alone to three places [*(i)* market, *(ii)* health facility, and *(iii)* outside the community] is less in Assam, Meghalaya and Nagaland. Similarly, the percentage of women having a bank or savings account that they themselves use is less in Assam, Manipur, Mizaoram and Nagaland than the national average (refer Table 4 9). *(table 4.9 on page 49)*

Table 4.8: Infant Mortality Rates (per 1000 live births) among Females (IMRF)

States	IMRF	Rank
Kerala	14	21
Goa	15	20
Manipur	16	19
Tamil Nadu	24	18
Nagaland	28	17
Tripura	29	16
Maharashtra	29	16
Delhi	31	15
West Bengal	32	14
Arunachal Pradesh	32	14
Sikkim	32	14
Punjab	35	13
Mizoram	39	12
Karnataka	39	12
Jharkhand	44	11
J and K	45	10
Gujarat	47	9
Andhra Pradesh	47	9
Himachal Pradesh	47	9
India	49	
Haryana	49	8
Bihar	50	7
Chattisgarh	54	6
Meghalaya	56	5
Rajasthan	57	4
Assam	60	3
Orissa	61	2
Uttar Pradesh	63	1

Source: Sample Registration System (SRS), 2012.

Table 4.9: Women's Participation in Decision-Making

States	Currently Married Women who usually Participate in Household Decisions (%)	Women of Age 15-49 who are Allowed to go Alone to three Places (Market, Health Facility, and Outside the Community) (%)	A Bank or Savings Account that they Themselves use (%)
1	2	2	4
Andhra Pradesh	40.4	37.3	18.0
Arunachal Pradesh	53.5	40.2	19.0
Assam	60.9	35.3	11.7
Bihar	32.7	25.2	8.2
Chhattisgarh	26.8	17.9	8.1
Delhi	52.0	36.6	30.4
Goa	47.0	56.8	42.4
Gujarat	36.6	47.3	19.9
Haryana	41.7	40.7	12.4
Himachal Pradesh	39.2	60.4	22.2
Jammu and Kashmir	25.2	51.0	21.9
Karnataka	35.2	30.6	22.1
Kerala	47.2	34.7	27.0
Madhya Pradesh	29.4	25.7	8.9
Maharashtra	45.4	40.2	20.3
Manipur	69.4	53.5	8.0
Meghalaya	77.3	28.1	16.9
Mizoram	70.4	75.4	8.1
Nagaland	73.1	25.4	7.4
Orissa	41.8	18.7	9.8
Punjab	37.4	39	14.6

Contd...

1	2	2	4
Rajasthan	22.8	31.6	7.6
Sikkim	58.7	50.9	20.9
Tamil Nadu	48.8	54.2	15.9
Uttar Pradesh	33.7	23.4	13.2
West Bengal	23.9	32.3	14.1
India	36.7	36.8	16.2
Tripura	30.2	36.8	18.7
Uttaranchal	36.0	42.8	20.1
Jharkhand	41.8	36.6	14.4

Sources: NFHS-3, Kishore and Gupta (2009).

Violence against Women

Since the practices such as dowry and bride burning are not very prevalent in NER, there arises the presumption that violence against women is not a major concern in the region. However, the data collected by the North East Network however suggests that violence against women, particularly domestic violence, is on the rise in the North-east (National Commission for Women, 2004). It is apparent from Table 4.10 that the violence against women is lowest in Meghalaya of North East. However, domestic violence is prevalent in Tripura, Assam and Manipur in comparison with other states of India.

Conclusion

From the foregoing discussion it is clear that the status of women in the states of NER is better in some indicators than the status of women in rest of India. However, puzzling contradictions occur within each state. For example, the sex ratio is high in the states of NER implying more females in the states. However, infant mortality rate for female is high in Assam. Similarly the literacy rate is high but at the same time high dropout rate shows a different picture of the states of NER. The female literacy levels are above average in Assam and Nagaland and the gap in literacy levels is strikingly low; however, enrolment rates for girls are low than the national average. Sometimes the different sources of data may create the problems of compatibility.

Table 4.10: Different forms of Violence Experienced by Women (%) of age 15-49, 2005-06

States	Physical Violence only	Sexual Violence only	Physical and Sexual Violence	Rank on the Basis of both Physical and Sexual Violence
Delhi	14.9	0.2	1.4	25
Haryana	23.4	1.4	4.3	15
Himachal Pradesh	4.1	0.3	1.1	26
Jammu and Kashmir	10.1	0.9	1.9	22
Punjab	25.0	1.0	4.9	13
Rajasthan	27.5	4.6	12.6	3
Uttaranchal	22.1	0.4	4.2	1
Chhattisgarh	24.0	0.8	5.3	12
Madhya Pradesh	37.0	1.4	8.4	7
Uttar Pradesh	30.3	1.1	6.7	11
Bihar	38.9	2.9	13.8	1
Jharkhand	23.5	2.1	9.2	6
Orissa	24.5	3.5	8.2	8
West Bengal	19.9	6.2	12.2	4
Arunachal Pradesh	25.1	2.8	7.5	10
Assam	24.7	2.2	9.6	5
Manipur	28.8	2.1	7.9	9
Meghalaya	14.6	0.4	1.0	27
Mizoram	22.9	0.5	2.1	21
Nagaland	12.9	3.1	3.0	17
Sikkim	16.8	1.6	2.4	20
Tripura	28.9	2.5	13.2	2
Goa	12.5	0.6	1.8	23
Gujarat	20.7	2.2	4.8	14
Maharashtra	27.2	0.3	1.7	24
Andhra Pradesh	29.9	0.5	3.4	16
Karnataka	16.7	0.2	2.9	18
Kerala	12.6	1.3	3.4	16
Tamil Nadu	36.1	0.0	2.5	19

Source: NFHS-3.

Workforce participation is only one of the variables to empower the women in the society. High female employment rate may satisfy 'Practical Gender Needs' (*e.g.*, provision of water, healthcare, employment etc.,) only not the 'Strategic Gender Needs' (*e.g.*, power and control, protection from domestic violence, equal wage, and control over own body etc.). The decision on what to cook, about their own healthcare, and staying with their parents/siblings, the extent of mobility and women's ability to make these choices to go to the market or visit friends/relatives without seeking permission are also important. This study shows that the percentage of currently married women who usually participate in household decisions is more in the states of the NER than the national average. However, the percentage of women who are allowed to go alone to the market, health facility, and outside the community is less in three states, namely: *(i)* Assam, *(ii)* Meghalaya and *(iii)* Nagaland. Similarly, the percentage of women having a bank or savings account that they themselves use is less in Assam, Manipur, Mizaoram and Nagaland than the national average. These indicators reveal that women have a very low degree of freedom of movement and low level of control over themselves and ability to make change in NER. Domestic violence is also prevalent in the states of NER.

Economic development does not guarantee gender equality. In informal sector the status of women is more vulnerable. Only gender aware policies of the policy-makers and change of the mindset of the people can help in this regard.

Although the FWPR has increased in some states of NER, however, in what type of work the women are engaged is a big question. The other study reflects more casualisation of the female employment in the states in both rural and urban areas which needs serious concern. There is a criticism that only highly qualified people are getting dignified jobs after economic reform in this competitive world and the people of the rural sector are lagging far behind. A rise in the share of regular wage employment could signify an improvement in the quality of female employment only if this rise is faster than the rise in the share of other two categories namely: *(i)* self-employed and *(ii)* casual worker (Sethuraman, 1998).

Therefore, it requires state specific own individual policy to achieve gender development and gender equality within its borders. A detailed examination of women's status even at the district level is necessary to have the right information for effective planning and implementation of government policy.

REFERENCES

Burman, J. J Roy (2012), 'Status of Tribal Women in India', *Mainstream*, Vol. L, No. 12, 2012, March 10.

Census of India (2011), Provisional Population Totals, Registrar General of India. New Delhi.

Government of Assam (2012-13), *Economic Survey Assam 2012-13*, Directorate of Economics and Statistics, Assam, 2010-11.

Government of India, *Women and Men in India 2000*, Central Statistical Organisation, Ministry of Statistics and Programme Implementation. New Delhi.

Government of India (2012), *Data for use of Deputy Chairman,* Planning Commission, 10 April.

Accessed from *Planningcommission.nic.in/data/datatable/0904/comp_data0904.pdf on 24-09-12.*

Hansdak, Eva Margaret (2012), The Status of Tribal Women, in Fr. Agapit Tirkey (ed.), *Responding to India's Social Challenges – Promoting Tribal Rights and Culture*. Accessed.

from http://www.holycrossjustice.org/pdf/Asia/IndiasSocialChallenges/PromotingTribalRights/TheStatusoftribalWomen.pdf on 07-10-12.

Kishor, Sunita and Gupta, Kamala (2009), *A Report on Gender Equality and Women's Empowerment* on the Basis of National Family Heath Survey (NFHS)-3, Mumbai, India.

Mandal, R. K and Minto Ete (2010), *Women in North East India: Role and Status of Arunachal Pradesh*, Mittal Publications, New Delhi.

Mohiuddin, Yasmeen (1995), Country Rankings of Women's Status: an Alternative Index, *Pakistan Development Review*, Winter.

National Commission for Women (2004), *Violence against Women in North East India: An Enquiry,* A Report Prepared by The North East Network, New Delhi.

NSSO (2010), *Employment and Unemployment Situation in India, 2007-08*, Report No. 531, NSS 64th Round, Ministry of Statistics and Programme Implementation, May.

Parwez, M. (2012), 'Customary Laws and Practices in North East India: Records and Reports.

Preserved in Law Research Institute (Lri), Gauhati', *Indian Journal of Applied Research*, Vol. 2, Issue 3, December, pp. 81-83. Accessed from http://www.theglobaljournals.com/ijar/file.php?val=ODY2 on 23-07-13.

Phukon, Dolly (2009), 'Status of Women in Assam-Continuity and Change', in Lalneihzovi (ed.) *Changing Status of Women in North-Eastern States*, Mittal Publications, New Delhi, pp. 17-28.

Rustogi, Preet (2004), Significance of Gender-related Development Indicators: An Analysis of Indian States, *Indian Journal of Gender Studies*, Vol. 11, No. 3, Sage Publications, pp. 291-343. Accessed from http://www.dise.in/Downloads/Use%20of%20Dise%20Data/Preet%20Rustagi.pdf on 26-02-12.

Sample Registration System (2012), *SRS Bulletin*, 46(1), December, New Delhi: Registrar General of India.

Swayam (2001), *The Status of Women: A Reality Check*, A Report Published by Swayam, A Women's Rights Organisation, Kolkata.

Zehol, Lucy Vashum (2010), Status of Tribal Women. Accessed from http://dspace.nehu.ac.in/bitstream/1/2733/1/Status.pdf on 07-10-12.

5

Violence against Women

Dr. M Dhanabhakyam
Nisamudheen. T

Abstract

Violence against women is partly a result of gender relations that assumes men to be superior to women. Given the subordinate status of women, much of gender violence is considered normal and enjoys social sanction. This article examines the problem of violence against women. The promotion of gender equality is an essential part of violence prevention. A range of school, community and media interventions aim to promote gender equality and non-violent relationships by addressing gender stereotypes that allow men more power and control over women. These include some well-evaluated interventions, but more evaluations are needed that use measures of actual violent behaviour as an outcome rather than improvements in attitude or knowledge, whose relation to violent behaviour may be unknown. Mainly two objectives are involved in this study. The tools used for this study is percentage analysis. The study focused on the violence against women in Calicut University.

Keywords: *Gender equality, violence, violence against women, women and violence.*

INTRODUCTION

Violence against women is a technical term used to collectively refer to violent acts that are primarily or exclusively committed against women. Similar to a hate crime, this type of violence targets a specific group with the victim's gender as a primary motive.

Cultural and social factors are interlinked with the development and propagation of violent behaviour. With different processes of socialization that men and women undergo, men take up stereotyped gender roles of domination and control, whereas women take up that of submission, dependence and respect for authority. A female child grows up with a constant sense of being weak and in need of protection, whether physical social or economic. This helplessness has led to her exploitation at almost every stage of life.

The law distinguishes several types of violence against women: psychological violence, physical violence, economical violence and sexual violence. Psychological violence is considered to be any act or omission that can hurt a woman's psychological stability, such as humiliation, negligence, abandonment, jealousy and threats and result in depression, isolation, devaluation of a woman's self-esteem or even suicide. Physical violence against women includes every act that inflicts no accidental damage by the use of physical force or some kind of weapon or object that can cause internal or external lesions. Patrimonial violence represents any act or omission that affects the victim's survival such as the transformation, destruction or withdrawal of objects, personal documents, patrimonial rights or damage caused to the common or private goods of the victim. Economic violence is every act or omission that affects economic survival of the victim, for example the control of income but also receiving less salary for the same type of work within the same organization. Sexual violence is every act that degrades or hurts the body or sexuality of the victim and is thus considered an assault against the woman's bodily integrity, dignity and liberty.

Statement of the Problem

Violence against women is increasing day-by-day. Because of the lack of a strong law victims are escaped easily through the loopholes of law. Women of all ages and backgrounds are at risk of many different types of violence. In fact, millions of women and girls in this country have experienced violence. Violence greatly affects the lives and health of women: the impact can last for year even a lifetime. But there are places to turn for help, ways to protect yourself, and hope for healing and a better future.

Objectives of the Study

1. To know the type of violence and effect of violence on women.
2. To analyse the factors influencing violence against women.

Scope of the Study

The scope of the study is limited to Female students in Calicut University, Calicut. The sample size of the survey is 50. The objectives are fixed based on the support of review available and analysis that has been made. In short the study has been conducted within the stipulated framework.

Research Methodology

The type of Research Method is adopted was descriptive research.. Both primary and secondary data are collected for the completion of this project. Primary data are collected using questionnaires and direct interview. Questionnaires are circulated among the Female students in Calicut University, Calicut. The sample size of the survey is 50.

Limitations of the Study

- The study is limited only to female students in Calicut University, which may fail to give a correct picture of the study.
- The researcher faces some difficulty due to the lack of co-operation from some respondents.
- The bias of respondents cannot be completely ruled out.

Types of Violence

(i) Domestic Violence

Women are more likely to be victimized by someone that they are intimate with, commonly called 'Intimate Partner Violence' or (IPV). The impact of domestic violence in the sphere of total violence against women can be understood through the example that 40-70 per cent of murders of women are committed by their husband or boyfriend. Studies have shown that violence is not always perpetrated as a form of physical violence but can also be psychological and verbal. In unmarried relationships this is commonly called dating violence, whereas in the context of marriage it is called domestic violence. Instances of IPV tend not to be reported to police and thus many experts believe that the true magnitude of the problem is hard to estimate. Women are much more likely than men to be murdered by an intimate partner. In the United States, in 2005, 1181 women, in comparison with 329 men, were killed by their intimate partners. In England and Wales about 100 women are killed by partners or former partners each year while 21 men were killed in 2010. In 2008, in France, 156 women in comparison with 27 men were killed by their intimate partner.

Though this form of violence is often portrayed as an issue within the context of heterosexual relationships, it also occurs in lesbian relationships, daughter-mother relationships, roommate relationships and other domestic relationships involving two women. Violence against women in lesbian relationships is about as common as violence against women in heterosexual relationships.

Diagnosis Planning

The American Psychiatric Association planning and research committees for the forthcoming DSM-5 (2013) have canvassed a series of new Relational disorders which include Marital Conflict Disorder Without Violence or Marital Abuse Disorder (Marital Conflict Disorder With Violence). Couples with marital disorders sometimes come to clinical attention because the couple recognises long-standing dissatisfaction with their marriage and come to the clinician on their own initiative or are referred by an astute health care professional. *Secondly*, there is serious violence in the marriage which is – "usually the husband battering the wife". In these cases the emergency room or a legal authority often is the first to notify the clinician. Most importantly, marital violence "is a major risk factor for serious injury and even death and women in violent marriages are at much greater risk of being seriously injured or killed (National Advisory Council on Violence Against Women 2000)". The authors of this study add that "There is current considerable controversy over whether male-to-female marital violence is best regarded as a reflection of male psychopathology and control or whether there is an empirical base and clinical utility for conceptualizing these patterns as relational".

Recommendations for clinicians making a diagnosis of Marital Relational Disorder should include the assessment of actual or 'potential' male violence as regularly as they assess the potential for suicide in depressed patients. Further, "clinicians should not relax their vigilance after a battered wife leaves her husband, because some data suggest that the period immediately following a marital separation is the period of greatest risk for the women. Many men will stalk and batter their wives in an effort to get them to return or punish them for leaving. Initial assessments of the potential for violence in a marriage can be supplemented by standardised interviews and questionnaires, which have been reliable and valid aids in exploring marital violence more systematically".

The authors conclude with what they call 'very recent information' on the course of violent marriages which suggests that "over time a husband's battering may abate somewhat, but perhaps because he has successfully intimidated his wife. The risk of violence remains strong in a marriage in which it has been a feature in the past. Thus, treatment is essential here; the clinician cannot just wait and watch". The most urgent clinical priority is the protection of the wife because she is the one most frequently at risk, and clinicians must be aware that supporting assertiveness by a battered wife may lead to more beatings or even death.

(ii) Mob Violence

In 2010 Amnesty International reported that mob attacks against single women were taking place in Hassi Messaoud, Algeria. According to Amnesty International, 'some women have been sexually abused' and were targeted "not just because they are women, but because they are living alone and are economically independent".

(iii) State Violence

War and Militarism

Militarism produces special environments that allow for increased violence against women. War rapes have accompanied warfare in virtually every known historical era. Rape in the course of war is mentioned multiple times in the Bible: "For I will gather all the nations against Jerusalem to battle and the city shall be taken and the houses plundered and the women raped..." Zechariah 14:2 "Their little children will be dashed to death before their eyes. Their homes will be sacked, and their wives will be raped". Isaiah 13:16.

War rapes are rapes committed by soldiers, other combatants or civilians during armed conflict or war, or during military occupation, distinguished from sexual assaults and rape committed amongst troops in military service. It also covers the situation where women are forced into prostitution or sexual slavery by an occupying power. During World War II the Japanese military established brothels filled with "comfort women", girls and women who were forced into sexual slavery for soldiers, exploiting women for the purpose of creating access and entitlement for men.

Another example of violence against women incited by militarism during war took place in the Kovno Ghetto. Jewish male prisoners had access to (and used) Jewish women forced into camp brothels by the Nazis, who also used them.

Rape was committed during the Bangladesh Liberation War by members of the Pakistani military and the militias that supported them. Over a period of nine months, hundreds of thousands of women were raped. Susan Brownmiller, in her report on the atrocities, said that girls from the age of eight to grandmothers of seventy-five suffered attacks. (See also: Rape during the Bangladesh Liberation War)

Violence in Empowerment Systems

When police officers misuse their power as agents of the state to physically and sexually harass and assault victims, the survivors, including women, feel much less able to report the violence. It is standard procedure for police to force entry into the victim's home even after the victim's numerous requests for them to go away. Government agencies often disregard the victim's right to freedom of association with their perpetrator. Shelter workers are often reduced themselves to contributing to violence against women by exploiting their vulnerability in exchange for a paying job.

(iv) Gender-based Violence by Male College Athletes

Violence against women is a topic of concern in the United States' collegiate athletic community. From the 2010 UVA lacrosse murder, in which a male athlete was charged guilty with second degree murder of his girlfriend, to the 2004 University of Colorado Football Scandal when players were charged with nine alleged sexual assaults, studies suggest that athletes are at higher risk for committing sexual assault against women than the average student. It is reported that one in three college assaults are committed by athletes. Surveys suggest that male student athletes, who represent 3.3 per cent of the college population, commit 19 per cent of reported sexual assaults and 35 per cent of domestic violence. The theories that surround these statistics range from misrepresentation of the student-athlete to an unhealthy mentality towards women within the team itself.

Controversy over Contributing Factors

Sociologist Timothy Curry, after conducting an observational analysis of two big time sports' locker room conversations, deduced that the high risk of male student athletes for gender abuse is a result of the team's subculture. [He states, "Their locker room talk generally treated women as objects, encouraged sexist attitudes toward women and, in its extreme, promoted rape culture. [He proposes that this objectification is a way for the male to reaffirm his heterosexual status and hyper-masculinity. Claims have been made that the atmosphere changes when an outsider (especially women) intrude in the locker room.

Response to Violence by Male College Athletes

In response to the proposed link between college athletes and gender-based violence, and media coverage holding Universities as responsible for these scandals more universities are requiring athletes to attend workshops that promote awareness. For example, St. John's University holds sexual assault awareness classes in the fall for its incoming student athletes. Other groups, such as the National Coalition Against Violent Athletes, have formed to provide support for the victims as their mission statement reads, "The NCAVA works to eliminate off the field violence by athletes through the implementation of prevention methods that recognise and promote the positive leadership potential of athletes within their communities. In order to eliminate violence, the NCAVA is dedicated to empowering individuals affected by athlete violence through comprehends.

Forms of Violence

Many terms are used to describe violence against women:

- Intimate partner violence.
- Domestic violence.
- Indecent exposure.
- Spouse or partner abuse.
- Voyeurism.
- Wife beating.
- Stalking.
- Rape, marital rape, date rape.
- Harassment.
- Family violence.
- Human trafficking.
- Sexual abuse, sexual violence, sexual.
- Exploitation.
- Molestation.
- Forced prostitution.
- Beating, battering.
- Forced pornography.

Effects of Violence on Women

Mental health	Women hurt by violence may have: • Depression. • Low self-esteem, loss of confidence. • Posttraumatic stress disorder (PTSD). • Guilt or shame. • Shock and disbelief. • Anxiety and panic attacks. • Emotional numbness. • Anger. • Self-hate or self-blame. • General sense of fear. • Fear of men, being alone, going out in public, intimacy, or anything that may trigger memories of the violence.

	• Suicidal thoughts. • Sense of being worthless or without hope.
Behaviour	Common physical injuries and health problems from violence include: • Increased risk of sexually transmitted infections (STIs) and HIV, which can lead to pelvic inflammatory cancer disease and a higher risk of cervical. • Unwanted pregnancies, or rapid, repeat pregnancies. • Miscarriages and other reproductive problems. • Vaginal bleeding or pelvic pain. • Injuries such as bruises, cuts, broken bones, or internal damage. • Back or neck pain. • Chronic pain syndrome. • Trouble sleeping and nightmares. • High blood pressure or chest pain. • Arthritis. • High stress and lowered immune system. • Central nervous system problems, such as headaches, seizures, or nerve damage. • Respiratory problems, such as asthma and shortness of breath.
Economic	Common financial struggles due to violence are: • Loss of income from missed work or a partner who withholds money. • Medical bills. • Legal fees. • Rent or moving costs of new housing. • Extra child care and protection costs.
Social	Common social issues due to violence include: • Stigma and discrimination. • Trouble getting medical, social, and legal services. • Strained relationships with friends and family. • Social isolation (from family, friends, and others who could help).

Analysis and Discussion

The number of students surveyed is 50. The questionnaire prepared on the basis of various factors which influence the women independence. The response of students in Calicut University, Calicut has given in Tables 5.1 to 5.3.

Age-based Classification of Respondents

Table 5.1 shows the age based classification of respondents. 46 per cent of the respondents are come under the age group of 22-24, 26 per cent of the respondents are come under the age group of 24-26 and 4 per cent, 24 per cent of the respondents are come under the age group of 18-20, 20-22 respectively.

Table 5.1: Age-based Classification of Respondents

Age	No. of Respondents	Percentage
18-20	2	4
20-22	12	24
22-24	23	46
24-26	13	26
Total	**50**	**100**

Source: Primary Data.

Sexual Abuse or Threats Against Women

Table 5.2 shows that majority of the respondents (68%) are not sexually abused by their boyfriends or others. But 20 per cent of the respondents are sometimes sexually abused by some persons, 12 per cent of the respondents are rarely abused and no one always abused sexually by boyfriends or others.

Table 5.2: Sexual Abuse or Threats

Opinion	No. of Respondents	Percentage
Never	34	68
Rarely	6	12
Sometimes	10	20
Always	0	0
Total	**50**	**100**

Source: Primary Data.

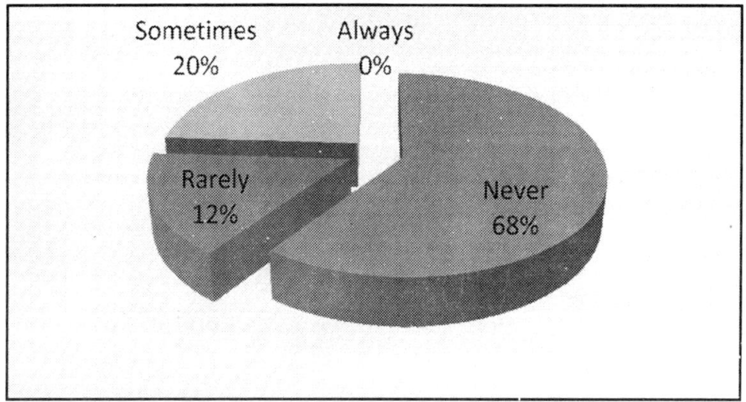

Fig. 5.1: Sexual Abuse or Threats

Psychological or Emotional Abuse Against Women

Table 5.3 shows the psychological or emotional abuse against women. Psychological or emotional abuse includes trace your phone calls, insult you and get angry about small things, accuse you of cheating, make fun of you, control how you spend your money or refuse to give you money, act jealous when you spend time with friends, blame you for his or her violence, use your children to manipulate you, follow you when you go out, try to make you afraid. 42 per cent of the respondents are rarely abused psychologically or emotionally from their boyfriends or others, 34 per cent of the respondents are sometimes abused psychologically or emotionally from their boyfriends or others, 14 per cent of the respondents are not abused and 10 per cent of the respondents are always abused psychologically or emotionally from their boyfriends or others.

Table 5.3: Psychological or Emotional Abuse

Opinion	No. of Respondents	Percentage
Never	7	14
Rarely	21	42
Sometimes	17	34
Always	5	10
Total	**50**	**100**

Source: Primary Data.

So we can conclude that most of the respondents have happening psychological or emotional abuse from someone.

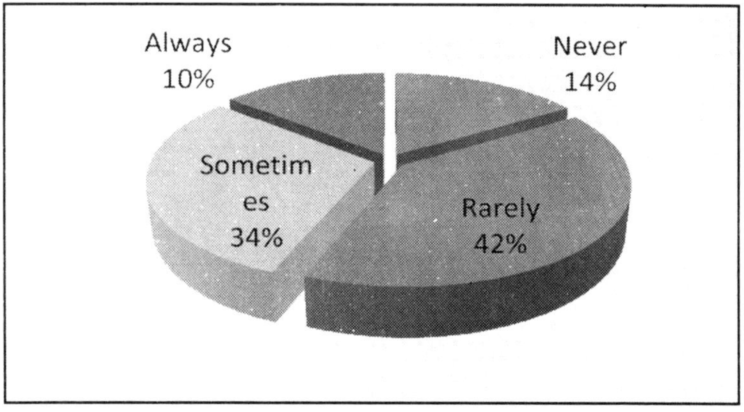

Fig. 5.2: Psychological or Emotional Abuses

Physical Violence or Threats Against Women

Table 5.4 shows the respondents opinion about physical violence or threats against women. Physical violence or threats includes hurt or threaten you – possibly with a weapon, become violent after alcohol or drug use, destroy your things etc. 40 per cent of the respondents are rarely happening physical violence or threats, 24 per cent of the respondents are sometimes happening physical violence or threats from their boyfriends or others, 16 per cent of the respondents are not happening physical violence or threats and 20 per cent of the respondents are always happening physical violence or threats. So we can conclude that most of the respondents have happening physical violence or threats.

Table 5.4: Physical Violence or Threats

Opinion	No. of Respondents	Percentage
Never	8	16
Rarely	20	40
Sometimes	12	24
Always	10	20
Total	**50**	**100**

Source: Primary Data.

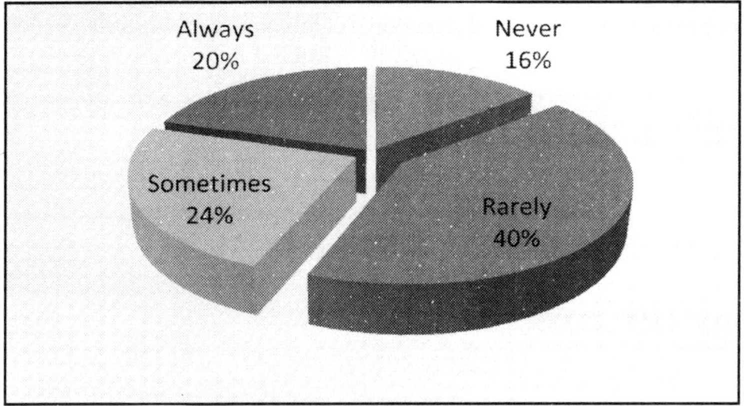

Fig 5.3: Physical Violence or Threats

Suggestions

- In this study some of the respondents are sexually abused by their boyfriends or others, to avoid this problem Government has to introduce a new scheme for giving awareness to girls about sexual matters.
- By reporting physical or sexual abuse against women to the concerned authority we can avoid this problem up to a limited extent.
- Government should introduce strict laws for the protection of women.

Conclusions

Violence against women is a technical term used to collectively refer to violent acts that are primarily or exclusively committed against women. Similar to a hate crime, this type of violence targets a specific group with the victim's gender as a primary motive. The promotion of gender equality is an essential part of violence prevention. A range of school, community and media interventions aim to promote gender equality and non-violent relationships by addressing gender stereotypes that allow men more power and control over women. These include some well-evaluated interventions, but more evaluations are needed that use measures of actual violent behaviour as an outcome rather than improvements in attitude or knowledge, whose relation to violent behaviour may be unknown. From this study we can clearly understood that violence against women are increasing day-by-day. When the government passed strong laws for the protection of women, also the violence against women are increasing.

REFERENCES

Barrett, K. A., O' Day, B., Roche, A., and Carlson, B. L. (2009), Intimate Partner Violence, Health Status, and Healthcare Access among Women with Disabilities. *Women's Health Issues*, 19, pp. 94-100.

Brittney N. Baack. (2008), Intimate Partner Violence and Women with Disabilities: The Relationship between Experience of Violence, Social Support and Mental Health.

Guptha C., Human Resource Management, Sulthan Chand and Sons, New Delhi, 2004.

Kothari C. R, Research Methodology, New Age International Privet Limited, New Delhi, 2004.

6

Rural Women's Development in India

R. Sathyakumar
Dr. M. Dhanabhakyam

Abstract

India is a land of villages and more than 74 per cent of population is living in the rural areas. In rural area, rural women constitute nearly 48 per cent of the country's population. The development India depends upon the development of rural masses and economic empowerment has changing the lives of many poor people including the women, by providing them economic gain on going and sustained basis. Entrepreneurship and literacy is suitable for economic empowerment of rural women. Women's economic empowerment is absolutely essential for raising their status in the society. Women have a good combination of entrepreneurial spirit, Ambition, discipline and restrains. Education provides women with the knowledge and skills to contribute to and benefit from development efforts and environment. The present study deals with the rural women's developmental activities like education and entrepreneurship in India and this study find out various motivating factors of rural women's in India.

Keywords: *Economic Empowerment, Entrepreneurship, Education, Rural Women.*

INTRODUCTION

Women in India constitute nearly 50 per cent of its population. According to 1991 census, there were 40.6 crores of women as against 43.7 crores of men. Roughly, there are 929 women for every 1000 men. Man considers woman to be frail and weak by nature. She is shorter and delicate compared to the strongly build man. But man forgets that a woman is made so, so to play a specific fro in nature which a man cannot play, that is the role of the mother. In intelligence both are equal. Man is aggressive and emotional. A woman is patient, calm and receptive. She can bear more pain and has more tolerance than a man. She is stronger in conviction and in perseverance. Yet women all over the world are playing a secondary role only. The position in India is no different. Women were overvalued in epics and puranas, for their service to their men. Serving a father first, secondly a husband, and later serving her children and grandchildren, had been her lot. Puranas mention the names of Seeta, Savitri and Anusuya and glorify them for their devote service to their husbands. They even say that a woman can easily get salvation by serving her husband. After Independence the Constitution of India gave equal rights to men and women in all walks of life. But even today one cannot say that all women in India enjoy equal rights with men in all matters.

The Following Reasons

- The customs and traditions prevalent for centuries.
- The high percentage of illiteracy among women.
- Ignorance of their rights.
- Patriarchal society.
- Economic system.
- Unchecked male domination in all walks of life.

In spite of all these problems mentioned above, one could see that the condition of India women has improved a lot. There are now adequate educational facilities for girls and women. Special incentives and reservations are there to encourage them to study. Even in employment there are special reservations.

Objectives and Methodology of this Study

The study is based on secondary data which is collected from the published reports of RBI, Census, Surveys, journals, websites, etc.

The Study was Planned with the Following Objectives

1. To study the literacy position of women's in India.
2. To study the rural women's entrepreneurship in India.
3. To study the opportunities and challenges faced by women entrepreneurs in India.

Empowerment of Women in India

Empowerment of women involves many things like economic opportunity, property rights, political representation, social equality, personal rights and so on. The need for women's empowerment arises from the subordinate position they have been accorded for a long time. The empowerment has been felt as a tool to bring about changes in their socio-economic condition. It has been felt on the part of nation as well as individual that no society can progress till women, a major constituent of society, lag behind. Empowerment of women needs to begin with her participation in different spheres of life. Education is a great determinant in this regard. To achieve empowerment women have to be educated to be aware of their rights and privileges in a modern society. It is education which can bring about awareness in them related to their social status, injustice and differentiation meted out to them. Besides, economic independence is a major factor which can contribute in empowering women. India in the very beginning realised this need.

Empowerment of Women in India is Conspicuous by Many Live Examples

Delegating power or an authority to a woman seemed astonishing to our governing bodies. Ironically, our country, our leaders and governing bodies in particular, are being ruled by Smt. Sonia Gandhi who is a woman. It is that woman who had been ranked 13th among world's most powerful women by Forbes magazine. It's a woman who is leading Indian National Congress as its president. Sonia Gandhi would be an epitome of women's leadership qualities. She did umpteen things what a male leader couldn't do. Smt. Mamta Banerjee is the next big name; she has managed to break the jinx of Communist Party in Bengal who has ruled there for more than half the century. She is the Railway minister of India and is working hard to improve the image of Indian railway. Smt. Mayawati who is the Chief Minister of Uttar Pradesh and president of the Bahujan Samaj Party is the most influential name in the Indian Politics. Smt. Pratibha Devisingh Patil is the first women President of India and is actively working for the upliftment of Indian women.

The year 2009 witnessed the History written moments when Smt. Meira Kumar became the first Indian women to hold the office of the Lok Sabha Speaker. She is an ex-IFS officer and hails from the Bhojpuri land clearly indicating the women power in politics. Women could really do more than what they actually think they can. The real power within a woman is exuded by the first woman IPS Officer Kiran Bedi. The ability of a woman to break the barriers and tread on a new path was proved by her. People usually get carried by the myth that men can do far better than women. Indian women dispelled the myth by making their footprints in almost every field of work.

Women are not only law-makers and law-controllers, but also Business magnates. Chanda Kochhar is the current CEO and MD of ICICI Bank. She was born in 1961 and now heads ICICI Bank. The CEO and Chairperson of PepsiCo, Indra Nooyi, born in 1955, sets the perfect model of a Business magnate. She carved out a niche for herself in Business. Nafisa Ali who was actress, model and politician is now an eminent social worker, with her crusade on HIV/AIDS being world recognised. She has been appointed as the Chairman of the Environment Committee of Commonwealth Games Delhi 2010. She is industrious in the area of health, women and child rights poverty and social development. She reached out to the masses and made a significant difference in lives of the people. Tennis star Sania Mirza and Badminton player Saina Nehwal made their mark representing India. Women have the inherent potential to overlook any impediments, to commit themselves to their ambitions and eventually drive the nation by fulfilling them. The real empowerment is attained only when they are wise-enough and highly-powered to make decisions and women, when authoritative, would turn into economic carriers of India.

Women's Education in India

For the past few centuries in India, the girl has been completely neglected even as a human being and she live as if only to support and satisfy men. In every home even today the boys are still pampered and given the best of everything and the girls of the same family are almost completely ignored.

Even in the basic requirement of education, girls are left out because it is felt that, they in any case have only to look after their homes and the needs of their families, so, where are the need to study? The only requirement of women is even today, to look after the needs of others and give birth to children, and no more they need to have. For this task of home keeping assigned to women, it is felt by all that there is no need for them to go to school. It is considered foolish to allow girls to waste their time in studies and this concept is widely accepted by the Indian society but now Indians are realised women's education is highly necessary for this society, so now a day they don't hesitate to send their daughters to schools. Now in India we find women professors, lady doctors, lady scientists, lady politicians and lady ministers.

Table 6.1: Female Literacy Rates in India (1951-2011)

Year	Urban %	Rural %
1951	22.33	4.87
1961	40.50	10.10
1971	48.80	15.50
1981	56.30	21.70
1991	64.00	30.00
2001	73.20	46.70
2011	79.95	58.82
CAGR	23.68	51.97

Source: Census of India.

Table 6.1 after the independence, an Indian woman's are mostly illiterate in rural people. The female literacy rate in India 1951 was 22.33 per cent in urban and 4.87 per cent rural areas. After that the women's are getting more aware about education and realised the essential of education. The government policies and schemes also motivating the rural women's in education. Currently the female literacy rate in India 2011 is 79.95 per cent in urban and 58.82 in rural areas. Overall growth of female literacy rate both urban and rural is showing positive growth rate, rural women's are getting fast growth in education compare with urban women's.

Women's Entrepreneurship in India

The country has undergone tremendous changes and has experienced higher rate of growth-economically industrially and technologically. Increasing educational facilities, industrialization, new economic policy, positive approach of government, availability of financial resources, entrepreneurship development, training facilities and changing socio-economic political environment encouraged women to enter into entrepreneurial activity. In India, numerically, though women are almost in equal numbers to men, and participating in all the lines of activity, including so called male dominated business, the number of women entrepreneurs is conspicuously low. In early 1970s women entrepreneurs were neglected and were not given much importance in economy.

Initially, women who entered into entrepreneurial activity were mainly involved in traditional items like handicrafts, food processing and food products. In 1975, after the declaration of 'International women's year' the women entrepreneurs begun to change and realising their role in economic and nation development.

Rural Women Entrepreneurs

Rural women entrepreneurs are those entrepreneurs who actually hail form reside in rural areas *i.e.*, either from a 'panchayat' and mobilise human resources requirements from those areas in which they live. "A rural women entrepreneur is a women or group of women who undertake to organize and run an enterprise in a rural area". The government of India notes women entrepreneurs as "an enterprise owned and controlled by women saving a minimum financial interest of 51 per cent of the capital and giving at least 51 per cent of the employment generated in the enterprise to women".

Policies and Programmes for Entrepreneurship Development among Rural Women

- Government Initiatives for Women Empowerment.
- Development Policies for Rural Women.
- National Machinery for Empowering Rural Women.
- Development of Women and Children in Rural Areas (DWCRA).
- Swarnajayanti Gram Swarojgar Yojana (SGSY).
- Rashtriya Mahila Kosh (RMK).
- National Commission for Women (NCW).
- Mahila Samridhi Yojana (MSY).
- Indira Mahila Yojana (IMY).
- Mahila Swayam Sidha Yojana (MSSY).
- Janani Suraksha Yojana (JSY).
- Raj Rajeshwari Mahila Kalyan Yojana (RRMKY).
- Maher Yojana.
- Annapoorna Yojana.
- Kamdhenu Yojana.
- Mahila Swavalamban Nidhi (MSN).
- Reception Centres and State Homes for Women.

Schemes of Indian Banks for Rural Women Entrepreneurs

- National Bank for Agriculture and Rural Development (NABARD).
- IDBI's Mahila Udyam Nidhi (MUN) and Mahila Vikas Nidhi (MVN).
- Priyadarshani Yojana of Bank of India.
- Stree Shakti Yojana of State Bank of India.
- Small Industries Development Bank of India (SIDBI).

Non-governmental Organizations (NGOs)

- National Alliance of Young Entrepreneurs (NAYE).
- National Association of Women Entrepreneurs and Executives (NAWEE).
- Self-employed Women's Association (SEWA).
- Federation of Indian Women Entrepreneurs (FIWE).
- International Centre for Entrepreneurship and Career Development (ICECD).

Opportunities and Problems Faced by Women Entrepreneurs in India

Opportunities for Rural Women Entrepreneurs

(i) *Integrated Rural Development Programme*: The main objectives of Integrated rural development Programme is to increase the income generating power of family who are below the poverty line to alleviate the poverty. They impart technical and entrepreneurial skills and raise the income level of the poor. Some of the major employment and anti-poverty programme are:

(a) *IRDP (Integrated Rural Development Programme)*: and its programmes:

- TRYSEM (Training Rural Youth for Self Employment).
- DWCRA (Development of Women and Children in Rural Areas).
- *JRY (Jawahar Rozgar Yojna)*: It is wage Employment programme. Implemented by Panchayats at Village, Block and District level in the ratio. 70:15:15 etc.

(ii) Regional Rural Development Centres.

(iii) Technology for Bank.

(iv) Fund for Rural Innovation.

(v) Social Rural entrepreneurship.

(vi) Entrepreneurship Development Institute of India.

Problem faced by Rural Women Entrepreneurs in India

Problems faced by women entrepreneurs Apart from the tacit assumption that women are frail and indecisive, women entrepreneurs encounter many problems in their efforts to develop the enterprises they have established. The main problems faced by the women entrepreneurs may be analysed as:

- *Shortage of Finance*: Women and small entrepreneurs always suffer from inadequate financial resources and working capital.
- *Inefficient Arrangements for Marketing and Sale:* For marketing their products, women entrepreneurs are often at the mercy of the middlemen who pocket large chunks of profit.
- *Shortage of Raw Materials:* Women entrepreneurs find it difficult to procure raw materials and other necessary inputs. The failure

of many women cooperatives in 1971 such as those engaged in basket-making was mainly due to the inadequate availability of forest raw materials. The prices of many raw materials are quite high.

- *Stiff Competition:* Many of the women enterprises have imperfect organisational setup. They have to face severe competition from organised industries and male entrepreneurs.
- *High Cost of Production:* Another problem which undermines the efficiency and restricts the development of women enterprises is the high cost of production.
- *Low Mobility:* One of the biggest handicaps for women entrepreneurs is mobility or travelling from place to place. Women on their own find it difficult to get accommodation in smaller towns.
- *Family Responsibilities:* In India, it is mainly women's duty to look after the children and other members of the family. Their involvement in family leaves little energy and time for business. Married women IJCEM.

Women's Contribution in Economic Activities

Although half the population of India comprises of women, yet the businesses owned and operated by them constitutes less than 5 per cent. This is a reflection of social culture as well as economic distortion in the decades of development. However, women's contribution and participation in economic activity and production of goods and services is much greater than statistics reveals, since much of it takes place in the informal sector and also in households.

Since the turn of the century, the status of women in India has been changing due to growing industrialization and urbanisation, special mobility, and social legislation. Over the years, more and more of women are going in for higher education, technical and professional education. Their proportion in the labour force has also increased. With the spread of education and awareness, women have shifted from the extended kitchen, handicrafts and traditional cottage industries to non-traditional higher levels of activities. During the 1970s – the decade of the international women's year, efforts to promote self-employment among women received greater attention from the government and private agencies. The new industrial policy of the government of India has laid special emphasis on the need to conduct special entrepreneurial training programmes for women to enable them to start their own venture.

Conclusion

In India, women's are play vital role in several sectors. They are contributed more in economic development. The government of India offering many facilities for rural women's development such as education facilities and financing to rural women entrepreneurs, but in some states rural women's are not so aware and literate as to handle all the legal and other formalities involving in loan taking and establishing an Industrial Unit and also some problems are faced by the rural women entrepreneurs. Compare with last two decades, now Indian women's are developed and showing positive growth in all activities.

REFERENCES

Charumathi, B., (1998), "Women Entrepreneur's Challenges and Prospects", in C. Swarajya.

Lakshmi, ed., Development of Women Entrepreneurship in India: Problems and Prospects (New Delhi, Discovery Publishing House).

Meenu Agrawal, Shobana Nelasco (2009), "Empowerment of Rural Women in India" Kanishka Publishers, New Delhi.

Ram Naresh Thakur (2009), "Rural Women Empowerment in India" in Empowerment of Rural Women in India Kanishka Publishers, New Delhi.

Dr. Suryani Motik, MGA President, Indonesian Businesswomen Association. "Significant Roles of Women Entrepreneurs in Economic Development".

Dr. Anita Mehta and Dr. Mukund Chandra Mehta (2011), "Rural Women Entrepreneurship in India: Opportunities and Challenges".

G. Sandhiyarani (2010), "Women's Education in India – An Analysis" *Asia Pacific Journal of Social Sciences.*

National Policy on Education, – POA, Ministry of Education, Government of India, 1986.

National Institute of Public Corporation and Child Development, Statistics of Women in India, 2010.

7

Empowerment of Rural Women in India

K. P. Bholane

Abstract

Empowerment of rural women has emerged as an important issue in recent times. Women's empowerment in India is heavily dependent on many different variables that include geographical location (urban/rural), educational status, social status (caste and class), and age. Policies on women's empowerment exist at the national, state, and locals (panchayat) levels in many sectors, including health, education, economic opportunities, gender-based violence, and political participation. This paper explained the areas of empowerment, approaches to empowerment and government of empowerment of rural women.

INTRODUCTION

"You can tell the condition of a nation by looking at the status of its women"

– Jawaharlal Nehru

A woman is the nucleus of the family, particularly, in rural India. She not only collects water, fuelwood, fodder and food but also plays a significant role in preserving the culture, grooming the children and shaping their destiny. Therefore Dr. Manibhai Desai always emphasised that although women represent only 50 per cent of the total population, they contribute 75 per cent to the development of our society while men contribute only 25 per cent. Unfortunately, in spite of their laudable roles, which cannot be substituted by machine or men, women have been neglected since generations. It is said in Manu Samhita (Chapter II, Para 145) that a Guru who teaches Veda is 10 times superior to an ordinary teacher and the father is 100 times more than a teacher, but the Mother is 1000 times more superior than the father.

For the rural women, the day starts early in the morning with the responsibilities of fetching water, fodder, fuel and cooking food. She takes care of the children and members of the family, their health, orientation and education and attends to various income-generation activities. She manages all the household matters, looks after the family assets and live-stock, handles the purchases and finance, works for almost 14-16 hours and is the last to sleep at night. Still, when you ask her children what their mother does? Most of them instantly reply 'nothing'. There is no recognition for their hard work, just because her work is not evaluated in terms of money. She often falls sick, but does not complain and this goes unnoticed by others in the family as they continue to work as usual for the sake of the family. Today women are the worst sufferers in the society due to drudgery, ill health, illiteracy, deprivation and humiliation. Backwardness of women is a sign of poverty. Lack of empowerment of women is a significant cause of poverty.

Areas of Empowerment of Women

- ***Drudgery Reduction***

The extent of burden and sufferings of the rural women in India vary widely with the social and economic status, local customs, size of family and many other factors. Hence, an intensive study with close interaction with women can help to identify suitable solutions for their problems. Following drudgery reduction measures can be introduced for women:

(a) Creation of safe drinking water sources closer to their houses.

(b) Maternal and child health and family welfare.

(c) Strengthening of traditional health care practices.

(d) Training of midwives and upgrading the skills.

(e) Awareness on health, hygiene and sanitation.

(f) Awareness of girl's education.

- ***Gender Equality***

Elder male members of the family always see women subdued and non-interfering. Therefore men should be sensitized about the benefits of women empowerment, particularly, with respect to development of children and enhancement of skills for income-generation. Recognition of their services to the family and society could empower them further and provide equal status in the society. Creation of awareness among men could enlist greater support for women participation in the various development programmes. In many regions, the men have taken a path contrary to tradition, to empower the women.

In Uttar Pradesh, some Village Panchayat Committees comprising of 5 men (Panch) announced that all the women in the village should be treated as daughters and sisters. This gave a boost to women's participation in various community development programmes. In Rajasthan, where many SHGs had decided to impose fine on members arriving late for the meetings, many men encouraged their wives to attend the meetings on time by taking the responsibility of cooking for the family on those days.

- ***Leaders in Community Development***

The community has recognised the status of the women and their contribution in not only managing their families, but also to the economic and social development of the entire community. Women have shown their capacity to play a major role in community development. With such significant contribution to the society, most women are participating in Gram Sabhas. Many active leaders of the Self-Help Groups have contested and been elected for various co-operative bodies and other village level organizations. The leadership of women has been recognised by the society. They are now able to influence the Panchyati Raj Institutions to work for the benefit of the communities. The dark days when they had to struggle for their rights and status in the society, are vanishing.

Approaches for Empowerment of Rural Women

The approaches for empowerment of rural women can be divided into four broad heads: *(i)* Educational Empowerment, *(ii)* Social Empowerment, *(iii)* Economic Empowerment and *(iv)* Technological Empowerment.

(i) ***Educational Empowerment:*** Education is the key which opens the door to life, develops humanity and promotes national development. Education can be an effective tool for women's empowerment. It enables rural women to acquire new knowledge and technology required for improving and developing their tasks in all fields. Therefore, at least one Functional Literacy Centre should be opened in each Gram Panchayat area with a view to make all and rural farm women functionally literate and adult education necessary.

(ii) ***Social Empowerment:*** Empowering women contribute to social development. Economic progress in any country whether developed or underdeveloped could be achieved through social development. Hence, women's empowerment cannot be ignored, while devising various policies for rural and socio-economic development.

(a) *Status of Women:* Even country has made progress in developing women's capabilities, but inequalities continue to exist between women and men. The low status of women is the outcome of a variety of causes in which patriarchal values reinforced by tradition, media and other socio-political institution play a major role. Thus, the institutional bases of women's oppression have to sensitize to accept the gender equality and moreover, women's perception of themselves would also need to be changed.

(b) *Cultural Bias:* Cultural traditions and economic necessity have always meant a significant role for women in agriculture. In India it is not uncommon that women do

not have control over the land. Even, where women constitute a larger share of a agricultural producers but, there are cultural constraints to easy communication between men and women, because almost all extension workers are men.

(c) *Health and Nutrition:* Health and nutrition are two very important basic needs for empowerment of rural women. To achieve real and quicker development in health sector, an extensive as well as intensive "Health Education and Awareness Campaign" (HEAC) needs to be given topmost priority and it should mainly stress on nutritional education, benefits of immunization, family planning etc.

(iii) Economic Empowerment: Empowering women with economically productive work will enhance their contribution to agricultural development.

(a) *Access to Resources*: The farm women need to have control over limited resources like land and livestock, so that they could take away decisions and implement them in any way that is required. Ownership and control over productive assets will create a sense of belonging and owning. It will thus help to take responsibility in family and local group activities. Other impact of control is to enhance their decision-making ability to meet some physiological needs like self-esteem and confidence.

(b) *Micro-Credit Programmes:* Micro-credit programmes extend small loans to poor people for self-employment projects that generate-income allowing them to care for themselves and their families. In most cases, micro-credit programmes offer a combination of services and resources to their clients in addition to credit for self-employment. Access to productive resources is critical for enhancing women's economic choices. Since, formal credit institutions rarely lend the poor, special institutional arrangement may become necessary to extend credit to those who have no collateral to officer their enterprises. In order to have access to credit, setting up self-help group, local banking system by women, Non Governmental

Organizations and provision of facilities by Government need to be established. The policy challenge is to support effective grass-roots credit schemes and intermediaries ad ensure that low-income have assured credit from the formal financial system. Access to Co-operatives – and Local Women's Organizations Collectivization has been recognised as a tenet of women's empowerment. It has been defined as a process of bringing a group of women together at a base to become an integral part 0 an economic activity. Organizational efforts should be made for integrating farm women into development. Organization of Mahila Mandals, Co-operatives, Societies and Discussion Groups will serve this purpose. The control of these organizations should be in the hands of womenfold themselves. Also, the present beneficiary to women's development should be replaced by participatory approach. Technological Empowerment: Through women are involved in almost all agricultural operations, in rural areas yet, they have inadequate technical competency due to their limited exposure to outside world. This has compelled them to follow the age old practices which in turn result in poor work efficiency and drudgery and needed computer, internet latest informations.

(c) *Capacity Building:* Capacity building and empowennent are important for which there should be decentralised capacity building among the rural women particularly farm women. Empowennent projects should go beyond the provision of basic social services for all. They should include components vital for enabling the poor to participate in economic activities. It is important to develop the skills among farm women in order to increase their productivity and to keep them abreast of modernization and technological changes for being competitive in the market.

(d) *Exposure to Mass Media*: The transfer of technology approach, which mainly includes mass media are also not paying due attention towards dissemination, of adequate and timely agricultural and marketing information to the farm rural women. Therefore, there is outmost need to provide adequate coverage to the programmes related to women and they must get exposure to mass media for improving their communication and meditation skills to strengthen their capacity to contact and mediate with external world.

(e) *Appropriate Training Programme*: Training is an important component of HRD which enhances knowledge, skill and attitude. For building technical competency among women, need-based skill oriented training programmes to reinforce their role in farm activities need special attention. The training programmes should initially be organized on their felt needs and then be switched over to unfelt but essential needs. To achieve this sacred task, infrastructural facilities in terms of more numbers of KVKs, FTCs and BRLP should be established in the district on priority basis.

(f) *Appropriate Technology for Women:* In order to cater the technological needs of farm rural women, women specific technologies should be developed. While evolving agricultural technologies, indigenous practices used by women should be paid due attention for blending with the frontier ones for greater adoption. Also there is need to strengthen linkage between research and extension organizations engaged in transfer of technology. Measures to strengthen women's empowerment and rural development: Empowennent of women is the prime objective of all development programmes and policies. These programmes could be planned properly and implemented effectively in order to attain self sufficiency and self-reliance.

Women Empowerment Programmes of Government

Government has been implementing various programmes which support women to take up new ventures and start self employment, which has been categorised under four heads:

1. *Empowering Strategies*: Indian Mahila Yojana, Mahila Samriddhi Yojana. The rural women's development and empowerment project now called as Swashakti Poject, development of women and children in rural area.
2. *Employment and Income-Generation*: Training of Rural youth for Self-Employment, Swayamsidha, Swawlamban, Support for Training and Employment Programme, Norwegian Agency for Development Co-operation Socio-Economic Programme. Condensed Courses of Education and Vocational Training, Swamjayanti Gram Swarozgar Yojna, Women's Vocational Training Programme, Swama Jayanti Shahari Rozgar Yojna, Urban Self Employment Programme, Development of Women and Children in Urban Areas, Jawahar Rozgar Yojna, Trade Related Entrepreneurship Assistance and Development, National Rural Health Mission, National Rural Employment Guarantee Scheme. Efforts are being made to merge support for Training and Employment Programme with other three programmes *i.e.,* NORAD, SEP and CCEVT thus bringing out an umbrella scheme of training and employment for women.
3. *Welfare and Support Services*: Hostels for working women, Swadhar, crèche house, day care centres for the children of working and ailing mothers.
4. *Other Enabling Measures*: Rashtriya Mahila Kosh, a national mechanism to meet micro-credit needs of poor and asset less women in the informal sector. Also known as the National Credit Fund for Women.

Initiatives of P.R.I.D.E. India

Two major initiatives taken by P.R.I.D.E. INDIA (Planning Rural-Urban Integrated Development through Education) with regard to the empowerment of women are the formation of various Self-Help Groups (SHG's) and the initiation of the Vipula Credit Co-operative Society. Since the financial services of the formal banking system have traditionally remained inaccessible to a majority of the poorer sections of the rural population, especially women, an initiative was made by P.R.I.D.E. INDIA to initiate a women's cooperative on the principle of mutual help. However, its success was limited as the operational area was in selected pockets only due to limited resources. Against this background, to meet the credit needs of rural women from the operational areas, P.R.I.D.E. INDIA initiated the creation of Self-Help Groups. The following are the core principles that apply to all P.R.I.D.E.'s micro-finance programmes:

(i) Serve the poorest clients, with a focus on women.

(ii) Promote solidarity and group guarantees.

(iii) Savings Mobilization.

(iv) Support capacity building/training.

(v) Increase productive assets.

(vi) Ensure a child-focused perspective.

(vii) Promote culturally appropriate program approaches.

(viii) Plan for sustainability.

Conclusion

With various women empowerment activities and training, there has been a significant increase in the confidence of women. There are various programmes conducted by governments and non-government organizations, but what is needed is that such programmes should be implemented properly, effectively and efficiently so that women will really be empowered.

REFERENCES

Empowerment of Women for Improved Quality of Life: BAIF's Approach, Retrieved on 2 August, 2013 from http://www.baif.org.in/doc/Empowerment_of_Women/Women%20Empowerment%20Approach%20Paper.doc.

Gupta K. (2009), Empowerment of Rural Women for Rural Development. Shodh, Samiksha aur Mulyankan, *International Research Journal*, Vol. II (6), pp. 869-871.

An Article "Much Needed to be Done to Empower Women" Published in *'The Hindu'* on April 21, 2013.

Upadhyay R. (2011), Women's Empowerment in India: An Analytical Overview, Retrieved on 30 June 2013 from http://asiafoundation.org/resources/pdfs/womensempowermentindiabriefs.pdf

8

A Study on Perspective of Women's Emerging Role, Status and Women's Rights

Anu Priya. M
Dr. M. Dhanabhakyam

Abstract

Women's roles in India have been changing and women are now emerging from the past traditions into a new era of freedom and rights. Women were considered inferior to men in practical life. But in scriptures they were given high position. Thus in past, the status of women in India was not clear. It was theoretically high but practically low. Women were prohibited to take part in domestic as well as in external matter. They were under the influence of their parents before marriage and their husbands after marriage. In spite of it, many women are suffering mental and physical tortures in their in-laws' houses. Their husbands demand more and more dowry. They consider their wives as good source of getting dowry. Bride-burning and bride – killing occur every day in India. This is how the status of Indian women is going down. The women can get back their rightful place in society if law is properly enforced to check male-superiority. The foundation of freedom, justice and peace in the world is the recognition that all men and women are born free and equal in rights and dignity. Women, like men, have individual and common roles, expectations and interests in society. In processes of democratization, conflict resolution, peace building, and security, sustainable solutions are not possible if women's voices are discounted or ignored. Study is designed to know the changing role of women and to find out the status of women in today's modern world and their respective women's rights. Three objectives are framed for the study. Surveys conducted by Census are used for the study. The necessity for educating women is not only for family, society and country, but also for their self-development and self-recognition and personal success.

***Keywords**: Equal in Rights, Emerging Role, Interests in Society, Self-development, Status of Women.*

INTRODUCTION

Emerging Role of Women World over

- Women have always been looked at as the care giver and as the home keeper.
- Being the symbol of the family, women have always been the home and have not been out in the other arenas of life.
- Women have played different roles in the family depending on their age and place in the household.
- When there is a sudden change in society, women have always stood up to assist and these moments have been recorded in history.
- After Second World War, there were important developments in education – the raising of the minimum school – leaving the age to 14 (1962), the entry of increasing numbers of girls and women into secondary and higher education.
- When women entered the work force, they then had a rallying point.
- When women started to be independent they wanted to wait on getting married and having children.

Women in India

- One of several factors that justify the greatness of India's ancient culture is the honorable place granted to women.
- Raja Ram Mohan Roy started a movement against the deprivation of women rights, inequality and subjugation.

- The contact of Indian culture with that of the British also brought improvement in the status of women.
- Another factor in the revival of women's position was the influence of Mahatma Gandhi who induced women to participate in the Freedom Movement.
- But in spite of this amelioration in the status of women, the evils of illiteracy, dowry, ignorance, and economic slavery would have to be fully removed in order to give them their rightful place in Indian society.
- Women continue to play a marginal and peripheral role in the overall national context despite constituting almost half the population with a critical role in production and social processes.

Objectives

1. To study the emerging role of women at different levels.
2. To study the status of women in present world.
3. To know about the various rights given to women's.

Methodology

This study is based on secondary data collected from various sources for the purpose of knowing the position of women in India. In addition to this supportive data is collected from various books, journals, libraries and news papers. Three objectives are framed for the study. Surveys conducted by Census are used for the study.

Women in India – Past and Present

- Mahatma Gandhi stressed, *"subjugation and exploitation of women was a product of man's vested teachings and women's acceptance of them*".
- There is need to resolve certain basic issues about the socialisation processes.
- *Evidently, E-components:* education, employment, earnings, empowerment, entitlement to property and effects of violence.
- Reservation of women at the village level but situational analysis reveal that majority of positions are acted upon by men.
- India today, a country where women are becoming more prominent. Yet increasing numbers, women are fighting long-standing prejudices.

- Women still faces enormous pressure to conform to social mores.
- Conforming to traditional roles within families poses as much of a barrier to business women in India as the still-too-thick glass ceiling at companies.
- Though women have made great strides in the corporate world in the last three decades, women from all income classes are still too often discouraged by family members from having careers that infringe too much on family life.
- The country's long history of valuing education, so women who achieve academically are seen as smart and savvy.

Women in India – Success and Oppression

Women in Banking and Finance

Lalita Gupte:
Former Joint MD of ICICI

Arnavaz Aga Popularly Anu Aga:
Former Chairperson of Thermax India

Women in Business and Technology

Neelam Dhawan
MD Hewlett Packard, India

Dr. Kiran Mazumdar Shaw
Chairman and Managing Director, Biocon Limited

Late Kalpana Chawla
(PH.D.) NASA Astronaut

Mayawati
Chief Minister
Uttar Pradesh Four Times

Status of Women

- Women have not achieved equality with men in any country.
- Women's life expectancy, educational attainment and income are highest in Sweden, Canada, Norway, USA and Finland.
- Their place is considered at home and public life is controlled by man.
- They play secondary role in decision-making.
- Their self-worth is undermined.
- Their self-concept is based on men's perception.
- Social institution socialise them into subordinate role.
- Parenting is primarily a women's concern.
- Women have less opportunities than men.
- They are treated as sex object: *(i)* prostitution, *(ii)* trafficking and *(iii)* pornography.
- There are unequal power relations between men and women in the family and society.
- Designation of male as 'head of household' for all social-economic and political purposes.

Women and Labour

- They are last to be hired and first to be fired.
- Their work is invisible and economic contribution is not recognised.

- They suffer triple burden of work and drudgery.
- No sharing of household work.

Women and Health

- Many women die due to unsafe and illegal abortion.
- Women are vulnerable to RTI and HIV/AIDS infection from men.
- Safe pregnancy care, rest, reduced workload beyond the reach.
- Girls and women face nutritional discrimination eating last and least.

Women in Difficult Circumstances

- Women in extreme poverty.
- Widow/deserted/separated.
- Forced prostitution and trafficking.
- Victim of rape and sexual harassment.
- Victim of domestic violence.
- Victim of marital disputes/conflicts.
- Women of alcoholic/drug addicts husband.
- Women with physical disabilities unwed mothers.
- Women in conflict with law and women prisoners.
- Women worker in bondage.
- Women used as drug peddlers.
- Women used in pornography.
- Victim of socially sanctioned practices-witch, prostitution, sati, genital mutilation.
- Victim of caste, class and gender.

Literacy Rate

The literacy rate is the number of educated people in a population, over the age of fifteen who can read and write.

As per Census of India statistics report, literacy rate has improved in last decade. As a result of free education system in the villages, the literacy rate has gone up tremendously, especially among females.

Literacy rate has increased from 64.83 per cent in 2001 to 74.04 per cent in 2011.

Male literacy -82.14 per cent

Female literacy -65.46 per cent

Number of Literates

Male and Female -778,454,120

Males 444,203,762

Females -334,250,358

Details of male and female literacy rates and the overall literacy rates in Indian States and Union Territories as per census data 2011.

India's Literacy Rate: Census

Sl. No.	State	2011 Census			2001 Census			
		Literacy (%)	Male (%)	Female (%)	Literacy (%)	Male (%)	Female (%)	Change (%)
1	2	3	4	5	6	7	8	9
–	**India**	**74.04**	**82.14**	**65.46**	**65.38**	**75.85**	**54.16**	**8.66**
1.	Kerala	93.91	96.02	91.98	90.86	94.24	87.72	3.05
2.	Lakshadweep	92.28	96.11	88.25	86.66	90.72	80.47	5.62
3.	Mizoram	91.58	93.72	89.40	88.80	92.53	86.75	2.78
4.	Tripura	87.75	92.18	83.15	73.19	82.42	64.33	14.56
5.	Goa	87.40	92.81	81.84	82.01	88.62	76.47	5.39
6.	Daman and Diu	87.07	91.48	79.59	78.18	86.14	67.42	8.89
7.	Puducherry	86.55	92.12	81.22	81.24	86.33	73.90	5.31
8.	Chandigarh	86.43	90.54	81.38	81.94	88.42	75.37	4.49
9.	Delhi	86.34	91.03	80.93	81.67	87.33	75.24	4.67
10. 11.	Andaman and Nicobar Islands	86.27	90.11	81.84	81.30	86.76	74.71	4.97
12.	Himachal Pradesh	83.78	90.83	76.60	76.48	85.35	65.61	7.3
13.	Maharashtra	82.91	89.82	75.48	76.88	85.97	67.03	6.03
14.	Sikkim	82.20	87.29	76.43	68.81	77.38	59.63	13.39
15.	Tamil Nadu	80.33	86.81	73.86	73.45	83.28	64.91	6.88
16.	Nagaland	80.11	83.29	76.69	66.59	76.04	56.87	13.52
17.	Manipur	79.85	86.49	73.17	70.53	80.33	61.46	9.32

Contd...

1	2	3	4	5	6	7	8	9
18.	Uttarakhand	79.63	88.33	70.70	71.62	81.02	63.36	8.01
19.	Gujarat	79.31	87.23	70.73	69.14	78.49	60.40	10.17
20.	Dadra and Nagar Haveli	77.65	86.46	65.93	57.63	68.82	43.53	20.02
21.	West Bengal	77.08	82.67	71.16	68.64	77.02	59.61	8.44
22.	Punjab	76.68	81.48	71.34	69.65	79.66	60.53	7.03
23.	Haryana	76.64	85.38	66.77	67.91	76.10	59.61	8.73
24.	Karnataka	75.60	82.85	68.13	66.64	76.06	57.80	8.96
25.	Meghalaya	75.48	77.17	73.78	62.56	71.18	50.43	12.92
26.	Orissa	73.45	82.40	64.36	63.08	71.28	50.51	10.37
27.	Assam	73.18	78.81	67.27	63.25	75.23	51.85	9.93
28.	Chhattisgarh	71.04	81.45	60.59	64.66	75.70	55.73	6.38
29.	Madhya Pradesh	70.63	80.53	60.02	63.74	75.35	54.61	6.89
30.	Uttar Pradesh	69.72	79.24	59.26	56.27	67.30	43.00	13.45
31.	Jammu and Kashmir	68.74	78.26	58.01	55.52	66.60	42.22	13.22
32.	Andhra Pradesh	67.66	75.56	59.74	60.47	71.16	50.29	7.19
33.	Jharkhand	67.63	78.45	56.21	53.56	63.83	38.87	14.07
34.	Rajasthan	67.06	80.51	52.66	60.41	70.32	43.85	6.65
35.	Arunachal Pradesh	66.95	73.69	59.57	54.34	65.43	40.23	12.61
36.	Bihar	63.82	73.39	53.33	47.00	59.68	33.12	16.82

The Literacy rate in India has improved a lot over the last one decade. Especially after the implementation of free education in the villages the literacy rate has gone up tremendously in states like Himachal Pradesh and Rajasthan.

India's literacy level has increased by 9.21 per cent in the past 10 years to reach 74.04 per cent, according to provisional data of the 2011 census.

According to the data, literates constitute 74 per cent of the total population, aged seven and above, and illiterates form 26 per cent. (*See both the figures on page no. 97*)

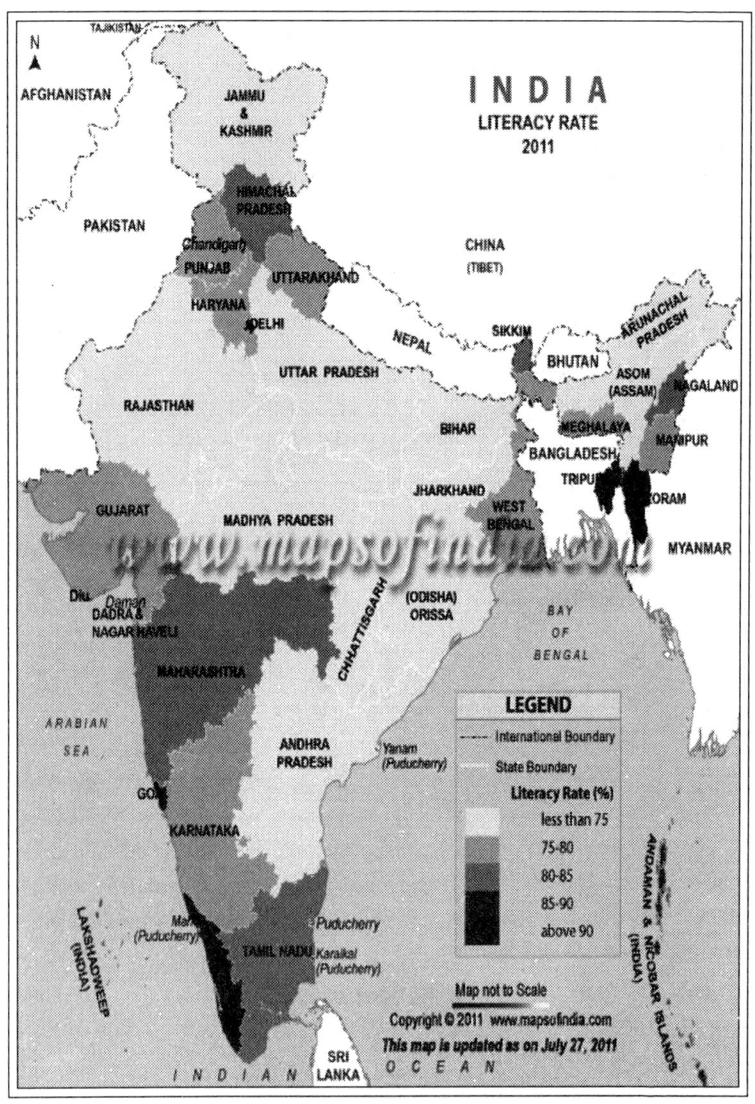
INDIA
LITERACY RATE
2011
N
TAJIKISTAN
AFGHANISTAN
PAKISTAN
CHINA
(TIBET)
NEPAL
BHUTAN
BANGLADESH
MYANMAR
SRI LANKA
JAMMU & KASHMIR
HIMACHAL PRADESH
Chandigarh
PUNJAB
UTTARAKHAND
HARYANA
DELHI
UTTAR PRADESH
RAJASTHAN
SIKKIM
ARUNACHAL PRADESH
ASOM (ASSAM)
NAGALAND
MEGHALAYA
MANIPUR
BIHAR
JHARKHAND
WEST BENGAL
GUJARAT
MADHYA PRADESH
Diu
Daman
DADRA & NAGAR HAVELI
MAHARASHTRA
CHHATTISGARH
(ODISHA) ORISSA
BAY OF BENGAL
ARABIAN SEA
ANDHRA PRADESH
Yanam (Puducherry)
KARNATAKA
LAKSHADWEEP (INDIA)
(Puducherry)
Puducherry
TAMIL NADU
Karaikal (Puducherry)
ANDAMAN & NICOBAR ISLANDS (INDIA)
INDIAN OCEAN
LEGEND
International Boundary
State Boundary
Literacy Rate (%)
less than 75
75-80
80-85
85-90
above 90
Map not to Scale
Copyright © 2011 www.mapsofindia.com
This map is updated as on July 27, 2011

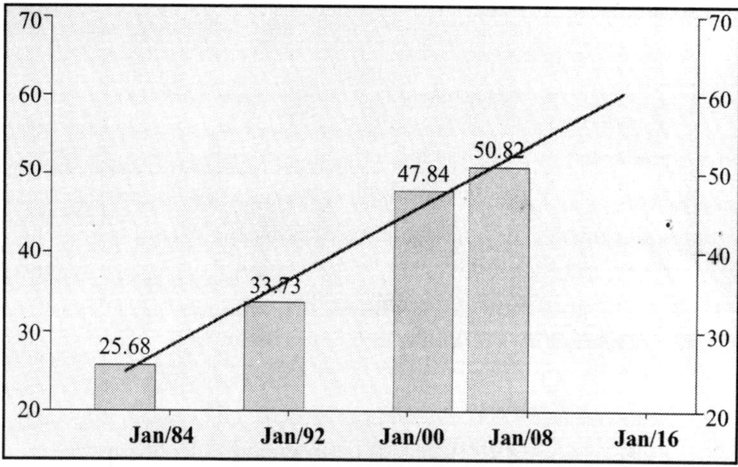

Fig. 8.1: Literacy Rate; Adult Female (% of Females Ages 15 and Above) in India

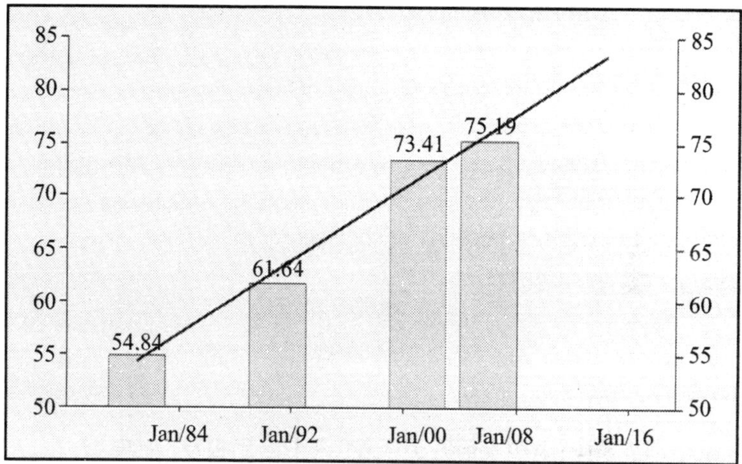

Fig 8.2: Literacy Rate; Adult Male (% of Males Ages 15 and Above) in India

The literacy rate went up from 64.83 per cent in 2001 to 74.04 per cent in 2011 showing increase of 9.21 per cent.

While female literacy in 2001 stood at 53.67 per cent, it has gone up to 65.46 per cent in 2011. The male literacy in comparison rose from 75.26 to 82.14 per cent.

Kerala with 93.91 per cent continues to occupy the top position among states in the field of literacy while Mizoram's Serchhip (98.76%) and Aizawl (98.50%) recorded highest literacy rates among districts.

Lakshadweep with a literacy level of 92.28 per cent, while Bihar remained at the bottom of the ladder with a literacy rate of 63.82 per cent followed by Arunachal Pradesh at 66.95 per cent.

Ten states and UTs *viz*; Kerala, Lakshadweep, Mizoram, Tripura, Goa, Daman and Diu, Puducherry, Chandigarh, NCT of Delhi and Andaman and Nicobar Islands achieved literacy rate of above 85 per cent, the target set by the Planning Commission to be achieved by 2011-12.

The gap of 21.59 percentage points recorded between male and female literacy rates in 2001 census has reduced to 16.68 percentage points in 2011. Planning Commission has set up target of reducing this gap to 10 percentage points by 2011-12.

Sex Ratio – A Social Indicator

Sex ratio is the number of females per 1000 males in the population. It is an important and useful indicator to measure gender equity in a society at a given point of time.

Census India usually brings out the sex ratio information. Changes in gender composition largely reflect the underlying social, economic and cultural patterns of the society in different ways.

Results of Census 2011

Total population of India is 1,21,01,93,422 which consists of 62,37,24,248 males and 58,64,69,174 females with the sex ratio of 940 females per 1000 males.

Sex Ratio and Child Sex Ratio (0-6 years) India

Year	Sex Ratio	Child Sex Ratio
1991	927	945
2001	933	927
2011	940	914

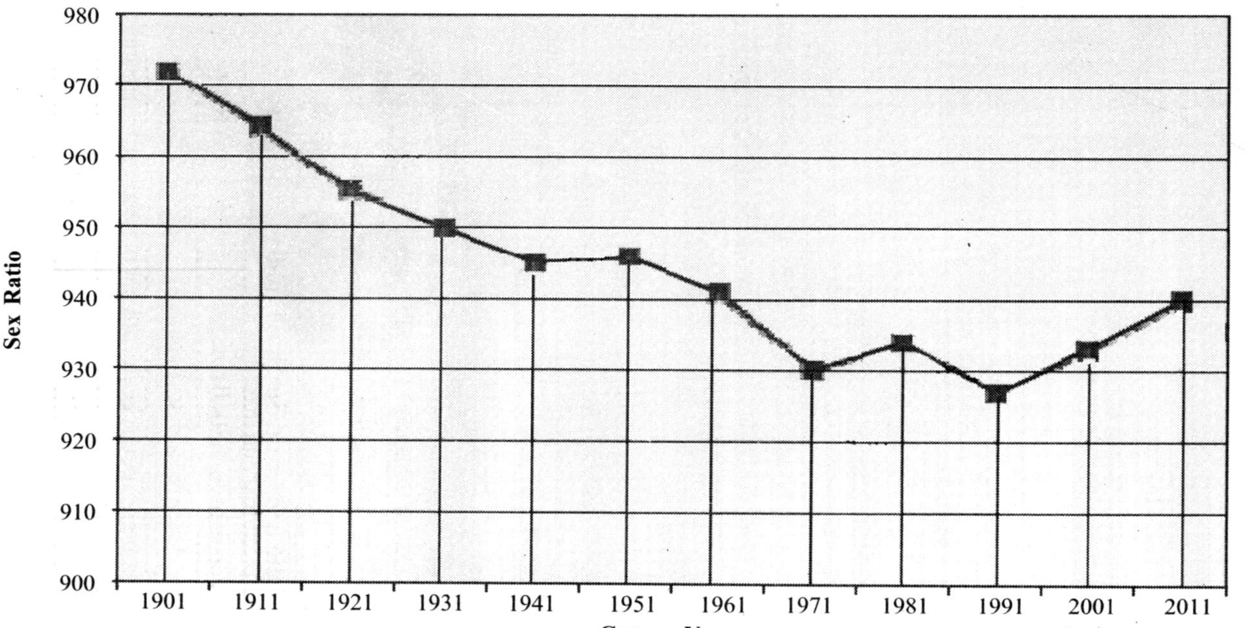

* :Provisional Population – Census 2011.

Sex Ratio is Defined as the Number of Females per Thousand Males

Fig. 8.3: Trends of Sex Ratio in India :1901-2011*

Top Five States/Union Territories with High Sex Ratios (females per 1000 males):

1. Kerela 1,084.
2. Puducherry 1,038.
3. Tamil Nadu 995.
4. Andhra Pradesh 992.
5. Chhattisgarh 991.

States/Union Territories with Low Sex Ratios (females per 1000 males):

1. Daman and Diu 618.
2. Dadra and Nagar Haveli 775.
3. Chandigarh 818.
4. NCT of Delhi 866.
5. A and N Islands 878.

In India, sex ratio is skewed in favor of males and has continued to rise and expand in various forms.

Trends in Sex Ratio

Historically sex ratio in India as remained favourable to males Sex ratio of total population has seen upward surge in the last two consecutive censuses In 2011 Census, Sex ratio in India increased to 940 from 934 recorded in the 2001 Census.

Women's Right

- Women are exposed to different kinds of violence.
- Women are at risk before birth, during their life and even after death.
- Living without fear and in a safe environment is a must.

The Preamble

We, The People of India, Having Solemnly Resolved to Constitute India into a Sovereign Socialist Secular Democratic Republic and to Secure to All its Citizens: Justice, Social, Economic and Political;

- *Liberty* of thought, expression, belief, faith and worship.
- *Equality* of status and of opportunity and to promote among them all.
- *Fraternity* assuring the dignity of the individual and the unity and integrity of the Nation.
- The Preamble assures dignity of individuals – which includes dignity of women.
- Equality of status and of opportunity to every man and women.

Fundamental and Women Rights

- Right to equality.
- Right to freedom.
- Right to equal opportunity.
- Right against exploitation.
- Right to freedom of religion.
- Cultural and educational rights.
- Right of women to economic development.

(a) Offences Affecting Life

(i) Dowry Death

- *Punishment:* Shall be punished with imprisonment of either description for a term which shall not be less than 7 years imprisonment which may extend to imprisonment for life time.

(ii) Abetment of Suicide

- *Punishment:* Shall be punished with imprisonment of either description for a term which may be extend to 10 years and shall also be liable to a fine.

(b) Cruelty by Husband or Relatives of Husband

- *Punishment:* Shall be punished with imprisonment of either description for a term which may extend to 3 years and shall be liable to fine.

(c) Wrongful Restraint and Confinement

- *Punishment:* Imprisonment for a term which may extend to 1 month or with a fine which may extend to 500/- Rs. or with both.

Equal Pay for Equal Remuneration

Duty of employer to pay equal remuneration to men and women workers for the same work or work of similar nature.

No discrimination to be made while recruiting men and women workers.

Maternity Laws

International Labour Organization adopted a convention in 1919 concerning the employment of women before and after child birth and gave the following conclusions:

- Women employee should have a right to a maternity leave with wages for 12 weeks.
- Should be provided half an hour break twice a day.

Restrictions

- No women shall work during the 6 weeks immediately following the day of her delivery.
- No employer shall employ a women during the 6 weeks immediately following the day of her delivery.

No women should be allowed to do any work:

- Which is arduous in nature.
- Which involves long hours of standing.
- That would interfere with her normal pregnancy.

Payment of Medical Bonus

Every woman entitled to maternity benefit to receive medical bonus of '250.

Leave of Miscarriage

On termination of pregnancy, women should be entitled for a leave of 2 weeks.

Nursing Breaks

Women returning to duty after delivery should be given interval for 2 breaks for nursing the child.

Mode of Advertising

- Conferences and Seminars.
- Workshops.
- Pamphlet and Magazines.

(d) Hurt and Grevious Hurt

- *Punishment for Hurt:* Shall be punished with imprisonment of either description for a term which may extend to 7 years and shall also be liable to fine.
- *Punishment for Grievous Hurt using Instrument:* Shall be punished with imprisonment of life, or with imprisonment either description for a term which may extend to 10 years and shall also be liable to fine.

Conclusion

- Women today are more practical and rational than earlier.
- Indian women have never been as expressive and independent as she is today.
- Women today, consider themselves as the true 'ardhangini' of their husbands. She is more cognizant of his world today and she understands his work pressures.
- Women-from being a care-taker/nurturer to a friend in the role of a Mother.
- It is widely felt that earning power allows them to voice their opinions on bigger decisions.
- Today's women no more feel that a career would be at the cost of neglecting the family and children.
- The Indian woman is also spending a lot more money on her personal appearance.

> *Civilization is a method of living and an attitude of equal respect for all people.*
>
> ***– Jane Addams***

Important to Understand

* Women are God's beautiful creation.
  - It is important to protect, treat and respect all women.
* The Government is making all efforts to protect the girl child. It has enacted various laws for their protection.
  - Every female citizen, should be aware of their rights.
* It is the duty of every man to stand by a woman and defend her rights and respect her dignity.

NOTES

Women and Law – Dr. S. R. Myneni.

Women and the Law – Dr. G. B. Reddy.

Women and Human Rights – Dr. Syed Maswood.

Justice for Women – A. S. Ahmed.

REFERENCES

Agnihotri, S. D. (2000), "Sex Ratio Patterns in the Indian Population: A Fresh Exploration", Sage Publications, New Delhi.

Bardhan P. (1988), *Sex Disparity in Child Survival in Rural India,* 473-480.

Mitra, A. (2008), "The Status of Women among the Scheduled Tribes in India", *Journal of Socio-Economics*, 37(3): 1202-1217.

Mitra, A. and Singh, P. (2008), "Trends in Literacy Rates and Schooling among the Scheduled Tribe Women in India", *International Journal of Social Economics*, 35, Issue 1 and 2.

Janaki R., Chandrasekarayya, T. and Murthy, P. (2011), "Declining Child Sex Ratios in India: Trends, Issues, and Concerns," *Asia Pacific Journal of Social Sciences* III(1): 183-198.

Jha, P., Kumar R., Dhingra, V. P., Thiruchelvam, D., Moineddin, R. (2006), "Low Female to Male Sex Ratio of Children Born in India: National Survey of 1.1 Million Households," Lancet 367: 211-18.

Singh, M. and Mohan, V. (2005), "The Rise of Sex Selection in India," Democracy at Large 2(1), 30-32.

Census of India (2011), *Final Population Totals Series 1: India Registrar General and Census Commissioner India.*

National Sample Registration Survey, 2011.

www.censusindia.gov.in

MAKE A DIFFERENCE, BRING A CHANGE,

KNOW YOUR RIGHTS, BE BRAVE AND FIGHT!!!!!!!!!!!

9

Rural Women Entrepreneurs

Motivational Factors Underpinning and the Encountered Problems

Anjan Kumar Bordoloi
Bishnu Prasad Chetry

Abstract

Indian women of today have taken many strides towards business ownership. The broad classification of women business owners include women who establish, inherit, or acquire a business; women who start businesses with spouses or business partners but are either at the forefront or behind the scenes; and finally, women who start fast-growing or part-time or slow-growing firms. Although earlier researches on women entrepreneurs have suggested that significant differences existed between female and male entrepreneurs. However, more recent studies have shown that there are far more similarities than differences between women and men entrepreneurs in terms of psychological and demographic characteristics. A series of researches have also shown that the workforce of women-owned businesses tend to be more gender balanced than the workforce of men-owned businesses, although women business owners are more likely to hire women. This study was carried out as the role of women entrepreneurs has gained significance in today's environment. Women, who succeed as entrepreneurs, are risk taking personalities. The women entrepreneurs have their own identity in the world of entrepreneurship as most of them are capable of fully identifying themselves in their new economic role in the society. The study highlighted the factors that have motivated women entrepreneurs in starting an entrepreneurial career with that of the encountered problems.

Keywords: *Rural, Women, Entrepreneurs, Motivational Factors, Problems, Assam.*

Prologue

An entrepreneur can be defined as one who initiates and establishes an economic activity or enterprise. Entrepreneurship thus refers to the general trend of setting up of new enterprises in a society (Begum, 1993). The International Labour Organization (ILO, 1984, cited in Islam and Aktaruzzaman, 2001) defines an entrepreneur as a person with a set of characteristics that typically includes: self-confidence, result oriented, risk taking, leadership, originality and future oriented. Khanka (2002) referred to women entrepreneurs as those who innovate, imitate or adopt a business activity. Given that entrepreneurship is the set of activities performed by an entrepreneur, it could be argued that being an entrepreneur precedes entrepreneurship.

Entrepreneurs play a very important role in the socio-economic welfare of the country. They identify needs of the business; purchase the other factors of production and coordinates with them for some productive purposes. They are the innovators, researchers and risk takers of the company. Due to mixed economy in India, both public and private entrepreneurship exist here. Large scale sectors are in public entrepreneurship and the middle and small-scale sectors are in private entrepreneurship. In order to develop entrepreneurship in India, Government of India has stepped towards Entrepreneurship Development Programmes.

Entrepreneurship plays an important role in developing and contributing to the economy of a country. It is related to the rapid industrialization. In India, entrepreneurship development has been accepted as a strategy for achieving the twin objectives of promoting entrepreneurship and also speeding up rapid industrialization. During the last two decades, Indian women have entered the field of entrepreneurship in greatly increasing numbers. With the emergence and growth of their businesses, they have contributed to the global economy and to their surrounding communities. The routes women have followed to take leadership roles in business are varied. Yet, most women business owners have overcome or worked to avoid obstacles and challenges in creating their businesses. The presence of women in the workplace driving small and entrepreneurial organizations creates a tremendous impact on employment and business environments.

Women entrepreneurs may be defined as the women or a group who initiate, organize and operate a business enterprise. Women constitute almost half of the population in the world. But their representation in gainful employment is comparatively low. But the global evidences supports that women have been performing exceedingly well in different spheres of activities like academics, politics, administration, social work and so on and now they have started plunging into industry also and running their enterprises successfully. Indian women business owners are changing the face of businesses of today, both literally and figuratively. The dynamic growth and expansion of women-owned businesses is one of the defining trends of the past decade, and all indications are that it will continue unabated. For more than a decade, the number of women-owned businesses has grown at one-and-a-half to two times the rate of all businesses. Even more important, the expansion in revenues and employment has far exceeded the growth in numbers.

The result of these trends is that women-owned businesses span the entire range of business life cycle and business success, whether the measuring sticks is revenue, employment or longevity. This strengthens the view that all Governmental programmes and policies should target at strengthening women's entrepreneurship in their native lands.

Rural Women Entrepreneurship

The phenomenon of women entrepreneurship is largely confined to metropolitan cities and big towns in India. Most of the women entrepreneurs also operate small-scale units. However, women entrepreneurs are also found in the rural areas too. A rural women entrepreneur is a women or a group of women who undertake to organize and run an enterprise in a rural area. The supply of rural women entrepreneurs may be classified into the following categories.

1. Women who take to entrepreneurship because of dire economic activity.
2. Women who take to entrepreneurship because they had the family background tradition in some skill or trade, hence they would like to have extra money for themselves and their families.
3. Women, who take it up because they have certain personality characteristics such as: need for achievement, need for power and influence, etc.
4. Women who take it up as leisure time activity.

Characteristics of Women Entrepreneurs

Indian women of today have taken many strides towards business ownership. The broad classification of women business owners include women who establish, inherit, or acquire a business; women who start businesses with spouses or business partners but are either at the forefront or behind the scenes; and finally, women who start fast-growing or part-time or slow-growing firms. Although earlier researches on women entrepreneurs have suggested that significant differences existed between female and male entrepreneurs. However, more recent studies have shown that there are far more similarities than differences between women and men entrepreneurs in terms of psychological and demographic characteristics. The dominant predictors of success in case of women entrepreneurs are work experience and years of self-employment.

Generally, women view their businesses as a cooperative network of relationships rather than as a distinct profit-generating entity. This network extends beyond the business into the entrepreneur's relationships with her family and the community. Certain cross-cultural studies on women entrepreneurs have reported that their management styles emphasise open communication and participative decision-making, and their business goals reflect a concern for the community in which the business operates.

The majority of women business owners operate enterprises in the service sectors, whereas the majority of male business owners operate enterprises in non service sectors, particularly manufacturing.

Women are not only achieving economic independence and wealth creation for themselves, but through job creation, they are also providing opportunities for others, particularly for other women.

A series of researches have shown that the workforce of women-owned businesses tend to be more gender balanced than the workforce of men-owned businesses, although women business owners are more likely to hire women. Put simply, an investment in women's entrepreneurship is an investment in the economic independence and well-being of all women.

This study was carried out as the role of women entrepreneurs has gained significance in today's environment. Women, who succeed as entrepreneurs, are risk taking personalities. The women entrepreneurs have their own identity in the world of entrepreneurship as most of them are capable of fully identifying themselves in their new economic role in the society. The study has highlighted many factors that have motivated women entrepreneurs in starting an entrepreneurial career. The Government schemes, incentives and subsidies have stimulated and provided support measures to these women entrepreneurs.

Objectives of The Study

The broad objectives of the study were:

1. To find out the motivational factors that persuade these women to became entrepreneurs.
2. To find out their level of awareness regarding different incentives.
3. To study the types of problems they have encountered in order to reach the level of success.
4. To discover the operational problems they are facing.
5. To provide suitable suggestions for future improvement.

Methodology

The study aims to test the status of rural women entrepreneurs with special reference to some selected locations at Tinsukia district of Assam. The study was carried during June-July, 2012. A structured questionnaire was prepared for the purpose of data collection covering the various aspects of the study and purposive sampling was applied to select 70 (seventy) successful women entrepreneurs to whom questionnaires were distributed and collected and later data so obtained has been tested. These women entrepreneurs were running *Beauty parlours, P.C.Os, Candle factories, Tailoring, Knitting and embroidery, Jute bag and carpet* manufacturing enterprises. The secondary information had been collected from books, journals and websites. The results arrived from the study do not reflect the views of the total population of successful women entrepreneurs. However, the results are indicative of the general trend in the motivation, identity and problems faced by the successful women entrepreneurs in the study area.

Analysis and Interpretation

1. A majority (52.2%) of the respondents were between the ages of 30-40 years.
2. From the sample, it was inferred that 78.3 per cent were married, 8.3 per cent were divorced, 8.3 per cent were widows, 5 per cent were single and these women entrepreneurs maximum (50%) were graduates too.
3. Of the total sample, the majority (63.3%) belonged to nuclear families. When analysed on the basis of number of children, the majority (84.2%) had upto three children.
4. Data clearly indicates that despite the common belief that joint families would more supportive to women who want to branch off on their own and enter businesses, the researchers found that it is the nuclear family that has produced more successful entrepreneurs. This may be due to fact that in a nuclear setup, the women has an equal say and is more open to new ideas.
5. 45 per cent of the children of these respondents were in the age group of 11-20 years. As children at this age does not required consistent attention so it provide these women engaged to doing something worthwhile to keep themselves busy and productive.
6. An analysis of the occupation backgrounds of the families-parents, in-laws and husbands occupation were also collected for study purpose. It is interesting to note that, while majority (44.6%) of the respondents originally came from service background, 41.4 per cent were mostly married to business families and the husband occupation was also businesses for

43.5 per cent of the respondents. Having lived in business environment after marriage, it seems that it became easier to these women to take new businesses rather taking any other vocations.

Motivational Factors for Women Entrepreneurs

The reasons for which women enter into business seems quite different from that of men to become entrepreneurs which has been reflected in this study. In order to arrive at an objective assessment, the respondents ranked 15 (fifteen) possible motivating factors in the order of priority. The first 3 (three) ranks were taken for score purpose. The reason ranked first was given 3 (three) points, the second received 2 (two) points and the third received 1 (one) point. It is evident from the study, most of women entered into business '*to keep busy*', and this factor ranked 1st amongst the motivational factors followed by the desire '*to fulfill ambition*', '*to pursue own interest*' was ranked 3rd, followed by '*by accident or circumstances beyond control.*' The above ranking indicates an interesting assemblage of reasons and factors that motivated the respondents. The research on entrepreneurship has provided that '*the need to excel and achievement*' and '*the ability to take calculated risks*' are the prime factors that motivate people. However, this study indicates different things from the accepted pattern of thinking. '*Keeping busy*' has emerged as the dominant factor motivating women entrepreneurs. The data reveals that while 60.8 per cent of the respondents have been taking help of their male counterparts in running their enterprises, 39.2 per cent are operating entirely in their own. However, when they were asked whether they could successfully run their enterprises in their own, 75 per cent respondents said yes.

This is further supported by the fact that majority of respondents were not under economic stress at the time of entering businesses. '*To earn money*' had been cited as fifth priority for entering into business. The fact that low priority had been given to '*giving good education to children*', '*securing social prestige*', '*making quick money*' etc., further substantiates that most of these entrepreneurs were from economically sound families. The second and third priorities had been identified as '*to fulfill ones' ambition*' and '*to pursue own interest*', which indicates their sense of independence. The fourth priority was '*by accident or circumstances beyond control*'. This is because of the death of their fathers/husbands. A larger percentage of women entrepreneurs were either married into business families, or had businessmen as husbands. This could be one of the reasons why despite having educational qualifications (50% entrepreneurs were graduates), none of them thought of taking up a job.

Awareness of Incentives

Training makes entrepreneurs more aware of their environment, and of the facilities and incentives offered by the Government, to give encouragement to women entrepreneurs. This is evident from the Table 9.1 given below:

Table 9.1:

Training	Awareness of Special Incentives			Total
	Aware	Partially Aware	Not Aware	
Trained	27.6	24.1	48.3	48.3
Untrained	19.4	6.5	74.2	51.7
Total	**23.3**	**15.0**	**61.7**	**100.0**

Source: Primary Data.

Of the trained entrepreneurs, 51.7 per cent were either aware or partially aware of the special incentives for women entrepreneurs; whereas, 74.2 per cent – an overwhelming majority of untrained women entrepreneurs, were not at all aware of the incentives meant for them. But it is surprising to note that very few had availed special incentives. After discussion with these respondents, the general feeling was that those incentives only existed in paper and that the formalities for availing them were too many and very complicated.

Operational Problems

The approach of entrepreneurs, who starts a new enterprise, would be varied, depending on the social and cultural settings. The personality, qualities, the values that sets goal towards the success, would vary. Every entrepreneur faces some problems in running business, and women in this study are no exception. In the sample, almost 15.7 per cent of the women said that they did not have any problems. The majority of the women (84.3%) indicated problems of varied nature. Some of the respondents said that problems arise when dealing with workers and the labourers. It seems semi-educated or uneducated class of workers cannot visualize a "*female boss*' in their field of work. The other factors, which have been indicated by the respondents, were marketing, recovery of payments from customers. The above three factors are related to outside or field jobs, which women generally find cumbersome. In the study an attempt has also been made to find out from the respondents, the problems which they faced while running their business, which are specific to their gender. Out of the total sample, 48 per cent did not feel that they faced any problems by virtue of being women. This indicates a good turning point, in the sense that women are developing confidence to undertake any work, thereby, shedding inhibitions. This would encourage many future women entrepreneurs to plunge into business.

Summary and Findings

1. Rural women entrepreneurs enter business mainly to keep themselves busy. Although the initial motivation was low, they tend to become high achievers once they actually get involved in it.
2. It was found that while majority of these women came from a family business as a core background as they were married to business families. The business environment seems to have prepared them mentally, thereby facilitating their entry in to business. Help and guidance was also available within the family in case of any operating problems.
3. Regarding seeking male help, while initially it was taken, a majority of respondents felt that they could manage entirely on their own.
4. Contrary to general belief, the choice of their business fields by women had not necessarily "*feminine*'.
5. The operational problems faced by the women were in the areas in dealing directly with the workers and the labourers; and also pertained to difficulties in carrying out the field work.
6. It was disconcerting to note that despite several incentives available to women entrepreneurs, not even single respondent

had availed of it. It was found that some women spent from their own sources without taking any financial help from Government agencies.

7. Majority of the women entered into business without any relevant training. The study indicates a direct association of knowledge about special schemes, etc. with training.
8. It has been proved, beyond doubt, that women entrepreneurs enjoy respect in the society.

Conclusion and Suggestions

Based on the findings, along with comments received from the respondents, the following suggestion has been put forwarded as concluded remarks:

1. The need for professionalism in women cannot be over stressed. Professionalism would help these women entrepreneurs to extract the maximum from the business and help to reduce grey areas.
2. There is a need for sufficient training facilities for these women entrepreneurs. The Government must make greater efforts to publicize the various schemes announced from time to time to attract women entrepreneurs.
3. The procedure for availing of special schemes for women entrepreneurs should be streamlined, so as to avoid unnecessary delays and thereby, dispelling the feeling that these schemes only exist on paper.

REFERENCES

Alvarez, S. A., and Meyer, G. D. (1998), Why do Women become Entrepreneurs? Frontiers of Entrepreneurship Research, Wellesley, MA: Babson College.

Anderson, Ellen (1984), "Why aren't there More Women Managers? World Executive Digest.

Anna, A. L., Chandler, G. N., Jansen, E., and Mero, N. P. (2000), Women Business Owners in Traditional and Non-traditional Industries," *Journal of Business Venturing.*

Ben-Yoseph, M., Gundry, L. K., and Maslyk-Musial, E. (1994), Women Entrepreneurs in the United States and Poland, Kobieta I Biznes.

Ben-Yoseph, M., and Gundry, L. K. (1997), Teaching about Women Managers and Women Entrepreneurs Across Cultures, *Journal of Developmental Entrepreneurship.*

Birley, Sue (1989), Female Entrepreneurs; Are they Really Different? *Journal of Small Business Management*, Summer.

Brush, C. (1992), Research on Women Business Owners: Past Trends, A New Perspective and Future Directions, Entrepreneurship: Theory and Practice. *Journal of Developmental Entrepreneurship.*

Brush, C., and Hisrich, R. (1988), Women Entrepreneurs: Strategic Origins Impact on Growth. Frontiers of Entrepreneurship Research. Wellesley, MA: Babson College.

Clark, T., and James, F. (1992), Women-owned Businesses: Dimensions and Policy Issues. *Economic Development Quarterly.*

Gundry, L. K., and Welsch; H. P. (1994), Differences in Familial Influence among Women-owned Businesses. *Family Business Review.*

Hisrich, R., Brush, C., Good, D., and DeSouza, G. (1997), Performance in Entrepreneurial Ventures. Does Gender Matter? Frontiers of Entrepreneurship Research. Wellesley, MA: Babson College.

Jagadeesh, N. (2006), "India's New Billionaires", Business World.

Kamau, D. G., McLean, G. N., and Ardishvili, A. (1999), Perceptions of Business Growth by Women Entrepreneurs. Frontiers of Entrepreneurship Research. Wellesley, MA: Babson College.

Lisowska, E. (1998), Entrepreneurship as a Response to Female Unemployment and Discrimination against Women in the Workplace, Kobieta I Biznes.

Moore, D. P. (2000), Careerpreneurs: Lessons from Leading Women Entrepreneurs on Building a Career without Boundaries. Davies-Black Publishers.

Moore, D. P. and Buttner, H. (1997), Women Entrepreneurs: Moving Beyond the Glass Ceiling. Thousand Oaks, CA: Sage Publications.

Patnaik, S. C. (1988), Industrial Development in Backward State: Dynamics of Policy, New Delhi, Asish Publishing House.

Roy, Rajeev (2008), "Entrepreneurship", Oxford University Press.

Salganicoff, M. (1990), Women in Family Business: Challenges and Opportunities. *Family Business Review.*

Schiller, B. R., and Crewson, P. (1997), Entrepreneurial Origins: A Longitudinal Inquiry. Economic Inquiry.

10

Domestic Violence
A Socio-legal Aspect

Dr. Pankaj Kumar

"The downfall of the nation is in its consistent neglect of the womanhood. However, the male folk of the Indian soil failed to sense it and advertently continued to turn blind eye to the same".

– Swami Vivekananda

Abstract

Violence against women is rooted in unequal power relations between men and women in society and can be understood within a gender framework. While gender roles prescribed a strict division of labour, women are expected to perform largely reproductive functions like maintenance of the household, child care etc. Women are judged and condemned by society if they go against the prescribed forms of behaviours for them. Unequal treatment and discrimination in child rearing and caring practices in the family, male preference and denial of right to health care and education to female are some of the factors that make women vulnerable and susceptible to different form of violence.

INTRODUCTION

Violence against women is rooted in unequal power relations between men and women in society and can be understood within a gender framework. While sex is a biological category, gender is a social construct and refers to widely shared expectations and norms within society about appropriate male and female behaviour and roles. While gender roles prescribed a strict division of labour, women are expected to perform largely reproductive functions like maintenance of the household, child care etc. Gender roles also prescribe characteristic of docility, unending patience and servility for women. Women are judged and condemned by society if they go against the prescribed forms of behaviours for them.

The construction of gender roles implies that women have far lesser access to productive resources and decision-making compare to men, resulting in unequal balance of power. Unequal treatment and discrimination in child rearing and caring practices in the family, male preference and denial of right to health care and education to female are some of the factors that make women vulnerable and susceptible to different form of violence. Gender based inequality exists in all stages of women's lives – from infancy to old age and manifests in the form of several acts of violence. Violence against women is not a myth, but a reality. It is an act of illegal criminal use of physical force and it also includes exploitation, discrimination, upholding of unequal economic and social structures, and the creation of an atmosphere of terror, threat or reprisal. This terror can be seen in domestic violence.

Conceptual Understanding of Domestic Violence

Domestic Violence is systemic and structural, a mechanism of patriarchal control of women that is built on male superiority and female inferiority, sex stereotyped roles and expectations, and economic, social, and political predominance of men and dependency of women. While the legal and cultural embodiments of patriarchal thinking vary among different culture and violence as a mechanism of enforcing patriarchal system. Through violence men seek and confirm the devaluation and dehumanization of women. It is a serious human right threat to women in every society-rich and poor, developed and industrialized. Particularly in patriarchal society, it is used as a weapon for subjugating women and suppressing their rights as equal partners in the family structure. NCW in its report, 'Violence Against Women in North East India', 2005, states that it is estimated that at least 3 out of every 5 women in India face domestic violence, reporting of such cases is extremely low. One of the major factors for this is the 'culture of silence' surrounding domestic violence.

In spite of the modernization of life, the basic patriarchal dynamic continues to express and replicate itself through violence in private sphere. The UN report, '*Violence Against Women in the Family*', 1989, concludes its analysis that there is no simple explanation for violence against women in the home. Certainly, any explanation must go beyond the individual characteristics of the man, the women and the family and look to the structure of relationships and the role of society in underpinning that structure. Violence against wives is the function of the belief, fostered in all cultures, that men are superior and that the women they live with are their possessions or chattels that they can treat as they wish and as they consider appropriate.

Domestic violence not only includes conduct which amount to cruelty on a women by her husband but also includes any act which is unbecoming of the dignity of women. This type of violence generally refers to torture, to injury, to harass somebody especially to suppress that person. It can be considered as a coercive method to assert one's will over another in order to prove one's power. Physical violence is just one form of the manifested violence which is legally punishable. The World Conference on Human Rights at Vienna held on June 25, 1993 for the first time recognised the violations of women's human right in many ways and held that they are inalienable, integral and indivisible part of the universal human rights and demanded equal status of women with men. It favoured eradication of all forms of discrimination against women. They are vulnerable to acts of violence in the family which include foeticide, infanticide, marital cruelty, dowry, murder, child abuse, marital rape, battering etc. The proposed Domestic Violence Bill, 2005 defines domestic violence as actual abuse or the treat of abuse that is physical, sexual, verbal, emotional or economic including dowry harassment.

Dowry Harassment

Dowry is one of the most obvious causes of domestic crime prevalent in India. It is defined as any property or valuable security given or agreed to be given, directly or indirectly, by one party to marriage, or by parents of either party to marriage, or by any person to either party to the marriage or to any other person at or before or at any time after the marriage, in connection with the marriage of said party. Being one of the most significant factors in violence against women it results in harassment, beating, and in many cases murder. Dowry violence against women, in which women are subjected to harassment by their husband and his family members, has been increasing since last one decade. In most of the cases dowry related violence goes unreported due to lack of awareness, fear of retaliation, distrust of legal instruments or inability to take legal measures prevent families from reporting to the police.

Wife Battering

Wife battering is the most common form of abuse in India. It has been often taken as physical assault on the wife and it undoubtedly includes the mental torture which is so subtle and its effects present very long time. Some feel the wife battering is the way in which man can express his anger and frustration, or it is an expression of inadequacy in man who feels the need to asserts him and gain control.

Sexual Abuse

Sexual abuse is an act done on a woman against her will, which may be treated as rape or an attempt to rape etc. Women are not safe even in their own families. Sexual abuse on women is not done by husband alone rather other family members are involved in it. But vast majority of abuses against women go unreported due to the social stigma attached to them. Sexual abuse takes many forms, including the insertion of objects into the woman's vagina, anal and oral sex, and forced sex with others. Sometimes women are threatened with mutilation of their breasts or genitals and suffer permanent disfigurement.

Child Abuse

Child abuse is yet another form of domestic violence which take various forms namely: physical abuse, emotional abuse, sexual abuse, neglect (physical, educational and emotional) and commercial abuse. Physical abuse includes inflicting physical injury by burning, hitting, punching, shaking, beating etc. Emotional abuse is also known as verbal abuse, mental abuse and psychological maltreatment. Neglect includes not providing adequate food or clothing or medical care, lack of emotional support and love. Sexual abuse is the involvement of child in any sexual activity, whether forced or consensual that occurs prior to the age of 18. It includes fondling a child's genitals, intercourse, incest, rape, sodomy and sexual exploitation. The impact of child abuse leads to impaired brain development, sleep disturbance, fear, anger, anxiety, depression, consuming alcohol and illicit drugs.

Marital Rape

Marital Rape, though not widely accepted as a crime by communities and law in India, is also experienced by a number of women within the four walls of the home. Women has to succumb themselves even without their will. It has often been found that most of the women are sexually abused not by her husband rather other male persons of the family. Women are forced to have sex with her husband even at the time when she is suffering in pain and agony during heavy menstrual falls. It is also seen that the men having anal sex with female results in various disease.

Female Foeticide and Infanticide

Female foeticide is one stream manifestation of violence against women. Female fetuses are selectively aborted after the determination of pre-natal sex and evading the birth of the girl. It is said to be one of the heinous crime posing threat both to the child who has every right to take birth and to the women who is bound to go for the termination even without her consent, thus violating human rights. Millions of girl children are been deprived of the basic rights to exists and strong intervention is needed to bring this brutality to end. This can be termed as new mode of infliction of 'cruelty' on women, and to the extent of eradication of fair sex.

Domestic violence has certain implications which are discuss in aforementioned paragraphs.

Psychological Implications

The emotional violence has far more psychological implications, as it erodes self-esteem and brings personality breakdown and total loss of functioning of an otherwise normal human being. Physical abuse also leads to emotional disorders. Depression, sexual dysfunction, eating problems and fear anxiety is the most common mental health problem experienced by women who are facing domestic violence. When women do not have proper support system at their family and community levels, they feel helpless and experience threat of death due to repeated violence. Such women suffer from acute anxiety disorder like obsessive compulsive disorder and Post Traumatic Stress Disorder (PTSD). Childhood sexual abuse, rape and domestic violence victims generally suffer from PTSD.

Physical Implications

Violence is a major cause of injuries to women. It ranges from minor cuts to bruises and welts to disability and sometimes death. Physical violence also leads to irritable bowel syndrome, gastrointestinal disorder and chronic pain. These health consequence become complexes when women fail to access timely health care due to various reason. Women who lack sexual autonomy are often powerless to refuse unwanted sex or use contraceptives. These women are at risk of unwanted pregnancy. Women who experiences sexual abuse are more likely to suffer from Sexually Transmitted Disease, AIDS etc. Generally women are afraid to raise the issue of use of contraceptives, as they are afraid of experiencing violence by their husband. Extreme stress and anxiety during pregnancy due to violence can reduce women's food intake and resulting in low birth weight. It can also lead to preterm delivery or foetal growth retardation. Any physical injury on abdomen leads to rupture of uterus and death of women. Women may go for unsafe and illegal abortion for unwanted pregnancies leading to maternal death.

Economic Implications

Domestic Violence against women has a serious impact on the economy within the household. It has been postulated that violence leads to decreased efficiency and productivity. The health costs of domestic violence impact both the public exchequer as well as household income. The Institute for Women's Policy Research made a pioneering attempt in 1996 to indicate how to map out direct and indirect societal costs of domestic violence which include direct costs like loss of income and productivity, health care and housings costs, and costs of social services and indirect cost like impact on child's well-being, female and child mortality, inter-generational social and psychological costs. In 2000, the International Centre for Research on Women undertook a household level study on the prevalence of domestic violence which illustrated that domestic violence can push economically fragile households into an economic crisis.

Legal Measures and Policies

Convention on The Elimination and Discrimination Against Women (CEDAW) is the first significant international legal document that pays specific focus to the violence that women suffer due to legal, social and cultural traditions. Recommendation 19 of CEDAW states "gender based violation is a form of discrimination that seriously inhibits women ability to enjoy rights and freedom on a basis of equality with men". The other international instrument is the *Convention on the Rights of the Child* (CRC), 1989. Article 2 of CRC prohibits discrimination on the basis of sex; Article 19 emphasises protection of the child from all forms of physical or mental violence, injury or abuse, neglect or negligent treatment, mal-treatment or exploitation including sexual abuse; and Article 34 calls for protection of children from all forms of sexual exploitation and sexual abuse. India ratified both the international instruments *i.e.,* CEDAW in the year 1993 and acceded to the CRC in 1992.

Though the *Dowry Prohibition Act* was enacted in 1961 to curb the menace of domestic violence but it did not bring much success as Section 3 and Section 4 of the Act criminalizes the giving and taking of dowry is punishable and existence of element of cruelty is not necessary. Brides often commit suicide due to dowry harassment. Section 305 and 306 of the *Indian Penal Code* (IPC) lays down that abetment of suicide of a delirious person is an offence punishable with death or life imprisonment. The irony lies in these sections are that these sections are beneficial to married women but it could not protect the widows, the children and the unmarried women from domestic violence.

Hence in 1980's two new sections were inserted under the Penal Laws Section 498A and 304B which to some extent proved beneficial to women in respect to dowry death. Matrimonial cruelty was introduced as an offence in IPC. It defined as "any willful conduct which is of such a nature as is likely to drive the women to commit suicide or to cause grave injury or danger to life or limbs or health (whether mental or physical) of the women". It includes harassment of women in connection with demands for property and like. Wrongful restraint or confinement of the spouse within her matrimonial house is also another common form of domestic violence which is punishable under Section 349 and 340 of the Penal Code.

Although child abuse is rampant, surprisingly India's has no separate legislation to deal with it. The legal remedies to protect child from child abuse include the law on rape (Section 375 of the IPC), sexual molestation (Section 354 of the IPC), and sodomy (Section 377 of the IPC). The sexual molestation law covers all sexual offences 'that outrage the modesty of the victim', other than penile penetration, punishments for which are maximum of two years in jail or a fine of few thousands rupee. Section 377 of the IPC is harsh. Though this section can be used in the case of child sexual abuse, its reference to unusual sexual offences makes it difficult for child victims to use this option as a legal remedy.

Again forced termination of female fetuses has been able to curb this menace by the statute of *The Pre-Natal Diagnostic Techniques (Regulation and Prevention of Misuse) Act,* 1994. Section 4 of the Act lays down that the pre-natal diagnosis test are permitted for the purpose of detecting certain specified abnormalities. Female infanticide is recognised as offence under 313 to 316 of the penal code.

Section 174 of the *Criminal Procedure Code*, 1973 was amended by the Criminal Law Act, 1983, to provide for investigation by the police of cases of suicide committed by women or death of women occurring in suspicious circumstances within seven years of marriage. Section 113A (Inserted by the Criminal Law 2nd Amendment Act, 1983) and 113B (Inserted by Act No. 43 of 1986) were inserted in *The Indian Evidence Act.* These provisions lay down that if a women commits suicide within seven years of her marriage due to 'cruelty' by her husband or his relatives, the court may presume that such suicide has been abetted by her husband or by his relatives.

Not only the criminal laws dealt with the acts of domestic violence rather the civil law also addresses the facets of domestic violence. Under Family Law, both under the *The Hindu Marriage Act,* 1955 and *The Dissolution of Muslim Marriage Act,* 1939 paves way 'cruelty' as a ground for divorce. Even the *Special Marriage Act*, 1954, *The Indian Divorce Act* and the *Parsi Marriage and Divorce Act* all allow 'cruelty' as a ground for divorce.

The Indian Penal Code and the Criminal Procedure Code did not adequately protect the woman against domestic violence. But *The Domestic Violence Bill*, 2005 seeks to protect the rights of women. The most salient features of the revised Bill are:

- Recognition of the fact that men and women live in relationships that might not always be legal.
- Recognition of the right of women to live in their marital homes.
- Provisions of positive entitlements – maintenance, protection from future violence, the right to custody over children as opposed to mere penalization of the husband.

Conclusion

The menace of domestic violence is beyond description as it is like as iceberg. In the present century, it would increase more due to change in life style. It is considered as a slow poison which is swallowing the ingredients of the family life as it strikes in various forms like physical, sexual, emotional and psychological and destroying personality completely. The unacceptable crime of female foetocide is increasing due to the misuse of technology such as ultrasonography, which immediately needs to be stopped as it is creating a gender imbalance in our population posing threat to both the nation and the society. The fact that this falling sex ratio is linked to increased dowry demands and expenditure on the marriages of daughters highlights the necessity for an intense campaign for social reform and gender equality. There should be strict enforcement of laws against sex determination tests and campaigns against clinics and hospitals were such tests are being carried out. Efforts must be made in providing proper nourishment and education to girl child.

The Domestic Violence against Women (Prevention and Protection) Bill, 2005 is helpful which provides victims to certain basic rights. One of the most important aspects of the bill is that *it enables women to get emergency and interim relief by obtaining a protection order within three days of application, a residence order to continue living in the shared household, monetary relief, custody of children and even compensation.* It also enables women to file an application for the protection of a child who may be abused – the first recognition of a child's right to live a violence free life.

Rape laws only recognise sexual crimes involving penile penetration and are totally dependent on medical evidence. Such evidence is very difficult to get in child abuse cases, as child sexual abuse is usually not an isolated incident but a series of incidents. With the growing number of cases on domestic violence and sexual abuse there is an urgent need for law and also for law reform. The new law must honour the basic dignity of human life making an unambiguous distinction between commodities, services on the one hand and human body and life on the other. The law enforcing mechanism should consider the phenomenon of domestic violence as a socio-legal and human problem. They should be strict, on one hand, with the persons involved in violating the rights of women and girls and on the other, be considerate and sensitive to those who become victims of circumstances. Justice to the aggrieved person is also hampered by the attitudes of the Indian society. Judges, lawyers, law makers, social workers, the police, doctors, mental health professionals and other medical personnel need sensitization and training to handle these cases and also to change the legal processes and mechanism. In the new millennium NGOs and the media must vigorously advocate this reform along with creating public awareness and sensitivity, as law is an instrument of social change capable of bringing about change along with other social institutions and organizations. It is time for us to become conscious of our rights. According to Ramkrishna Paramhansa, entire world bears various colours of God, but woman has been its best colour. Henceforth, by providing rights to the women in sphere of social, economic and political would give the real colour to women.

REFERENCES

Ahuja, Ram, (1987), *Violence Against Women*, Rawat Publication, Jaipur.

Ashraf, Nehal, (1997), *Crimes Against Women*, Commonwealth Publication, New Delhi.

Agarwal, B. D. (2002), *Legislating Domestic Violence*, *Criminal Law Journal,* Vol. 108.

Anand, A. S. (2003), *Justice for Women,* Universal Law Publishing Co. Pvt. Ltd., New Delhi.

Goel, Aruna, (2004), *Violence and Protection Measures for Women Development and Empowerment*, Deep and Deep Publications Pvt. Ltd., New Delhi.

Malavika, Karlekar, (2003), *Domestic Violence, Veena* Das (Ed) Sociology and Social Anthropology, Oxford University Press.

Mishra, Saraswati (2002), *Violence Against Women and Status of Indian Women,* Gyan Publishing House, New Delhi.

Nigam, Shalu (1998), *Right of Women*, Legal News and View, November, Social Action Trust, New Delhi.

Paranjape, N. V. (2005), *Criminology and Penology* Central Law Publications, Allahabad.

Sehgal, Singh, B. P. (2004), *Human Rights in India: Problems and Perspective,* Deep and Deep Publications Pvt. Ltd., New Delhi.

Verma, J. S. (2004), *The New Universe of Human Rights,* Universal Law Publishing Co. Pvt. Ltd. New Delhi.

Vasudha Nagraj and Suneetha, (2005), *A Domestic Violence Bill that fits the Bill*, The Asian Age, New Delhi: 18 June.

Reports

Domestic Workers, NCW, Jan, 2005.

Ending Violence against Women and Girls in South Asia, UNICEF, 1998.

Justice to Women Victims of Crime and Violence, NCW and ISS, 2003.

Violence Against Women in North East India: An Enquiry, NCW, Jan, 2005.

Women Initiated Community Level Responses to Domestic Violence, International Centre for Research on Women, 2002.

Women get Extra Cover from Domestic Violence, The Times of India, New Delhi, Friday, June 24, 2005.

Legislations

Convention on The Elimination and Discrimination Against Women (CEDAW), 1979.

Convention on the Rights of the Child (CRC), 1989.

Criminal Procedure Code, 1973.

Dowry Prohibition Act, 1961.

Indian Penal Code, 1860.

The Pre-Natal Diagnostic Techniques (Regulation and Prevention of Misuse) Act, 1994.

The Indian Evidence Act, 1872.

11

Participation of Women in Retail Business
A Study on Twin Capital Cities of Arunachal Pradesh

Dr. Philip Mody

Abstract

In the 21st century women are no longer a mere piece of attraction at home or simply a home-maker. The same happen to the women in capital region of Arunachal Pradesh, India. They geared up to contribute to the home and lead the business as well. Infact, the study area is experiencing boom in retail business due to mass participation of women burying age old tradition of running home only. In the study area, women aged between 25 to 30 years old are most active in retail business but they are mostly illiterate. In addition, most women retailers of the study area conceive ideas of doing business through family members and relatives. They also enjoy economic liberty over their business and spend most of business income to meet family expenses. They rely mostly on own capital to start off pretty retail business to their best choice. However, institutional financing is least heard story of women retailers of the study area. The present study makes an attempt to study nature of women' participation in retail business in the twin cities of Arunachal Pradesh.

Keywords: *Arunachal Pradesh, Business, Retail Business and Women in Retail Business.*

INTRODUCTION

In recent times, entrepreneurial activity among women is higher in emerging economies with a share of 45.5 per cent off 100 per cent. However, the proportion of women entrepreneurs vary considerably among the economies from 16 per cent in the Republic of Korea to 55 per cent in Ghana – the only economy with more women than men entrepreneurs. In addition, in many emerging economies women are now starting business at a faster rate than men do, making significant contributions to job creation and economic growth. Spirits of entrepreneurship is very intense among women even in developed economies. As a matter of facts that the number of women-owned businesses in the United States is growing at twice the rate of all firms in the recent times. Currently around 30 per cent and 15 per cent of American and British firms are owned by women. Moreover, women make up 40 per cent of the world's work forces. Interestingly, many of the sectors critical for economic growth in some of the poorest countries rely heavily on women employees, such as agri-business, tourism, textiles and garments so on and so forth.

It is very true of women that they contribute towards empire building of retail business around the world not at the cost of non-fulfillment of family responsibilities. In recent times, women have made entry into retail business in a massive ways which was supposedly an area mainly and predominantly occupied by men. Fascinatingly, retail business is at a boom and is experiencing active participation of women in the twin cities of Arunachal Pradesh (herein after called the Study Area). It is a lucrative profession and there is an urge seen in women of the study area to join retail business without any qualms thereby spoiling the age old tradition of running homes and killing therein their capabilities.

Objectives

The paper-makes an attempt to:

1. Analyse Gross Income of Women Retailers in the study area.
2. Discuss Financing of Retail Business own by women in the study area.
3. Assess Economic Liberty of Women over their Retail Business in the study area.
4. Draw Sources of Idea of doing Retail Business by Women of the study region.

Research Methodology

The present study is carried over the two major cities of Arunachal Pradesh namely: *(i)* Naharlagun and *(ii)* Itanagar. Infact these cities constitutes capital region of the state. The facts and figures pertaining to women retail business during the year 2012-13 has been taken to for present study.

During the present study an effort has been made to make the study empirical based on survey and statistical methods. The work is purely based on both primary and secondary data. For the collection of primary data a sample survey was conducted over three major towns that represent capital complex of Arunachal Pradesh. Altogether, 40 women undertaking retail business have been selected at random basis. Eight samples each from grocery shop, garment store, vegetable vendor, meat vendor and beauty parlor have been taken to for present study. Interview method with the help of well-designed schedules is used for current study. As regard to secondary data, published books, research papers, journals and articles, have been referred to. However, internet has been one of the most used sources of secondary data for the present study. Data have been analysed, interpreted and summarised with the help of various types of statistical tools like percentage and diagram. Audio-visual tools *viz;* tape recorder and digital camera have also been used to facilitate the collection and visual representation of data.

Analysis and Interpretation of Data

Observations made on present study have been analysed and interpreted under following major heads which are as follows:

(i) Age of Women Retailer in the Study Area

It is observed from Table 11.1 and Fig. 11.1 that women's falling under age category from 25 to 30 years is found most active in retail business. This age group constitutes 55 per cent of total samples taken from the study area. Age group above 30 to 35 years is found to have snatched the second places sharing 25 per cent of total respondents.

Table 11.1: Age of Women Retailer in the Study Area

Age Group	Below 25 Years	From 25 to 30 Years	Above 30 to 35 Years	Above 35 Years
Total 40	0	22	10	8
Percentage	0	55	25	20

Source: Field Data.

However, it is unveiled from Table 11. 1 and Fig. 11.1 that none of women retailer is of the age below 25 years. Fascinatingly, degree of women entrepreneurship in retail business in the study area is found to be on decrease with increase in their ages. Only eight off 40 sample women retailers that constitute 20 per cent of total samples are found to be older women into retailing business.

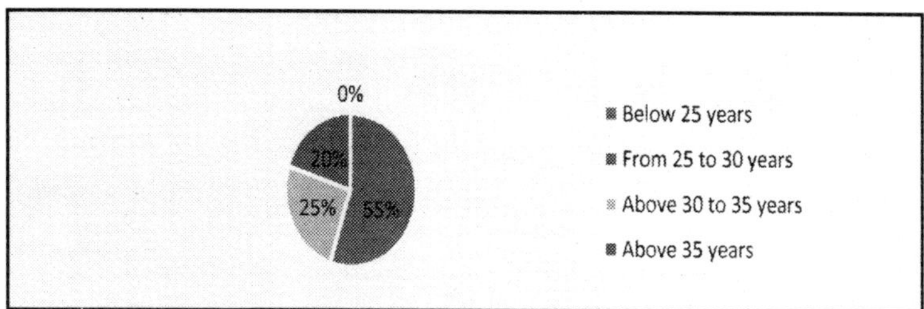

Fig. 11.1: Age of Women Retailer

(ii) Education Level of Women Retailers in the Study Area

It is revealed from Table 11.2 and Fig. 11.2 that most of the women retailers in the study area are illiterate. Illiterate women retailers constitute 35 per cent of total samples. Second in the row, matriculated women retailers are found to have managed their business in the study area. Likewise, literate but not matriculate and high school passed women retailers have occupied the third and fourth slots in the order. To great dismay, none of women retailer is found to have either graduated or did any equivalent or above.

Table 11.2: Education of Women Retailers in the Study Area

Level of Education	Illiterate	Literate but not Matriculate	Matriculate	High School Passed	Graduate and Above
Total 40	14	8	12	6	0
Percentage	35	20	30	15	0

Source: Field Data.

Interestingly it is clear from Fig. 11.2 that illiterate and matriculate women are found most active in this business sector. Towards mass women participation in retail business, the states Government need to encourage illiterate women retailers through various informal modes of education. This would sure to let illiterate women retailers to understand mosaic and dynamic of business in a better ways. Moreover, it ensures better management and profitability of their business.

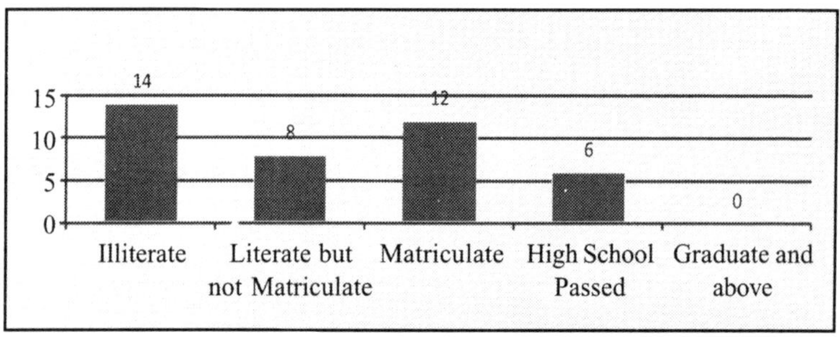

Fig. 11.2: Education Level of Women Retailers

(iii) Sources of finance of Women Retailers in the Study Area

It is observed from Table 11.3 that non-institutional sources of finance (relatives, own capital, money lenders etc.,) has been the major sources of finance to women retailers in the study area.

Table 11.3: Sources of Finance of Women Retailers in the Study Area

Institutional Sources				Non-Institutional Sources			
Co-operative Bank	Regional Rural Bank	SBI	Others (NEDFi)	Money Lender	Relative	Own Capital	Others
0	0	0	3	0	8	29	0

Source: Field Data.

On the side of institutional financing, only North East Development and Financial Corporation (NEDfi) is found to have financed only three sample women retailers in the study region. It is revealed that 29 samples have capitalised on own capital to start off with their business. However, relatives are also found to be one of the major sources of finance to their business. Unfortunately, none of the women retailer has reported to get finance from either Regional Rural Bank or State Bank of India.

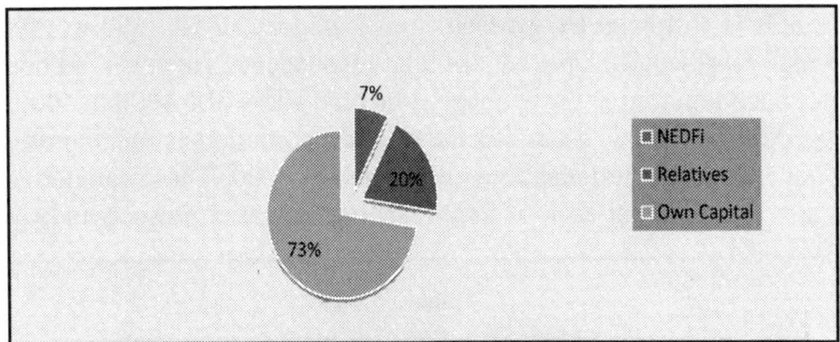

Fig. 11.3: Sources of Finance

In addition, it is apparent from Fig. 11.3 that 73 per cent, 20 per cent and seven per cent of total women retailers under present study have been financed by own capital, relatives and NEDfi respectively.

(iv) Per day Gross Income of Women Retailers

It is revealed from Table 11.4 and Fig. 11.4 that most women retailers earned per day gross income above Rs. 5000. In this category, 12 women off 40 *i.e.,* 30 per cent women are reported to have earned more than Rs. 5000 in a single day from their retail business.

Table 11.4: Per day Gross Income of Women Retailers in the Study Area

Categories of of Income	No. of Respondents	Percent
Below Rs. 300	2	5%
From Rs. 300 to 500	9	22.5%
Above Rs. 500 to 1000	6	15%
Above Rs. 1000 to 2000	5	12.5%
Above Rs. 2000 to 3000	4	10%
Above Rs. 3000 to 4000	2	5%
Above Rs. 4000 to Rs. 5000	0	0%
Above Rs. 5000	12	30%
Total	**40**	**100%**

Source: Field Data.

It is followed by gross income category of Rs. 300 to 500 which represent 22.5 per cent of total respondents. However, no one has been reported to have amassed income above Rs. 4000 to 5000. In addition, per day gross income of women retailers is found pretty poor below Rs. 300 and above Rs. 3000 to 4000. These categories share five per cent each of total respondents under present study.

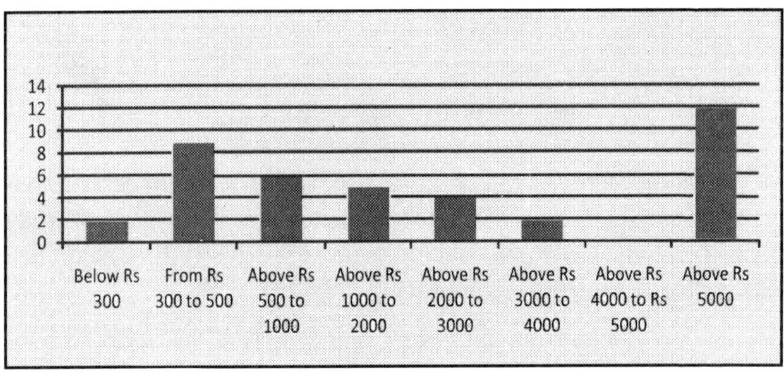

Fig. 11. 4: Per day Gross Income of Women Retailers

(v) Economic Liberty over Business by Women Retailers

In the study area, most of the women retailers enjoy economic liberty over their business as evident from Table 11.5 and Fig. 11.5. 37 respondents off 40 that constitute 92 per cent of total samples are reported to have enjoyed economic liberty over their business. They are not being faced with interventions in any form either from husband or relatives.

Table 11.5: Economic Liberty over Business by Women Retailers in the Study Area

	Yes	No	Partial
No of Respondents	37	0	3
Percent	92	0	8

Source: Field Data.

They takes own business decisions – savings, purchasing and expansion of business etc. During the field study, it is found that only eight per cent of respondents are reported to have partial liberty over their business. It implies partial business decision-making. It construes partial influences on their decisions by either their husbands or family members. Fortunately, none of the women under current study has reported to have under complete influence of others while making vital decision-making as evident from Table 11.5 and Fig. 11.5 respectively.

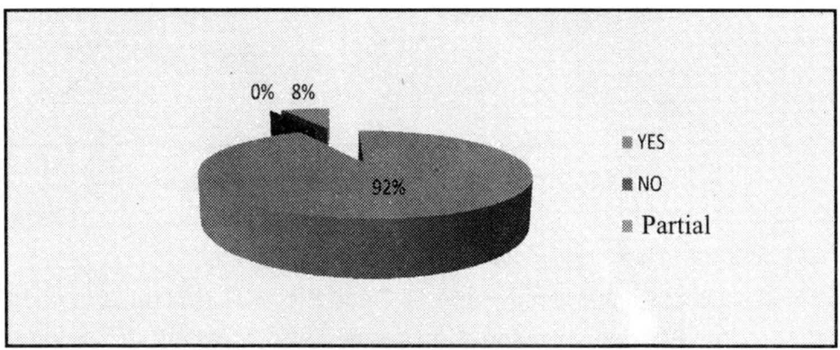

Fig. 11.5: Economic Liberty over Business

(vi) Application of Business Income by Women Retailers

It is revealed from Table 11.6 and Fig. 11.6 that women retailers have used most of their business income toward family expenditures. 19 off 40 samples *i.e.*, 47 per cent of total samples are found to have met their family financial requirements through business income. It is also clear from Table 11.6 that 28 per cent of women under present study have devoted business income towards expansion.

Table 11.6: Application of Business Income by Women Retailers in the Study Area

Application of Income	Bank Deposit	Family Expenditure	Expansion of Business	Others
No. of Respondents	8	19	11	2
Percent	20	47	28	5

Source: Field Data.

In addition, only 20 per cent of observed samples has made direct bank deposits of business income. It portrays growing consciousness of women on banking business in the study area. However, only 5 per cent of observed samples are found to have channelized business income into other domains.

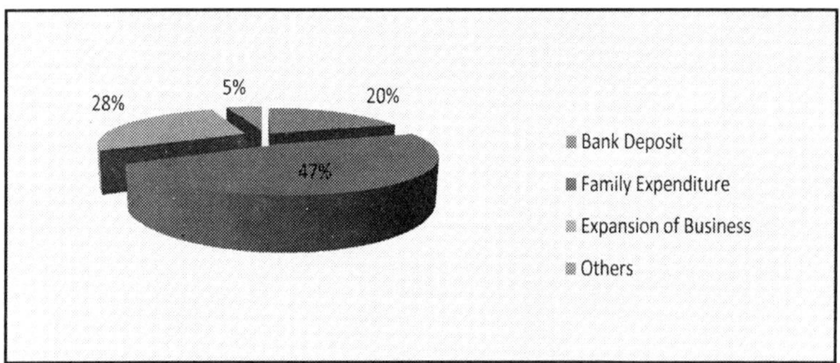

Fig. 11.6: Application of Business Income

(vii) Source of Idea of Retail Business by Women

It is crystal-clear from Table 11.7 and Fig. 11.7 that most women retailers have received inspiration or ideas of doing retail business from their family and close relatives. 19 off 40 samples that represent 47.5 of total samples are in receipt of ideas from their family members and other close relatives.

Table 11.7: Source of Idea of Retail Business by Women in the Study Area

Sources	Family and Relative	Friends	Neighbors	Outside Exposure	Self	Others
No. of Respondents	19	14	3	0	4	0
Percent	47.5	35	7.5	0	10	0

Source: Field Data.

Moreover, friends have been one of major sources of idea or motivation behind doing retail business by women of the study area as it share 35 per cent of total samples. In addition, neighbors and own self have booked third and fourth places as being sources of idea of doing retail business. However, none of the woman has reported to have drawn ideas of doing retail business either from others or outside exposures.

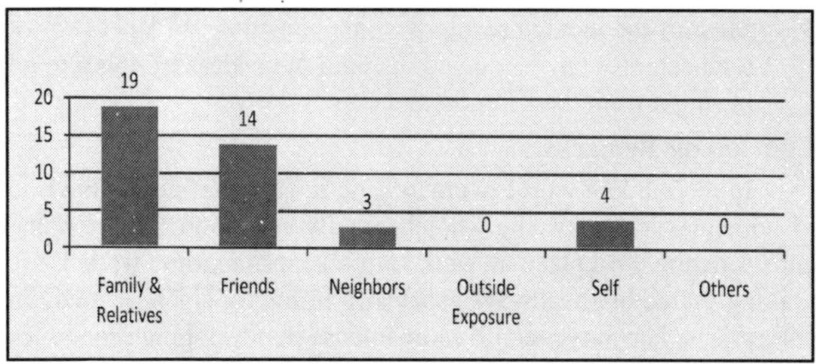

Fig. 11.7: Source of Idea of Retail Business

Major Findings

1. The present study reveals that women under age group from 25 to 30 years are most active in retail business. This age group constitutes 55 per cent of total samples taken from the study area.
2. Degree of women entrepreneurship in retail business in the study area is found to be on decrease with increase in their ages.
3. Most of the women retailers in the study area are illiterate that constitute 35 per cent of total samples.
4. None of women retailer in the study area is found to have either graduated or did any equivalent degree or above.
5. Non-institutional sources of finance have been the major sources of finance to women retailers in the study area of which 72.5 per cent is in a form of own capital.
6. None of the women retailer has reported to get finance from either Regional Rural Bank or State Bank of India.
7. Only seven per cent of the observed samples have been financed by North East Development and Financial Corporation (NEDfi) under institutional sources of financing.
8. 30 per cent of the total samples are reported to have earned more than Rs. 5000 in a single day from their retail business.
9. 92 per cent of total samples are reported to have enjoyed economic liberty over their retail business.
10. 47 per cent of total samples are found to have met their family financial requirements through business income.

11. Most of the women retailers which constitute 47.5 per cent of total samples have received inspiration or ideas of doing retail business from their family and close relatives.

Concluding Remarks

In the modern world, woman is no longer confined to the role of homemaker. Today, she wholeheartedly contributes to the home and leads the workplace as well. Into business regime, women are making incredible headways especially in micro, small or medium enterprises. The movement is more intense in developing economies and they enjoy financial empowerment. Moreover, women' participation in retail business is on rise all over the world as the same happens in capital region of Arunachal Pradesh. The present study confirms age group of women between 25 to 30 years as most active but mostly illiterate in the releam of retail business. In addition, most women retailers of the study area conceive ideas of doing business through family members and relatives. They also enjoy economic liberty over their business and spend much of business income for family members. However, institutional financing is least heard story of women retailers of the study area. They rely mostly on own capital to start off pretty retail businesses. However, maintaining balance between family commitments and business, excessive credit sales, stiff competition, inconsistency of income and too much of family members to support at home are some of the key nightmares they are being faced with.

Nevertheless, retail business helps in cementing common platform for women that facilitates close interaction and helps in combating their frustration arisen out of unemployment and mind-numbing family life.

REFERENCES

Balakrishnan, K., (2011), 'Present Status of Women Entrepreneurship in India' Oppaper.com, free Essay and Research Papers.

Kickul, J. R. and Thomas, C., (2007), 'Women Entrepreneurs Preparing for Growth: The Influence of Social Capital and Training on Resources Acquisition', *Journal of the Canadian Council for Small-business and Entrepreneurship.*

Kilgallen, K. and Hardie, C., (2007); *'Women in Retail: It's a Man's World'*, Retail Weeks, 22 November.

12

Women and Education in India

Dr. Surajit Kumar Bhagowati
Rupali (Goswami) Sarma

Abstract

Women play a vital role in the overall development of the country. It not only helps in the development of half of the human resources, but in improving the quality of life at home and outside. Educated women not only tend to promote education of their girl children, but also can provide better guidance to all their children. In addition to this, educated women can also help in the reduction of infant mortality rate and growth of the population. Education is a reasonably good indication of development and the right of every individual to education is one of the first provisions of the Universal Declaration on Human Rights. But education is often neglected in societies struggling to meet the needs of their people. Recently education has received greater priority as Planners and Policy-makers finally recognised it as a key factor in determining the pace of development. Only 65.46 per cent of women are literates as per 2011 census. Even though the education system expanded very rapidly, the gender gap in literacy remains conspicuous by its presence. The Constitution of India confers on women, equal rights and opportunities in all fields. The Government of India has endorsed the same through its Plans, Policies and Programmes. In spite of all these, women in India have not been able to take full advantage of their rights and opportunities in practice for various reasons. Therefore in this paper an attempt has been made to highlight the literacy status of Indian women as well as the International and National initiatives to promote women's education in India.

Keywords: *Women, Education, Gender Sensitization, Literacy, Low Literacy.*

INTRODUCTION

Although efforts have been taken to improve the status of women in India, the constitutional dream of gender equality is miles away from becoming a reality. Even today, 'the mainstream remains very much a male-stream'. The dominant tendency has always been to confine women and women's issues in the private domain. The traditional systems of control with its notion of 'what is right and proper for women' still reigns supreme and reinforces the use of violence as a means to punish its defiant female 'offenders' and their supporters.

Women in India constitute almost 50 per cent of the country's human resources and their contributions are vital for the nation's progress. Women's development is regarded as an important approach to raise the levels of productivity and to break the vicious circle of poverty, for which better health and education forms important. These factors not only improve the physical well-being of the individuals directly, but also enhance their productivity and ability to contribute to the 'National Income'.

In any society, education is a reasonably good indicator of development. Spread and diffusion of literacy is generally associated with essential trait of today's civilization such as modernization, urbanisation, industrialization, communication and commerce.

Therefore to acquire a better quality of life, education is highly essential. The word 'education' implies the characteristics of both the types of knowledge, material as well as spiritual. Mahatma Gandhi said that "education is a means for an all round drawing out of the best in child and man-body, mind and spirit. Literacy is not the end of the education or even the beginning. It is one of the means where man and woman can be educated". Thus Gandhiji's concept of education stands for the balanced and harmonious development of all the aspects of human personality. Moreover, the 'Human Rights' concept also tells that each human being has right to live with human dignity (Universal Declaration of Human Rights, 1948, Articles 14-26.

The Constitution of India also confers on women, equal rights and opportunities in all fields – political, social, economic and legal. The Government of India has endorsed the same through its Plans, Policies and Programmes launched at different points of time. The article 15 of the Constitution of India prohibits any discrimination on grounds of sex (Constitution of India Article 15(1) (3)). In spite of these, women have not been able to take full advantage of their rights and opportunities in practice for various reasons.

The magnitude of illiteracy among women in India is very high. Only 65.46 per cent of women are literates as per 2011 census. It reflects that India is not utilising the potential workers in a proper way. There is either un-utilisation or under utilisation of women's capacities and skills. Therefore in this paper an attempt has been made to highlight the International as well as National responses towards women's education. At the end of the article some measures are suggested to overcome the problem of illiteracy among women and to foster their journey towards a dignified and decent life.

Methodology

The data for the present study have been gleaned from various sources which have been duly acknowledged. Information on women's enrolment at different levels of University and professional colleges was obtained through the reports of the University Grants Commission, New Delhi and The Report on Selected Educational Statistics, Published by the Statistics Division, Ministry of Human Resource Development, New Delhi.

Observation and Data Analysis

- *Women's Right to Education*: It is nearly six decades since the UN General Assembly adopted the Declaration of Human Rights – on 10th December 1948. This declaration listed 30 Articles. Out of which the Article 26 states that:

"Everyone has the right to education. Education shall be free, at least in the elementary and fundamental stages. Elementary education shall be compulsory. Technical and professional education shall be made generally available and higher education shall be equally accessible to all on the basis of merit. Education shall be directed to the full development of the human personality and to the strengthening of respect for human rights and fundamental freedoms. It shall promote understanding, tolerance and friendship among all nations, racial, religious groups and shall further the activities of the United Nations for the maintenance of peace. Parents have a prior right to choose the kind of education that shall be given to their children".

- *The Reality in India*: In Independent India, education acquired special significance and has been supported by the Government from time to time through its policies and programmes. Therefore in recent years the education system expanded rapidly. But the gender gap in literacy rate remains conspicuous by its presence. The following facts and figures throw light on the gravity of the problem which is a reality and the seriousness of the task ahead.

According to the Table 12.1 the pre-Independence time literacy rate for women had a very poor spurt in comparison to literacy rate of men. This is witnessed from the fact that literacy rate of women has risen from 0.7 per cent to 7.3 per cent where as the literacy rate of men has risen from 9.8 per cent to 24.9 per cent during these four decades.

In the post-independence period the percentages of literacy rates among males and females grown in a faster mode. But the gap between male and female literacy which was 18.30 per cent in 1951 increased to 25.05 per cent in 1961 and 26.62 per cent in 1981 (Table 12.1). After that there was a slow decrease in the gap as the literary rate among women started gradually increasing after 1991 (54.16% in 2001 and 65.46% in 2011) due to the interventions taken by the government. But still nearly 35 per cent of women are illiterates. From this analysis one can infer that still the female literacy rate is wadding behind male literacy rate. This higher rate of illiteracy of women is undoubtedly attributing for women dependence on men and to play a subordinate role. The lack of education is the root cause for women's exploitation and negligence. Only literacy can help women to understand the importance in educating them to accomplish their goals in par with men in different spheres of life.

Table 12.1: Literacy Rates in India Since 1901 to 2011

Year	Persons	Males	Females	Difference of Male Female Literacy Rates
1901	5.3	9.8	0.7	9.1
1911	5.9	10.6	1.1	9.5
1921	7.2	12.2	1.8	10.4
1931	9.5	15.6	2.9	12.7
1941	16.1	24.9	7.3	17.6
1951	18.33	27.16	8.86	18.30
1961	28.30	40.40	15.35	25.05
1971	34.45	45.96	21.97	23.99
1981	43.57	56.38	29.76	26.62
1991	52.21	64.13	39.29	24.84
2001	65.38	75.85	54.16	21.69
2011	74.04	82.14	65.46	16.68

Source: Census of India 2011.

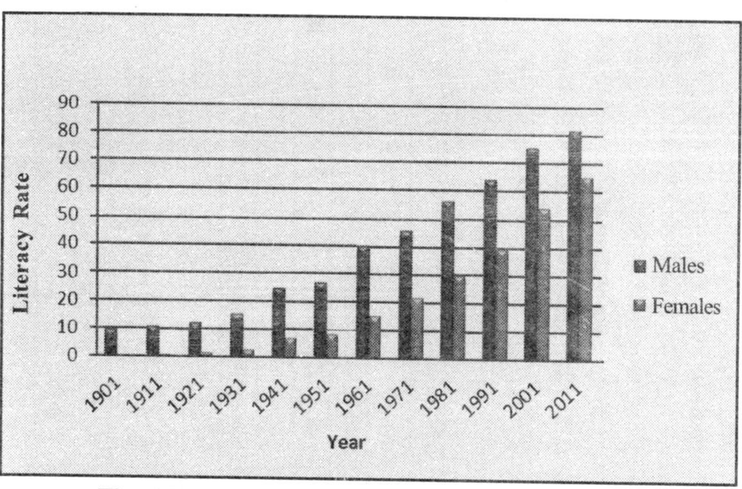

Fig. 12.1: Literacy Rates in India 1901 to 2011

Table 12.2 shows that the state-wise female literacy rate had an average of 65.46 per cent in all India basis in 2011 census with Kerala state in highest literacy with 91.98 per cent and among Union Territories, Lakshadweep occupies first place with 88.25 per cent. In Uttar Pradesh only 52.66 per cent women are literate followed Bihar with 53.33 per cent. Similarly, out of 35 states six (6) states have recorded female literacy below 60 per cent while nine (9) states have recorded more than 80 female literacy (2011 census).

Table 12.2: Literacy Rates State-wise, Gender-wise in India (2011 census)

	States/ UT	Total Literates	Male Literates	Female Literates	Total Literacy Rate	Male Literacy Rate	Female Literacy Rate
	1	2	3	4	5	6	7
	India	77,84,54,120	44,42,03,762	33,42,50,358	74.04	82.14	65.46
1.	Jammu and Kashmir	72,45,053	43,70,604	28,74,449	68.74	78.26	58.01
2.	Himachal Pradesh	51,04,506	27,91,542	23,12,964	83.78	90.83	76.60
3.	Punjab	1,89,88,611	1,06,26,788	83,61,823	76.68	81.48	71.34
4.	Chandigarh	8,09,653	4,68,166	3,41,487	86.43	90.54	81.38
5.	Uttarakhand	69,97,433	39,30,174	30,67,259	79.63	88.33	70.70
6.	Haryana	1,69,04,324	99,91,838	69,12,486	76.64	85.38	66.77
7.	NCT of Delhi	1,27,63,352	72,10,050	55,53,302	86.34	91.03	80.93
8.	Rajasthan	3,89,70,500	2,41,84,782	1,47,85,718	67.06	80.51	52.66
9.	Uttar Pradesh	11,84,23,805	7,04,79,196	4,79,44,609	69.72	79.24	59.26

Contd...

1		2	3	4	5	6	7
10.	Bihar	5,43,90,254	3,27,11,975	2,16,78,279	63.82	73.39	53.33
11.	Sikkim	4,49,294	2,53,364	1,95,930	82.20	87.29	76.43
12.	Arunachal Pradesh	7,89,943	4,54,532	3,35,411	66.95	73.69	59.57
13.	Nagaland	13,57,579	7,31,796	6,25,783	80.11	83.29	76.69
14.	Manipur	18,91,196	10,26,733	8,64,463	79.85	86.49	73.17
15.	Mizoram	8,47,592	4,38,949	4,08,643	91.58	93.72	89.40
16.	Tripura	28,31,742	15,15,973	13,15,769	87.75	92.18	83.15
17.	Meghalaya	18,17,761	9,34,091	8,83,670	75.48	77.17	73.78
18.	Assam	1,95,07,017	1,07,56,937	87,50,080	73.18	78.81	67.27
19.	West Bengal	6,26,14,556	3,45,08,159	2,81,06,397	77.08	82.67	71.16
20.	Jharkhand	1,87,53,660	1,11,68,649	75,85,011	67.63	78.45	56.21
21.	Orissa	2,71,12,376	1,53,26,036	1,17,86,340	73.45	82.40	64.36
22.	Chhattisgarh	1,55,98,314	89,62,121	66,36,193	71.04	81.45	60.59
23.	Madhya Pradesh	4,38,27,193	2,58,48,137	1,79,79,056	70.63	80.53	60.02
24.	Gujarat	4,19,48,677	2,39,95,500	1,79,53,177	79.31	87.23	70.73
25.	Daman and Diu	1,88,974	1,24,911	64,063	87.07	91.48	79.59
26.	Dadra and Nagar Haveli	2,28,028	1,44,916	83,112	77.65	86.46	65.93

Contd...

1		2	3	4	5	6	7
27.	Maharashtra	8,25,12,225	4,62,94,041	3,62,18,184	82.91	89.82	75.48
28.	Andhra Pradesh	5,14,38,510	2,87,59,782	2,26,78,728	67.66	75.56	59.74
29.	Karnataka	4,10,29,323	2,28,08,468	1,82,20,855	75.60	82.85	68.13
30.	Goa	11,52,117	6,20,026	5,32,091	87.40	92.81	81.84
31.	Lakshadweep	52,914	28,249	24,665	92.28	96.11	88.25
32.	Kerala	2,82,34,227	1,37,55,888	1,44,78,339	93.91	96.02	91.98
33.	Tamil Nadu	5,24,13,116	2,83,14,595	2,40,98,521	80.33	86.81	73.86
34.	Puducherry	9,66,600	5,02,575	4,64,025	86.55	92.12	81.22
35.	Andaman and Nicobar Islands	2,93,695	1,64,219	1,29,476	86.27	90.11	81.84

Source: Census report 2011.

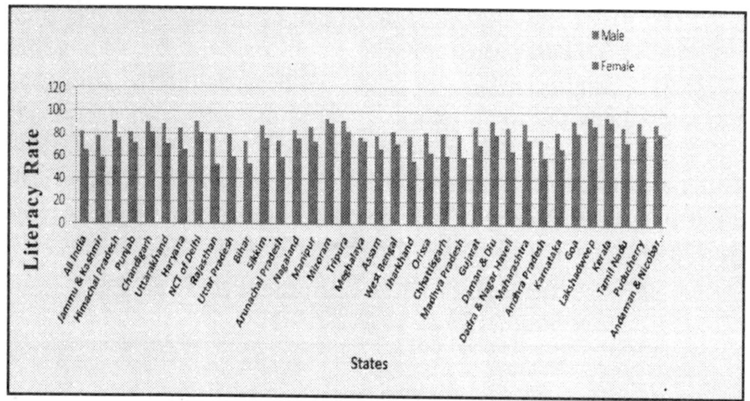

Fig. 12.2: Literacy Rates State-wise: 2011

As per the census 2011, the positions of female literacy in different districts of the country (top/bottom five districts) are as below:

Top Five Districts According to Female only Literacy Rate in India are:

1. Serchhip in Mizoram with 98.28 per cent female only literacy rate.
2. Aizawl in Mizoram with 98.00 per cent female only literacy rate.
3. Mahe in Puducherry (U/T) with 97.61 per cent female only literacy rate.
4. Pathanamthitta in Kerala with 96.26 per cent female only literacy rate.
5. Kottayam in Kerala with 95.67 per cent female only literacy rate.

Bottom Five Districts According to Female only Literacy Rate in India are:

(i) Alirajpur in Madhya Pradesh with 30.97 per cent female only literacy rate.

(ii) Bijapur in Chhattisgarh with 31.56 per cent female only literacy rate.

(iii) Dakshin Bastar Dantewada in Chhattisgarh with 32.88 per cent female only literacy rate.

(iv) Jhabua in Madhya Pradesh with 34.29 per cent female only literacy rate.

(v) Shrawasti in Uttar Pradesh with 37.07 per cent female only literacy rate.

The participation of girls at all stages of education has been increasing steadily through the years as may be seen from Table 12.3. Since 1950-51 to 2010-11, the girls' participation has increased many folds in Primary, Upper Primary, Sec./Sr. Sec. stages and Hr. Education levels from 28.1 per cent to 47.9 per cent, from 16.1 per cent to 47.1 per cent from 13.3 per cent to 44.7 per cent and from 10.0 per cent to 40.1 per cent respectively. However, the girls' participation is still below fifty per cent at all stages of education.

Table 12.3: Percentage of Girls Enrolment to Total Enrolment by Stages, 1950-51 to 2010-11

Year	Primary I-V	Upper Primary VI-VIII	Sec/Sr. Sec/ Intermediate IX-XII	Higher Education Degree and above
1950-51	28.1	16.1	13.3	10.0
1960-61	32.6	23.9	20.5	16.0
1970-71	37.4	29.3	25.0	20.0
1980-81	38.6	32.9	29.6	26.7
1990-91	41.5	36.7	32.9	33.3
2000-01	43.7	40.9	38.6	39.4
2010-11	47.9	47.1	44.7	40.1

Source: Reports of the Ministry of HRD, Government of India.

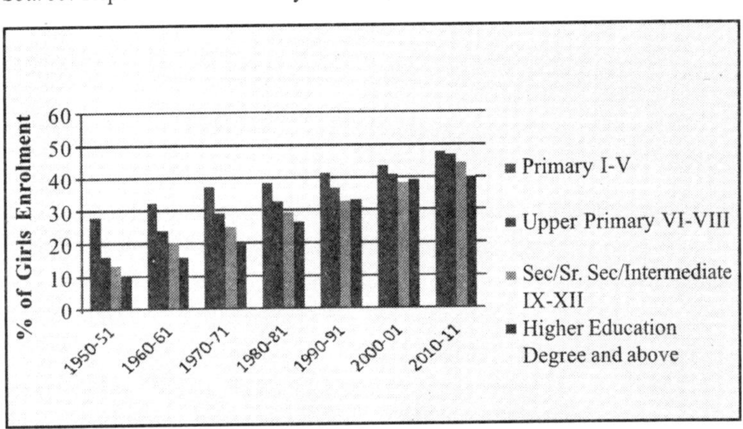

Fig. 12.3: Percentage of Girls Enrolment in Different States of Education

Responsible Factors for Low Literacy Rates among Women in India

The literacy rate in the country has increased from 18.33 per cent in 1951 to 74.04 per cent in 2011 census. The female literacy rate has also increased from 8.86 per cent to (in 1951) to 65.46 per cent (in 2011). It is noticed that female literacy during the period 1991-2011 has increased by 26.17 per cent where as male literacy has rose by 18.01 per cent. Though there is an increase in female literacy rate, still 34.54 per cent of women are illiterates in India. (2011 census). Since 2001 the difference between male and female literacy has been in decreasing trend *viz;* 21.69 per cent in 2001 to 16.68 per cent in 2011.

In spite of a number of National and International Programmes are in implementation to eradicate illiteracy from our country, especially among women, the gap between male and female literacy still persists. In this context, the factors responsible for low female literacy rate in India are identified and listed below:

- Gender based inequality.
- Social discrimination and economic exploitation.
- Occupation of girl child in domestic chores.
- Low enrolment of girls in schools.
- Low retention rate and high dropout rate.
- Deprived of access to information and alienated from decision-making processes.
- Absence of female teachers in schools.
- Schools established in faraway places etc.

Barriers to Education: (past findings)

There are several reasons for the low levels of literacy in India, not the least of which is the high level of poverty. Over one-third of the population is estimated to be living below the poverty line (The World Bank, 1997a). Although school attendance is free, the costs of books, uniforms, and transportation to school can be too much for poor families. Poor families are also more likely to keep girls at home to care for younger siblings or to work in family enterprises.

If a family has to choose between educating a son or a daughter because of financial restrictions, typically the son will be chosen. Negative parental attitudes toward educating daughters can also be a barrier to a girl's education. Many parents view educating sons as an investment because the sons will be responsible for caring for aging parents. On the other hand, parents may see the education of daughters as waste of money because daughters will eventually live with their husbands' families and the parents will not benefit directly from their education. Also, daughters with higher levels of education will likely have higher dowry expenses as they will want a comparably educated husband. However, education sometimes lowers the dowry for a girl because it is viewed as an asset by the husband's family.

Another barrier to education in India is the lack of adequate school facilities. Many states simply do not have enough class-rooms to accommodate all of the school-age children. Furthermore, the classrooms that are available often lack basic necessities such as sanitary facilities or water. In Uttar Pradesh, a recent survey found that 54 per cent of schools did not have a water supply and 80 per cent did not have latrines (The World Bank, 1997b). Lack of latrines can be particularly detrimental to girls' school attendance.

In some states, the inadequate supply of classrooms is further compounded by the large increase in the number of school-age children due to high population growth rates.

Lack of female teachers is another potential barrier to girls' education. Girls are more likely to attend school and have higher academic achievement if they have female teachers. This is particularly true in highly gender-segregated societies such as India (Bellew and King, 1993; King, 1990). Currently, women account for only 29 per cent of teachers at the primary level (MHRD, 1993). The proportion of teachers who are female is even lower at the university level, 22 per cent of instructors (CSO, 1992). These proportions reflect the historic paucity of women with the educational qualifications to be teachers. However, the proportions are likely to change in the future as women currently account for nearly half of those being trained as teachers. Again there are differences among the states; the states with the highest literacy rates are also the states with the highest proportion of female teachers. As long ago as 1965, the Indian government agreed to rewrite text-books so that men and women would not be portrayed in gender-stereotyped roles. However, a study of Indian text-books done in the 1980s found that men were the main characters in the majority of lessons. In these lessons, men held high-prestige occupations and were portrayed as strong, adventurous, and intelligent. In contrast, when women were included they were depicted as weak and helpless, often as the victims of abuse and beatings (Kalia, 1988). These depictions are strong barriers for improving women's position in society.

Although, most of these limitations in women education have been minimized by the Government of India but still the threats persists.

Women's Education – The International and National Initiatives

- *International Initiatives*: India has ratified various International Conventions and Human Rights instruments committing to secure equal rights of women. Key among them is the ratification of the Convention on Elimination of All Forms of Discrimination Against Women (CEDAW, 1979) in 1993. CEDAW was adopted by United Nations General Assembly (UNGA) in December 1979, and there are more than 150 states parties to the convention.
- *CEDAW – 1979:* This Convention calls for equal rights for women regardless their married status in all fields – political, economic, social, cultural and civil. It appeals for a national legislature to ban discrimination; recommends temporary special measures to spread equality between men and women and actions to modify social and cultural pattern that perpetuates discrimination (CEDAW – 1979).

UNICEF, Report in 1992 Conference on Education for All Girls

Programmes of Women's Studies have attempted to dismantle stereotypes and build up women's esteem. Special studies reveal both the extent to which women have been deprived and oppressed and elements in the tradition of all civilization that promote positive images to and ease the conflicts experienced by many women in pursuit of their advancement and new roles in society.

The UAC's programme for promoting Women's Studies envisages assistance to Universities for setting up centres and cells for Women's Studies. The centres and cells are required to undertake research, develop curricula and organize training and extension work in the areas of gender equality, economic, self-reliance of women, girl's education, population issues, issues of human rights and social exploration (Vina Mazumdar, 2003).

- *Beijing Conference: Platform for Action 1995:* The Mexico Plan of Action (1975), the Nairobi Forward Looking Strategies (1985), the Beijing Declaration as well as the Platform of Action (1995) and the outcome Document adopted by the UNGA (United Nations General Assembly) Session on 'Gender Equality and Development and Peace for the 21st century', titled Further actions and initiatives to implement the Beijing Declaration and the Platform of action have been unreservedly endorsed by India for appropriate follow up.

Beijing Conference adopted a Declaration and Platform of Action on the concluding day. The Platform of Action is addressing the unequal access to and inadequate educational opportunities to women suggested the following strategies to be adopted by the Governments.

Strategic objective 1: Ensure equal access to education.

Strategic objective 2: Eradicate illiteracy among women.

Strategic objective 3: Improve women's access to vocational training, science and technology and continuing education.

Strategic objective 4: Develop non-discriminate education and training.

Strategic objective 5: Promote lifelong education and training for girls and women (Beiging Platform of Action – Five Years After 2002).

- *Education for All:* The World Conference on Education for All, sponsored by UNESCO, UNICEF, the World Bank and the UNDP, held in 1990 took stock of the persistence and dimensions of the gender gap. Its final Declaration stated that drawing attention to poor environments experienced by hundreds of millions of girls, it calls for ensuing that all learners receive the nutrition, health care and general physical and emotional support they need.

- *National Initiatives:* The development strategy in Independent India in the 1950s depended heavily on planning. Therefore the development plans prepared for Five years are referred as the Five-year Plans. The first two plans referred to the problems of women's education and occupation. The Report of the Committee on the 'Education of Women' 1959, made extensive recommendations which led to a more focused thrust in the subsequent plans. But disparities in the literacy rates between men and women continued. These were amply substantiated by the Report of Committee on the 'Status of Women, 1974'. This led to a broader perspective and the Sixth Plan linked education to the participation of women in the development process (Status of Women, 1974).
- *The National Policy on Education (NPE)* – 1986 revised in 1992 took an even broader view in underscoring the role of education in empowering women in order to overcome inequalities and disparities. It has been regarded as a land mark in the approach to women's education and also attempted for the first time to address itself to the basic issues of women's equality.

Education will be used as an agent of basic change in the status of women. In order to neutralize the accumulated distortion of the past, there will be a well conceived edge in favour of women. The National education system will play a positive, interventionist role in the empowerment of women. It will foster the development of new values, through redesigned curricula, text books, training and orientation of teachers, decision makes and administrators.

The NPE also provided detailed information about the recommendations of the Rammurthy Committee and Education for All by 2000 AD. This has presented an over view on the status of women's education in India since 1995 in all its aspects, particularly empowering women through 'Mahila Samakya Programmes'. These programmes are directed to create a learning environment where women can collectively affirm their aim, the strength to demand information and knowledge and move forward towards attaining a quality life (New Education Policy, 1986, 1992).

The Eighth Five-year Plan marked the adoption of two National Plans for Action in 1992. One for children and the other one exclusively for the girl child (VIII Five-year Plan, 1992-97).

In the Ninth Plan the thrust was on strengthening the early joyful period of play and learning in the young child's life to ensure a harmonious transition from the family environment to the primary school. Towards this, special efforts were made to develop linkages between ICDS (Integrated Child Development Scheme) and primary education. Their operational linkage aimed at reinforcing co-ordination of timings and location based on community appraisal and micro planning at grass root level. Girl's education was viewed as a major intervention for breaking the vicious inter-generational cycle of gender and socio-economic disadvantages. The effective expansion of day care services, linkages of child care services and primary schools was a major input to promote developmental opportunities for the girl child for participation in primary education and supportive services for women (IX Five-year Plan, 1997-2002).

During X Five-year Plan a programme called 'Sarva Siksha Abiyan' was launched with an objective – that all the children in the school going age (below 14 years) in India , must be in schools and should complete five years of schooling by 2007 (X Five-year Plan, 2002-07).

Dr. Manmohan Singh, Prime Minister of India has termed the XI Five-year Plan as India's Educational Plan. The NDC (National Development Council) in December 2007, places the highest priority on education as a central instrument for achieving rapid and inclusive growth. It aims at:

1. Increase literary rate for persons of age 7 years or more to 85 per cent.
2. Lowering gender gap in literacy to 10 percentage points.
3. Reduction of dropout rate of children from elementary school from 52.2 per cent to 20 per cent by 2011-12.
4. Developing minimum standards of education attainment in elementary school, and by regular testing, monitoring the effectiveness of education to ensure quality (XI Five-year Plan, 2007-12).

Education for All (EPA): Education for all, means extending educational opportunities to all, regardless of race, colour, creed, sex or ability. In the Indian context, EPA implies the following:

- Universalisation of Elementary Education – UEE.
- Expansion of Early Childhood Care and Education – ECCE.
- Equalization of Educational opportunities for women.
- Removal of regional and gender disparities
- A systematic programme for Non-Formal Education
- Imparting basic education
- Providing vocational training etc.

Gender Sensitization: Government attaches greater importance to those efforts which trigger changes in social attitudes towards women. The women's development division of the National Institute of Public Cooperation and Child Development, New Delhi, organizes training programmes with a focus on gender issues. These programmes include para-legal training, training of elected women representatives of panchayats, leadership and organization, training of voluntary agencies reaching women awareness and gender sensitization programmes, incorporation of gender issues in development programmes etc.

In addition to this the Women's Studies Centres established in various Institutions and Universities have been imparting training on Gender Sensitization to different target groups (students, officials, administrators, police personnel, Panchayat Raj functionaries etc.)

The programme of education for prevention of atrocities against women was started in 1982. Based upon the recommendations made in the National Perspective Plan (1988), and the National Policy for the Empowerment of Women (2001) the proposal for setting up 'National Resource Centre's for women is now at an advanced stage.

Strategies Adopted by the Government for Increasing Female Literacy in the Country

The main strategies adopted by the Government for increasing female literacy in the country include (National Literacy Mission, 1988):

1. National Literacy Mission for imparting Functional Literacy.
2. Universalisation of Elementary Education.
3. Non-Formal Education.

Contribution of Literacy Campaigns to Female Literacy

The provision of educational opportunities for women has been an important part of the national endeavour in the field of education since India's Independence. Though these endeavours did yield significant results, gender disparity persists with uncompromising tenacity, more so in the rural areas and among the disadvantaged communities. This is not only a matter of national anxiety and concern but also a matter of national conscience. It is with this concern that the Government of India launched the National Literacy Mission in 1988 for eradication of adult literacy. Since women account for an overwhelming percentage of illiterates, the National Literacy Mission – Mission of imparting functional literacy to women was launched in 1988. The total Literacy Campaigns launched since 1988 under the aegis of the National emphasis are making efforts to:

> *"Create an environment where women demand knowledge and information, empowering themselves to change their lives. Inculcate in women the confidence that change is possible, if women work collectively. Spread the message that education of women is a pre-condition for fighting against their oppression. Highlight the plight of the girl child and stress the need for universaliation of Elementary Education as a way of addressing the issue".*

Some of the significant ways in which the literacy campaigns have contributed to the promotion of female literacy and women's empowerment are as follows:

- Heightened social awareness among women.
- Increased school enrolment rate of girls.
- Increased self-confidence and personality development.
- Promoted gender equity and women's empowerment.
- Improved the status of women in the family.
- Educational equity – Gender gap in literacy levels have gradually reduced.
- Encouraged Women to take up entrepreneurship.
- Increased household savings and access to credit.
- Provided awareness about health and hygiene.

Some of the significant ways in which the literacy campaigns have contributed to the promotion of female literacy and literacy campaigns have heightened social awareness among women regarding the importance of education, both for themselves as well as for their children. Large numbers of women have been participating whole-heartedly in the literacy campaigns as learners and volunteers. Because of the campaign mode and creation of a positive environment for literacy, women receive a social sanction to participate in the literacy programmes. As women came out of their homes and take part in the campaigns with great enthusiasm, they acquire a heightened sense of self-awareness and desire to gain knowledge of host of women's issues.

The literacy campaigns have also motivated and encouraged women learners to educate their children, particularly girls by enrolling them in formal schools. An evaluation study of the literacy campaign in Birbhum District of Bihar has shows that the biggest achievement of the adult literacy programme in Birbhum has been its impact on girls' education. The confidence of the girls, as they perform drill or play football, is the result of the awareness among neo-literate parents that girls need to be educated and outgoing. The need to provide equal opportunity to both girls and boys has also had effect of generating greater demand for the quantity to both girls and boys has also had effect of generating greater demand for the quantity and quality of primary schooling.

In our neighboring Country Bangladesh, more than 90 lakh women are being empowered by the Grameen bank to restart their basic level of education and understanding of economic system of the country through micro-credit. Even the most illiterate women, who have not seen the school in life, are being considered as most respected member of their families by their orthodox husbands. Therefore, no one can avoid education, and no one should be allowed to run out of the education system, if a country needs to be developed socially and economically.

Considering the above, the following are the some strategies recommended to encourage girls/women's education in India.

- Involving women's groups like DWCRA and Self-Help Groups in promoting women's literacy.

- Providing free and compulsory education for all girls up to 20 years.
- Establishment of more number of primary school.
- Bringing out changes in the attitudes of parents and in the society.
- Inclusion of Literacy programmes in all governmental schemes.
- Effective implementation of follow up programme.
- Removal of gender bias in the school curriculum.
- Establishment of more number of NFE (Non-Formal Education) schools to enroll girls and women of different age groups.
- Widening the scope of Distance Education Programme to cover all categories of people especially rural women.

Conclusion

The right of every individual to education is one of the first provisions of the Universal Declaration on Human Rights. But education is often neglected in societies struggling to meet the many needs of their people. Recently education has received greater priority as Planners and Policy-makers finally recognised it as a key factor in determining the pace of development. Creating educational opportunities for girls and women is strongly emphasised in the work of the UN. CEDEW suggests 'ençouraging co-education' as one way of eliminating the stereotyping of women. Education, being the most powerful instrument for empowering women assumes special priority in the recent plans and programmes of National and International action. Concerted efforts are also made to bring more women into the purview of education. In spite of these many provisions, still there is a wide gap between male and female literacy levels in India. Keeping this in view the programme of action for future has to be formulated so as to reduce the gender gap as well as illiteracy rate among girls and women.

REFERENCES

Beijing Platform for Action, Five Years After, Department of Women and Child Development, Ministry of Human Resource Development, Government of India, June, 2000.

Census of India – 2001, Government of India, Part III, NSS 61st Round Survey Report, 2004-05, p. 24.

Constitution of India, Article 15(1)(13).

Five-year Plans, Government of India, Planning Commission (1992-2012).

Government of India, Selected Educational Statistics, 2004-05, Ministry of Human Resources Development, Department of Higher Education, Statistics Division, pp. 146-147, 2007.

Mazumdar, Vina, Evolution of Women's Studies in India. Dialouge with Researchers: Linking Policy and Research – A Consultation on Women's Studies, New Delhi: Centre for Women's Development Studies, pp. 47-49, 2002.

National Perspective Plan, Department of Women and Child Development, Government of India, pp. 67-80.

National Policy for the Empowerment of women, Department of Women and Child Development, Ministry of Human Resource Development, Government of India, 2001.

National Policy on Education, POA – Ministry of Education, Government of India, 1986.

Recommendations of the Committee on the Status of Women in India, and Views of the Empowered Committee (Inter-Ministerial), Government of India, Ministry of Education and Social Welfare, 1974.

Statistics on Women, National Institute of Public Cooperation and Child Development, New Delhi, 2007.

Universal Declaration of Human Rights, 1948.

The World Bank, 1997a, India: Achievement and Challenges in Reducing Poverty, Washington, DC.

The world Bank 1997b, Primary Education in India, Washington, DC.

Bellew, Rosemary T. and Elizabeth M. King, 1993, "Educating Women: Lessons from Experience," in Elizabeth M. King and M. Anne Hill, eds., Women's Education in Developing Countries, Baltimore.

King, Elizabeth M., 1990, Educating Girls and Women: Investing in Development, Washington, DC.

Ministry of Human Resource Development, 1993, Selected Educational Statistics, 1991-92, New Delhi.

(CSO) Central Statistical Organization, 1994, Statistical Abstract India 1992, New Delhi.

Kalia, Narendra Nath, 1988, "Women and Sexism: Language of Indian School Text-books," in Rehana Ghadially, ed., Women in Indian Society , New Delhi.

13

Drop-out of Girls

The Achilles Heel of the Indian Educational System

Arundhati Bhattacharyya
Soma Dhar

Abstract

India is an emerging power in the 21st century. Education is a very important resource for overall development of the personality of the individual and holistic development of the country. Swami Vivekananda has rightly stated that education is the manifestation of the perfection already in man. It is only with the support of education that an individual can develop all his faculties. Studies have shown that girls' education is consistently associated with positive development outcomes such as reduced maternal mortality, smaller families and healthier children. Moreover, when a mother is educated, inter-generational poverty is broken, children are more likely to be sent to school and infant and child mortality is reduced, among other benefits.

INTRODUCTION

India is an emerging power in the 21st century. From time immemorial, education was given utmost importance in the Indian civilization. A civilization cannot survive without the strong structure of education. Education is a very important resource for overall development of the personality of the individual and holistic development of the country. The format of education may be different for different countries, but there is no iota of confusion that all countries of the world have given utmost importance to educational enrichment of its citizens. Swami Vivekananda has rightly stated that education is the manifestation of the perfection already in man. It is only with the support of education that an individual can develop all his faculties.

According to Population Census of India 2011, the literacy rate of India has shown as improvement of almost 9 per cent. It has gone up to 74.04 per cent in 2011 from 65.38 per cent in 2001, thus showing an increase of 9 per cent in the last 10 years. It consists of male literacy rate 82.14 per cent and female literacy rate is 65.46 per cent. The ideal situation towards which all countries are striving is 100 per cent enrolment of both boys and girls, and 100 per cent retention at least up to the end of the primary school stage of education, usually a minimum of five years. This is the presupposition upon which is based the drive for universal primary education (UPE). Countries striving to attain UPE have to eliminate wastage and in particular drop-out. It is not possible in an educational system where drop-out exists. By its presence, it proclaims that UPE has not been attained. Drop-out represents a staggering loss.[1]

Studies have shown that girls' education is consistently associated with positive development outcomes such as reduced maternal mortality, smaller families and healthier children. Moreover, when a mother is educated, inter-generational poverty is broken, children are more likely to be sent to school and infant and child mortality is reduced, among other benefits. Education is one of the most effective strategies for combating child marriage, especially as girls progress to secondary school. According to a World Bank report, a one percentage point increase in female education raises the average level of GDP by 0, 3 percentage points.[2]

Indian Constitution

Universalization of elementary education of children up to the age of 14 was envisaged under Article 45 of the Constitution, which was under Directive Principles of State Policy. With a view to making right to free and compulsory education a fundamental right, the

Constitution (Eighty-third Amendment) Bill, 1997 was introduced in Parliament to insert a new article, namely, article 21 A conferring on all children in the age group of 6 to 14 years the right to free and compulsory education. The said Bill was scrutinized by the Parliamentary Standing Committee on Human Resource Development and the subject was also dealt with in its 165th Report by the Law Commission of India. After taking into consideration the report of the Law Commission of India and the recommendations of the Standing Committee of Parliament, the proposed amendments in Part III, Part IV and Part IVA of the Constitution are being made which are as follows:

(a) To provide for free and compulsory education to children in the age group of 6 to 14 years and for this purpose, a legislation would be introduced in Parliament after the Constitution (Ninety-third Amendment) Bill, 2001 is enacted.

(b) To provide in article 45 of the Constitution that the State shall endeavour to provide early childhood care and education to children below the age of six years.

(c) To amend article 51A of the Constitution with a view to providing that it shall be the obligation of the parents to provide opportunities for education to their children.[3]

The NPE of 1986 itself has suggested not only periodic reviews of the policy but also a revision in the long-term. It was also a major departure from the national policy adopted on the recommendations of the Education Commission under Professor D. S Kothari, which in 1966 had called for a common school system as well as for a Plus-Two stage of schooling beyond Class X. Strengthening of research in the university system was another major recommendation.[4]

The most notable development has been the acceptance of common structure of education throughout the country. The 10+2+3 structure was accepted by most of the states. In the school curricula, a common scheme for studies was allotted to boys and girls. Science and mathematics were incorporated as compulsory subjects.[5]

In the Programme of Action 1992, the rural girls are doubly disadvantaged. On the one hand, there is non-availability of proper educational facilities and on the other hand, they have to be engaged in paid and unpaid work, since childhood.[6]

. In 2001, the Government of India (GOI) launched the Sarva Shiksha Abhiyan ((SSA), now the programmatic vehicle for the delivery of the RTE) with a mandate that expenditure decisions be taken based on plans made at the school level through Village Education Committees (VEC). These plans are then aggregated at the district and state levels. Drawing on this model, the RTE mandates the creation of School Management Committees (SMCs) tasked with similar responsibilities. Despite this bottom-up planning structure, the centralized delivery system has disempowered these committees and in fact created disincentives for parental participation in a number of ways: *First*, teachers, as pointed out already, are not accountable to SMCs. *Secondly*, committees have spending powers over very little money. In 2010-11, committees had spending powers over just about 5 per cent of SSA funds. School grants rarely reach schools before October (the PAISA district studies found that on average school grants reach school bank accounts toward the end of September/ early October). These delays in fund flows mean that needs at the school often remain unmet owing to lack of money. Expenditures even for school grants are based on formal or informal orders received from district and block officials.[7]

Education of Girl Children

Education is the most powerful tool for change and can put girls on the path to economic and social empowerment. Education develops manpower for different levels of the economy. It is also the substrate on which research and development flourish, being the ultimate guarantee of national self-reliance. Education is a unique investment in the present and the future. Awareness of the inherent equality of all will be created through the core curriculum. The purpose of holistic education is to remove prejudices and complexes transmitted through the social environment and the accident of birth.[8] The United Nations Gender Inequality Index has ranked India below several sub-Saharan African countries. Gender disparities are even more pronounced in economic participation and women's business conditions in India. In India, the Sarva Siksha Abhiyan (SSA) which held a survey on the Gender Disparity and drop-out rates in India has revealed the record which explains that in a typical India family, the son almost gets special interest and care. According to the status of education in India, it also highlights that parents prefer to send their sons to private schools whereas the girl is sent to government schools.[9]

The National Council of Educational Research and Training (NCERT) released data for its 8th All India Education Survey, a survey which covers over 13 lakh recognised schools across the country. The NCERT released data for its 8th All India Education Survey, a survey which covers over 13 lakh recognised schools across the country. Collected for the period 2002-09, the survey reveals that even though there was a 19.12 per cent increase in girl's enrollment, girls enrolled in the primary school stage, drop-out as they move to higher classes. However, the survey also revealed that 40 per cent of primary schools have two teachers in each school. It also said schools in rural areas are still deprived of basic facilities like drinking water, usable urinal and playgrounds. The data reveals that one-fifth of the total primary schools in rural areas do not have drinking water, three out of ten schools are without usable urinal facilities and about half of the schools do not have playgrounds.[10]

In the year 2011 the National Commission for Protection of Child Rights (NCPCR) conducted a pilot of Social Audit of RTE Act in one district each in ten states of India namely: *(i)* Assam, *(ii)* Andhra Pradesh, *(iii)* Bihar, *(iv)* Delhi, *(v)* Haryana, *(vi)* Madhya Pradesh, *(vii)* Maharashtra, *(viii)* Rajasthan, *(ix)* Tamil Nadu and *(x)* Uttar Pradesh. The post facto Social Audit exposed that poor infrastructure and dismal teacher-pupil ratio are the characteristic features of most government schools in these 10 states. When many states like Delhi and Uttar Pradesh are accommodating more than 80 students in one class, the state of Haryana and Rajasthan lack basic amenities like drinking water and toilet facilities.

Many reports published in recent times have indicated a high drop-out rate by female students due to unavailability of toilets in school premises. These schools visited for the pilot social audit by NCPCR expressed anguish over government's non-responsiveness for construction of toilet facilities. The social audit conducted by the NCPCR found out that the quality of education is shamefully low in all the 10 states as most of the six and seventh graders were even unable to read their text-books.[11]

Activists say that Andhra Pradesh reports one of the highest numbers of school drop-outs among girls. If the net enrolment rate of girls in primary education is 96 per cent, it gradually dips to 60 per cent in secondary education. Activists have stated that a primary reason is that Andhra Pradesh has the least number of usable toilets in the country. Activists say that around 47,000 of the 76,000 government schools do not have usable toilets. A UNICEF-backed survey in 2010-11 had revealed that around 42.6 per cent of government schools have toilets but they are not usable. Where toilet facilities are available, maintenance is a big problem. Adequate sanitation staff are unavailable. Every third girl born in India dies in the first year of life. One in four does not live to celebrate their 15th birthday. Two out of five girls are malnourished. Every second adolescent girl is anaemic. Seven out of 10 girls drop-out of school before they reach 10th standard.

Six out of ten girls become child brides. Four out of 10 have their first child before they turn eighteen. [12]

Steps to be taken for Retention of Girl Child

Poverty is one of the main determinants of school drop-out. Family economic circumstances are important to meet the hidden and upfront costs of schooling, failure of which leads to many temporary as well as permanent drop-outs of children. Hidden costs of schooling include opportunity cost, travel cost, uniform, daily expenditures, while upfront costs include admission fee, examination fee, tuition fees etc. [13] So, it is very necessary that support from the government should be available, so that the poor parents do not have to pay for the hidden cost for education of the children, especially girl children. Apart from school education, children have to undertake private tuition. This additional expenditure of the poor parents can be nipped in the bud, if proper education is available in the school itself. For it, the teacher-student ratio has to be improved, infrastructure of the school, including class rooms, black boards, library, play grounds etc., have to be improved. Overall, sensitization of the teachers regarding their role in carving the lives of the future generations of India should be focused on.

Women and Child Development Ministry had mentioned economic disadvantage, workload within and outside the household, sibling care duties, social attitude towards girls' education and disability as the main reasons for high drop-out rates of girl students. The Ministry had also mentioned that the steps taken by it for retention of girl child in schools include provision of a neighbourhood school, two sets of uniforms for all girls within a ceiling of Rs. 400 per child per annum, free text-books for all girls at primary and upper primary levels. Transport and escort facility is also provided to children from remote habitations with sparse population where opening of school is not viable. Residential schools for drop-outs and vulnerable girls have been opened in Educationally Backward Blocks, the ministry had said.[14]

Some initiatives have been undertaken by State governments. The Chief Minister of Tripura stated that the state government has decided to give free bicycles to 50,000 poor girl students in a bid to boost women's education and reduce the school – drop-out rate. The state government has been providing free school text-books to students up to Class IX. To give some more assistance to poor girl students to reduce drop-out rates, 50,000 girl students living below poverty line would get free bicycles in addition to existing benefits. Girl students in Class IX to XII with an annual family income up to Rs. 1.25 lakh would get the benefit.

The new scheme will cost Rs. 15 crore in the first year and Rs. 6 crore in subsequent years.[15]

In order to control the drop-out rate of girl students in schools, text-books need urgent revisions. They need to start from what children can do and be more realistic and developmentally appropriate in what children are expected to learn, with clear learning goals and sequence. Systems must be put into place to track attendance, not just enrollment, and ensure regular reporting and monitoring of this attendance. Mother tongue instruction and programmes for language transition need to be introduced and expanded. Teacher recruitment policies need to assess teachers' knowledge, but more importantly their ability to explain content to children, make information relevant to their lives and to use teaching learning materials and activities other than the text-book. State teacher education plans should invest in the human resource capacity of academic support structures, like Block and Cluster Resource Centres (BRC/CRC) and District Institutes of education and Training (DIET), to enable them to help improve teaching and learning quality via in-service training and classroom visits. As per Right to Education, indicators for child-friendly education need to be defined and measured regularly as a part of the markers of quality. Libraries, with take home books for reading practice at the household level, should be monitored as part of RTE indicators. Family reading programmes could also be part of innovations to help support first generation school goers.[16]

In an effort to minimize incidences of dropping out when students from the Scheduled Castes are promoted from elementary classes to secondary education, the state government has decided to introduce pre-matric scholarships for students of standard IX and X. A government notification to this effect was issued on Saturday for all schools in the state of Maharashtra. According to the scheme, all day scholars will get an amount of Rs. 150 per month, while students studying in residential schools will receive an amount of Rs. 350 per month. Day scholars will get Rs. 750 for books and stationery, while residential students will get Rs. 1,000. The students will receive this amount for a period of 10 months in an academic year. The scheme is directly aided by the union government.[17]

Conclusion

It is the need of the hour that drop-out of girls should be minimized, other-wise, India will have to face its repercussions in the future. On the one hand, Indians are dreaming to be a Super Power in the future. On the other hand, the socio-economic indicators reflect the hard truth regarding high drop-out of girls, rising crimes against women, high maternal mortality and child mortality rates etc. Indian government should be serious in rooting out the evil of high drop-out rate of girls in schools. The support of the civil society, non-government organizations, activists can be enriching for the whole society. Nelson Mandela has stated that education is the most important weapon that can be used to change the world. It is all the more necessary that girls get an opportunity to use this weapon positively to build a wonderful world of tomorrow. Otherwise, lack of education of girls may turn to be the Achilles heel for the whole nation.

REFERENCES

1. Sattar, Ellen 'Drop-out in Primary Education: A Regional Overview,' *The Drop-out Problem in Primary Education: Some Case Studies*, UNESCO Regional Office for Education in Asia and The Pacific, Bangkok, 1984, 1-2.
2. Mutavati, Anna, 'Keep the Girl Child in School for Positive Development', October 13, 2013 http://www.thestandard.co.zw/2013/10/13/keep-girl-child-school-positive-development/,Retrieved 13.10.13.
3. http://indiacode.nic.in/coiweb/amend/amend86.htm Retrieved 1.10.13.
4. Aarti Dhar, 'New National Policy on Education Coming,' The Hindu, August 18, 2011. http://www.thehindu.com/news/national/new-national-policy-on-education-coming/article2366743.ece Retrieved 10.9.13
5. National Policy on Education 1986.
6. http://mhrd.gov.in/sites/upload_files/mhrd/files/NPE86-mod92.pdf Retrieved 15.9.13.
7. http://mhrd.gov.in/sites/upload_files/mhrd/files/POA_1992.pdf Retrieved 15.9.13.
8. Madhavan, M. R., 'Bringing Hard Evidence to the Table', Annual Status of Education Report (Rural) 2011 Provisional, January 16, 2012, 14-15 http://indiagovernance.gov.in/files/status_of_education_report_2011.pdf Retrieved 2.5.13
9. http://www.ncert.nic.in/oth_anoun/npe86.pdf Retrieved 1.6.13
10. 'SSA's Survey on Gender Disparity and Drop-out Rates in Schools', July 9, 2013. http://education.oneindia.in/news/2013/07/08/ssa-survey-on-gender-disparity-drop-out-rate-in-schools-005682.html Retrieved 9.7.13
11. 'Girls' Enrolment Jumps up but Drop-out Rate Still High,' January 22, 2013.
12. http://www.dnaindia.com/india/1791233/report-girls-enrolment-jumps-up-but-drop-out-rate-still-high Retrieved 10.5.13
13. Baruah, Ajupi 'on Right Based Approach to Education and Certain Issues of Inclusion' http://indiagovernance.gov.in/files/inclusive-education.pdf Retrieved 10.10.13.
14. Baseerat, Bushra, 'Andhra Tops in Girl School Drop-outs: Activists', Oct 11, 2013. http://timesofindia.indiatimes.com/city/hyderabad/

Andhra-tops-in-girl-school-drop-outs-Activists/articleshow/23937897.cms Retrieved 11.10.13.

15. Basumatary, Rupon 'School Drop-out Across Indian States and UTs: An Econometric Study,' *International Research Journal of Social Sciences*, Vol. 1(4), 28-35, December (2012), 28.
16. 'Girl Students Drop-out a Serious Problem, Says Parliament Panel,' August 23, 2013, http://indiatoday.intoday.in/story/girl-students-drop-out-a-serious-problem/1/300882.html Retrieved 1.8.13.
17. 'Free Bicycles to Boost Women's Education in Tripura,' August 16, 2013. http://indiatoday.intoday.in/story/free-bicycles-to-boost-womens-education-in-tripura/1/299723.html, Retrieved 18.8.13.
18. Bhattacharjea, Suman, Wadhwa, Wilima, Banerji, Rukmini, 'Inside Primary Schools: A Study of Teaching and Learning in Rural India,' ASER, Pratham Mumbai Education Initiative, October 2011, 8 http://indiagovernance.gov.in/files/education-in-rural-India.pdf Retrieved 11.10.13.
19. Aid to Scheduled Castes Students may Stem Drop-out Rate, October 7, 2013 http://articles.timesofindia.indiatimes.com/2013-10-07/pune/42793146_1_pre-matric-scholarship-day-scholars-new-scheme Retrieved 7.10.13.

14

Positive Steps towards Women

M. Jahnvi
Shanthi V

Abstract

Women place in Indian society has a historical perspective we call her the Goddess (Devi), The Mother, The Sister, The wife their own dreams, and becoming equal financial contributors within their households. Now we believe it's time for them to lead the way forward. The term empowerment refers to increasing the spiritual, political, social or economic strength of an individual. It's all about Power, Morale, self-image, Growth, learning, positive thinking, access etc. Women Empowerment India is an initiative to take practical steps to make Women of India financially independent through various initiatives. There are many schemes and policies developed to empower the women in the society some of which are discussed below in detail.

INTRODUCTION

From the beginning of the era, Women place in Indian society has a historical perspective we call her the Goddess (Devi), The Mother, The Sister, The wife. Women started to learn about some of the finest human qualities like compassion, self awareness, sacrifice, service, devotion by observing their own mothers, grandmothers and other women in their lives... For many centuries, the role of woman was to be the nurturing institution for her children, to be the solid foundation for her spouse, and to be the soldier fighting against the world's sufferings. Then came the times when Women got to the space of equality in the work place, achieving their own dreams, and becoming equal financial contributors within their households. Now we believe it's time for them to lead the way forward. The term empowerment refers to increasing the spiritual, political, social or economic strength of an individual. It's all about Power, Morale, self-image, Growth, learning, positive thinking, access etc. It is the process by which a women takes the challenge against the gender-based discrimination against them in all the institution and structure of society. The values or specialty or changes of an empowered women.... It improves the personal knowledge, self-defining power, authenticity, creativity physical strength, equality, identification, economic independence, freedom from oppression, have a women power in society. Women Empowerment India is an initiative to take practical steps to make Women of India financially independent through various initiatives. We believe that Financial Independence is one of the most powerful ways for Women Empowerment... this will define herself as a complete, whole human person, not a helpmate to man, a mother, a housewife or server of other's needs etc., by which she develops self governing skills and positive self image. There are many schemes and policies developed to empower the women in the society some of which are discussed below in detail.

Schemes to Prevent Female Infanticide

Killing of infant girls intentionally is called as female infanticide. Government of India undertaken various measures to minimize this but still it leads to baby girl negligence, discrimination leading to death and sex selective abortion. It is happening in most of the families where the status of the women is low. The rate of female infanticides is more in India and China throughout the world. Year by year the rate is increasing although government initiates different types of programmes, human rights organizations striving high to put an end by imparting education, financial incentives, and threat of punishments. Mullahera showed a birth ratio of 1,188 girls to 1,000 boys in 2009.

That's way ahead of the latest figures for the district (an 853 to 1,000 ratio), the state (an 877 to 1,000 ratio), and India (a 914 to 1,000 ratio).

The main reason in India is ours is a patriarchal society where cultural bias against women exists which contributes to female infanticides. In India, Tamil Nadu is the state where we can find more number of female infanticides that to especially Salem, Dharmapuri, Dindigul and Madurai. It is a major constraint which supports an imbalance in the sex ratio. According to Indian census statistics, the number of female children per male children dropped from 973 girls per 1000 males in 1901 to 929 girls per 1000 males in 1991, and continues to decrease. The main reason for this instance is the way of thinking, Indian people feels that "Sons are called upon to provide the income; they are the one's who do most of the work in the fields, they are believed to secure the family's economic future". "They look female children as a burden to the family because of dowry system in which a bride's family is expected to give large sums of money and goods to the husband's family.

The Tamil state government taken some steps to minimize female infanticide and sex selective abortions. In the year 1992, they launched 'Jayalaitha Protection Scheme for the Girl child' – under this scheme the poor family with one or two girl Childs and no sons are eligible for monetary incentives in the form of fixed deposit, the deposit is in the name of female girl, which will expire at the age of twenty one years for the girl. The Tamil Nadu government also launched another scheme named as 'Cradle Babies', rather than killing the female infants the families abandon their unwanted baby in cradles set up in government health centres. However, both of these programmes failed to eradicate female infanticides in Tamil Nadu. In addition to these the government can add some more schemes like Marriage Law and Women's protection Law and prohibits the discrimination against women who give birth to daughters, Sex Selective Abortion Law and Maternal Health Care Law, prohibiting the medical technology to determine the gender of fetus to minimize the impact of female infanticides in addition to that education to both men and women, strategies to improve the status of women and access to family counseling and healthcare also plays a vital role in minimizing female infanticides.

Economic Empowerment of Women

To empower women the vital importance goes to education which is considering as a main aspect of human security. In 21st century women is enjoying more freedom and power than ever before. But still according to the United Nations women actually performs only 53 per cent of the work whereas men are credited in performing all three quarters of economic activities. Female economic power enhances the wealth of the nation, in terms of fewer children, fertility rates (which are inversely related to national income), giving equal education to both son and daughter. The major factors affecting women's economic empowerment are sexual violence, human trafficking, lack of adequate access to education, responsible health care, finance, knowledge about rights and laws, less importance in decision-making.

Most of the researches show that women are interested in reinvesting their profits back into human capital. Economic power to the women leads to gaining equality, control over their own lives, and direct contribution to the children development in terms of nutrition, health and education which in turn indirectly to the nation's income growth. The women economic empowerment erases corruption and violence, promote greater environmental sustainability and through education, lower fertility rates, minimize the rate of HIV/AIDS. But, recently the World Economic Forum stated that 58 countries to assess the size of the gender gap. Those countries are not taking any initiation to minimize the gender gap. Countries like United state, Mexico, Jordan and Egypy are in the race in minimizing the gender gap. Poverty elimination is possible only unless women's economic security is strengthened. The research shows that:

- There are 135 million children in the world, in the age group of 7-18 who are not receiving any education at all, out of which 60 per cent are girls approximatelys.
- Of the girls who do begin primary school, only 1 in 4 is still in school four years later.
- The gender gap increases at higher levels of education.
- Two-thirds of the 880 million illiterate adults around the world are women.

- When women's income increases, money is more likely to be channeled back into families and they are more likely to educate daughters.
- Each additional year in school raises a woman's earnings by about 15 per cent compared to 11 per cent for a man.

Government Announces Major Incentives for Education of Single Girl Child

New Scholarships of CBSE and UGC Institutes

In major initiatives for girl education in the country, the Government has decided that every single girl child will be eligible for free education from standard VI to XII from current financial year.

The UGC will also launch another Post-graduate Scholarship scheme for the single girl child, is eligible to receive a scholarship of Rs. 2000 per month to pursue her Post-graduate education in any recognised institution. Total number of girl students benefiting under the scheme would be about 2400 from its second year, onwards. These will spur our young women and men to strive towards higher levels of excellence and do themselves and the country proud.

Similarly, if the only two children in a family are girls, both of them will be entitled to a concession in fees to the extent of 50 per cent. Fees for this purpose will include tuition fee and all other fees, by whatever name charged, but excluding money charged, if any, for transport and food.

Promotion of Women's education has been one of the cornerstones of the educational policy. Unfortunately, girls still face discrimination in our society. Son preference has led to various abhorrent practices including female foeticide. Participation of girls in education also suffers because of societal attitudes. New initiatives have, therefore, become necessary to give the girl child her due, and to empower her for a life of equality and dignity.

To perpetuate Indiraji's memory and make her a source of inspiration for our girls, it has been decided that all female students at the college/university level, who are single girl children will be called 'Indira Gandhi Scholars' and would receive recognition and support throughout their educational careers.

CBSE will offer 550 scholarships based on its Class XII examinations, purely on merit basis @ Rs. 500 per month for pursuing Under-graduate education in non-medical and non-engineering courses in recognised colleges. CBSE also conducts entrance exams for medical and engineering students, *viz*; AIPMT and AIEEE. CBSE will offer 500 scholarships every year, 350 for engineering students and 150 for medical students, for pursuing these courses. The rate of scholarship would be Rs. 1000 per month. From fourth year onwards, a total of 2000 students will be getting these scholarships at any given point of time. The scholarships will be based on the top ranks received in these exams.

The UGC will implement two Post-graduate Scholarship Schemes. The First and Second rank holders of B.A., B.Sc., and B.Com and First rank holders in 18 identified Honours Courses of all recognised Universities and Deemed to be Universities will be given scholarship of Rs. 2000 per month for pursuing their Post-graduate education in any recognised institution of higher learning in the country. Total number of students benefiting from this scheme would be nearly 5000 from its second year, onwards.

Women Entrepreneurship

One of the important sources of economic growth is recognised as women entrepreneurship. They provide and create new jobs for themselves as well as for others but still they are considered as minority of all the entrepreneurs. Women entrepreneurs faces gender-based barriers at the time of starting the business and also at the time of growing their businesses, like discriminatory property, matrimonial and inheritance laws and/or cultural practices; lack of access to formal finance mechanisms; limited mobility and access to the information and networks, etc.

The southern states of India as well as in Maharashtra if we observe that almost 50 per cent of women are leading small scale industrial units. To promote women entrepreneurship government of India offered different schemes and policies, it is as follows:

Policies and Schemes for Women Entrepreneurs in India

1. To cater the needs of potential women entrepreneurs, various state small industries development corporations and Micro Small

Medium enterprises conducts various development programmes because they have inadequate educational background.

2. Government of India started a new cell called as Women cell, the main motive of this cell is to take care of women specific problems.
3. Both state and central government launches several schemes which provides assistance for setting up training cum income generating activities. SIDBI also launched special schemes for women entrepreneurs.

Under Prime Minister's Rozgar Yojana (PMRY) they are giving preference to women beneficiaries. To facilitate the participation of women in beneficiaries of the scheme, the government of India made several relaxations. Under MSE Cluster Development programme by ministry of MSME, in case of hard intervention the contribution from the ministry of MSME varies between 30 per cent 80 per cent, but the contribution of MSME is upto 90 per cent in the case of clusters owned and managed by women entrepreneurs. The government guarantees upto 75 per cent of the loan extended under the Credit Guarantee Fund Scheme for Micro and Small Enterprises and other type of incentives are as follows:

Incentives to Women Entrepreneurs

1. 100 per cent reimbursement of Stamp duty and transfer duty paid by the industry on purchase of land meant for industrial use.
2. 100 per cent reimbursement of Stamp duty for Lease of Land/ Shed/Buildings.
3. 100 per cent reimbursement of Stamp duty and transfer duty paid by the industry on financial deeds and mortgages etc.
4. 25 per cent rebate in land cost in IEs/IDA's limited to Rs. 5.00 Lakhs.
5. Power cost will be reimbursed @ Rs. 0.75 per unit during the first year of the policy and thereafter for the remaining four years the rate of reimbursement would be so regulated on yearly basis keeping in view of the changes in the tariff structures to ensure that power cost to the industry is pegged down to the first year's level.

6. 15 per cent investment subsidy on fixed capital investment will be given to SSI/Tiny Units subject to a maximum of Rs. 15.00 lakhs.
7. 5 per cent Additional Investment subsidy on fixed capital investment limited to Rs. 5.00 Lakhs.
8. Another 5 per cent investment subsidy on fixed capital investment limited to Rs. 5.00 Lakhs for women belongs to SC/ ST Community.
9. Upto 25 per cent of the tax paid during one financial year will be ploughed back to Industries as a grant by the Government towards the payment of tax during next year. However, such grant shall not remit in net cash outflow to Government. Benefit will be available for 5 years from the date of commencement of production *i.e.,* up to 6th year.
10. 5 per cent of project cost will be provided as seed capital assistance to SSI/Tiny Units as a grant for industries, which were sanctioned seed capital assistance by Prime Lending Institutions under National Equity Fund Scheme limited to Rs. 5.00 Lakhs.
11. 5 per cent interest subsidy on Prime Lending Rate (PLR) will be given on the term loan taken by new Tiny/SSI industrial units subject to a maximum of Rs. 5.00 lakh per year for a period of 5 years.
12. 8 per cent subsidy on capital equipment for technology up-gradation.
13. 50 per cent subsidy on the expenses incurred for quality certification limited to Rs. 1.00 Lakh.
14. 25 per cent subsidy on cleaner production measures limited to Rs. 5.00 Lakhs. 3.2.15. 50 per cent subsidy on the expenses incurred for patent registration limited to Rs. 5 Lakhs.

Government bodies and allied institutions provide special schemes for women entrepreneurs, it follows as:

- Schemes of Ministry of MSME.
    - Trade related entrepreneurship assistance and development (TREAD) scheme for women.

  - Mahila Coir Yojana.
- Schemes of Ministry of Women and Child Development.
  - Support to Training and Employment Programme for Women (STEP).
  - Swayam Siddha.
- Schemes of Kerala State Women's Development Corporation.
  - Self-employment loan programmes.
  - Educational loan schemes.
  - Single women benefit schemes.
  - Job oriented training programmes.
  - Marketing support for women entrepreneurs.
  - Autorickshaw/school van's driver scheme.
- Kerala Government's Women Industries Programme.
- Delhi Government's Stree Shakti Project.
- Schemes of Delhi Commission for Women (Related to Skill development and training).
- Incentives to Women Entrepreneurs Scheme, 2008, Government of Goa.
- Magalir Udavi Scheme, Pudhucherry Government.
- Financing Schemes by Banks/Financial Institution's.

Women Entrepreneur Associations

The efforts of government and its different agencies are supplemented by NGOs and associations. These associations also plays an equal role in facilitation women empowerment. Various women associations in India is listed as follows:

1. Federation of Indian Women Entrepreneurs.
2. Consortium of Women Entrepreneurs.
3. Association of Lady Entrepreneurs of Andhra Pradesh.
4. Association of Women Entrepreneurs of Karnataka.
5. Self-Employed Women's Association.
6. Women Entrepreneurs Promotion Association.
7. The Marketing Organization of Women Enterprises.
8. Bihar Mahila Udyog Sangh Bihar Mahila Udyog Sangh.

9. Mahakaushal Association of Women Entrepreneurs.
10. SAARC Chamber Women Entrepreneurship Council.
11. Women Entrepreneurs Association of Tamil Nadu.
12. Ti E Stree Shakti.
13. Women Empowerment Corporation.

Government offers Paid Incentives for Pregnant Women

To improve the maternal health, government of India offer cash incentives to pregnant women, through the Project named as Indira Gandhi Matritva sahyog Yojana. The main motive of the project is to improve the health and nutrition of pregnant, lactating women and infants. It implemented first in 52 districts across the country at a cost of Rs. 1,000 crore.

As per the scheme, each and every pregnant woman and lactating woman in the target districts will receive a total cash incentive of Rs. 4,000, but in three installments between the periods from second trimester to the child attaining the age of six months. From this scheme all central and state government employees are excluded because they are enjoying the benefits of paid maternity leave. An estimation of around 13.8 lakh pregnant women receives benefit from the scheme at initial stages, at first the project implemented at Anganwadi centres.

Janani Suraksha Yojana (JSY)

The JSY is the Hindi words which literally mean 'Pregnant Women Safety Scheme'. The main aim of this scheme is to reduce maternal and neonatal mortalities through promoting institutional deliveries. This scheme is modified from the earlier scheme called as National Maternity Benefit Scheme (NMBS) nowadays it is popularly called as NRHM. NMBS was introduced in the year 2001 for providing nutrition support to the pregnant womens. The pregnant women under BPL receives an amount of Rs. 500/-prior to the delivery especially eight to twelve weeks prior to due data. The scheme is specifically targeted for scheduled casts/scheduled tribes and poor population. In India it considered as a large scale conditional cash transfer programme, which is launched government of India in the year 2005. It provides financial incentive to a pregnant women delivering either in a government hospitals or in accredited private health facility. Throughout India an only woman from low income a household

In addition to the above government offers different types of incentives to promote women, some of them are:

Schemes	**Benefits To Scheme**	**Description**
1	**2**	**3**
Delivery Huts	To All Pregnant Women	• 24 Hours Delivery Services, Free Referral Transport Facilities Available For All Pregnant Women, Immunization to New born (O Dose Polio and BCG).
Ladli (Non-ICDS Areas)	Financial Assistance of Rs. 5000 @ 2500 per Girl on Birth of 2nd Girl Per Annum for Five Years	• Having Haryana Domicile Whose 2nd Girl is born on or after 20th August 2005 for this Incentive Irrespective of their Caste, Creed, Religion, Income and No. of Sons, the Birth of Both the Girls Should be Registered.
Tailoring Training To SC Widows/ Destitute Women/ Girls	Benefits to SC Widows	• Rate of stipend 100/- PM, Rs. 50/- for purchase of raw material, payable of all days of attendence, sundays and sanctioned holidays.
Pension to Widows and Destitute Women	Women Unable to Sustain themselves from their own sources and in need of financial assistance from State	• A woman domicile of Haryana or residing in Haryana for the last one year at the time of submission of application, Age 18 or Above Widow or unmarried, Own income from all sources is less than Rs. 10,000/- per annum or decided by the Government time to time, is eligible for pension, Amount of pension is 350/- Per Month or decided by the State Government time to time.

1	2	3
Ladli Social Security Pension Scheme	Families Having only one Girl Child and no son biological or adopted and age between 45 to 60 years	• Domicile of Haryana or working for Government of Haryana, The amount of the pension is to be Rs. 500/- per month or decided by the Government time to time. Applications are invited under this scheme in every month on second Wednesday in Tehsils in Distt. and in Distt. Social Welfare office Ambala.
Socio-economic Upliftment of Women	Women	• To provide Financial assistance for income-generating scheme to women of target group, to provide training to women to improve/enhance their skill.
Promotion and Strengthening of Mahila Mandals	Registered Mahila Mandals	• The Mahila Mandals do work for the promotion of Nutrition education, family welfare, food storage, immunization of children, small saving accounts of women, provision of bathrooms, smokeless chulhas, women crafts centre, and balwadis etc. The registered Mahila Mandals have representative of all classes of society, and have their own executive committee. The women and Child Development Department provide grants for the training of upto 5 members of each Mahila Mandals. For basic equipments and Stationery etc., cash grant of Rs. 1500 is paid to newly registered Mahila Mandals. After two years of getting the first grant, the Mahila Mandal can be given a second matching grant of Rs. 750 for starting some income-generating activities.

Contd...

1	2	3
		The schemes, namely: Mahila Mandal Sammelan, Inter State Study Tour of Mahila Mandals, Incentive Awards to Mahila Mandal have been clubbedunder the scheme promotion and strengthening of Mahila Mandal.
Kishori Shakti Yojna (Adolescent Girls Scheme)	Adolescent Girls between 11-18 years of age	• Improving the nutritional and health status of adolescent girls between 11-18 years of age, to train and equip them to improve home-based and vocational skills, to promote awareness of health hygiene, nutrition, home management, child care, and take all measures as to facilitate their marriage after attaining the age of 18 years and even later. This scheme is being implemented through Anganwadi Centres. The girls are also provided supplementary nutrition at Rs. 2.50 per girl, per day. The expenditure on supplementary nutrition is being borne by the State Government.
Special Employment to educated/semi educated young men/women of Rural areas through diary development by establishment of Mini Dairy Units	Unemployed educated/ semi-educated young men/women, He/she should have sufficient arrangement for growing green fodder for the milch animals	• To provide self-employment to the educated/uneducated unemployed men/women, widows of the all categories, exservicemen, to raise socio-economic standard of weaker sections of the society, To increase the production of milk at lower cost fulfilling the requirements of consumers in general and milk plants of the State in particular, To gradually replace the poor quality animals with good quality animals.

are eligible for the cash incentives, but in ten high focus states offers the benefits to all women irrespective of their socio-economic status. Women who delivered in health facility receives Rs. 600 whereas thousand rupees in high focus especially in urban areas. In rural areas it is around Rs. 700 for health facility and Rs. 1400 for high focus states. The implementation of the scheme is not uniform in all the districts. The statistics showed that after the implementation of this programme , there is a reduction in the rate of perinatal mortality by 3.7 deaths per 1000 pregnancies and neonatal mortality by 2.3 deaths per 1000 live births. In the current financial year upto June 2013 12,000 pregnant woman benefited under Janani Suraksha Yojana. The main motive and objective is to reduce maternal and neonatal mortality by promoting institutional deliveries among the pregnant women. One more scheme for the pregnant women's named as Janani Shishu Suraksha Yojana (JSSK) also known as 'Maa Tujhe Salaam', through this scheme the government of india offering free treatments. Nearly till now two lakh pregnant women got benefited especially in jammu Kashmir along with that the Health Minister launched Sick New born Care Units at district level, stabilization units at community health centre level and Baby care units at delivery points including primary health centres and sub centres at district level for New born care.

One can say JSY is people centric health programme in the country. The scheme implemented in a stratified manner among the states on the basis of performance on maternal mortality in LPS and HPS.

Conclusion

If women choose to be ignorant then all the efforts taken by the Government and women activists will go in vain. Even in twenty-fifth century, they will remain backward and will be paying a heavy price for their dependence, So, it is a wake-up call for women to awake from their deep slumber and understand the true meaning of their empowerment. In the end we would like to conclude with the following quotation by Sri Sri Ravishankar. "The role of women in the development of the society is of utmost importance. In fact, this is the only thing that determines whether the society is strong and harmonious or otherwise. Women are the back bone of society".

REFERENCE

Google Search – Weblink: http://www.dcmsme.gov.in, http://business.gov.in

15

Women Empowerment
A Womb to Tomb Process

Mary Princess Lavanya

Abstract

Women empowerment is possible only when it is been given importance from womb to tomb. Empowerment is not an over night miracle or a phenomenon, but definitely it is a process. Women empowerment is an integrated aspect, not just biological, but, social, cultural, financial, religious, political construct attached to it. Women's issues are perceived to be linked to social issues. Women form an important social category. The basis of this category is not simply the biological entity but also the socio-cultural construct. Social status and roles of women are defined not only in terms of the gender dimension but also in terms of the norms, values, beliefs, traditions, and customs of the society.

INTRODUCTION

Women empowerment is possible only when it is been given importance from womb to tomb. Empowerment is not an over night miracle or a phenomenon, but definitely it is a process. The empowerment of a woman begins from the moment of conception, also for man, but while concentrating on women that moment of conception should be given more importance. Because, every emotion that the mother experiences has an impact on the child. According to Erik Erickson's psycho-social development theory, every stage of a human needs development, especially women, failing in any of the stages, will collapse the development. After the conception is the developmental milestones which is crucial in everyone's life, then is the puberty an important stage of blooming, marriage, pregnancy which is second birth for a woman and finally menopause, followed by gracefully approaching the second childhood. Women empowerment is an integrated aspect, not just biological, but, social, cultural, financial, religious, political construct attached to it. Women's issues are perceived to be linked to social issues. These issues are especially focused on women's unequal access to productive resources, decision-making bodies, health care facilities, education, employment opportunities and social justice.

Women form an important social category. The basis of this category is not simply the biological entity but also the socio-cultural construct. Social status and roles of women are defined not only in terms of the gender dimension but also in terms of the norms, values, beliefs, traditions, and customs of the society. Women as a social category cut across the boundary of caste, class, race, estate etc., social groupings. They belong to diversified socio-economic groups and are also divided in terms of spatial considerations like rural and urban.

Prenatal Development as a Foundation

The Fetal life begins at ovum fertilization. The three stages of pre-natal development include, germinal, embryonic and the fetal period, each period is a process of empowerment which depends on the bio-psycho-social conditions of the mother. Every emotion that she experiences affects the development of the fetal; it can be positive or negative. Positive emotion brings forth a happy, sociable and emotionally healthy child into this world. The nature of the biological condition is that, it prepares itself for the Birth of the child, how much more the parents needs to prepare themselves psychologically to receive this precious gift of a child. But unfortunately if it is found that the fetus is going to be a female, the joy is totally gone and people consider it as a curse and try to abort the child, all these emotional aspects convey the untold message to the fetus inside the womb. This definitely has an adverse impact on the fetus. Good prenatal care makes a difference.

According to Erik Erickson's theory, the stage one is more to do with the psychological basic belief in oneself and others. He terms it as, Trust *vs.* Mistrust. This stage starts from birth to one year and it is the most important stage in one's life framing the foundation for the entire life. Infants are completely dependent on others, trust can be established when babies are given adequate warmth, touching, love, and physical care. Mistrust is caused by inadequate or unpredictable care and by cold, indifferent, and rejecting parents. If the girl child experiences positive emotions like happiness and everything relating to trust, she is going to be an achiever all through her life, come what may because the virtue over here is hope. The hope that the little child develops at that early years of life will pay way for hope throughout her life span. This development is the first step towards women's empowerment. Empowering girl baby in this stage will definitely begin a real transformation in the society.

Developmental Milestones

Every parent looks forward to the first time to see their baby smile and look into their eyes. Some keep detailed journals of baby's progress and others call grandma with every milestone achieved. Because most children develop at different paces it is difficult to say what is 'normal' and what is not. There are five primary developmental areas that professionals monitor. These are: *(i)* physical development; *(ii)* language and speech development; *(iii)* social and emotional development; *(iv)* adaptive development; and *(v)* cognitive development. Children may experience mild to severe delays in one or all the areas depending on the situation. The parents should know if their child is on schedule, if not, it is important to seek the advice of a professional early. Early intervention can make a world of difference in the child's later development. It's disheartening to know that most parents ignore this when it comes to the girl baby, for no fault of hers.

Physical Development

In the early days, a newborn do not have control of her movements. The baby will likely lie as if still in uterus until the second month when she may start to relax and stretch out. By the sixth month the baby will likely be sitting up and reaching for objects. By the twelfth month baby will be crawling and possibly even walking. By two years the child should be able to jump in place or off a step. There is no concern if these skills don't emerge right at the second year. However, if they are not evident at thirty months, consulting a professional is must. In India there's always disparity that exists between girls and boys. When delay in the milestones occur, girls are not given immediate attention as it is given to boys, this is one of the reason, why when she is in her adulthood, she never ever bothers about her health, if it's for the husband or for her children immediate care is given.

Language and Speech Development

Babies are communicating long before actual words come out of their mouths. The first months their interactions may be limited to cries of hunger and cries to be held and cuddled. Responding to the baby's need is important. This is the foundation by which language develops. If the child seems unusually silent or has not cooed or squealed by the third of fourth month, it has to be discussed with the doctor. But least importance to such an issue may worsen the disability, and early intervention can lessen the problems.

Social and Emotional Development

Social skills start as early as the second month when the baby may start smiling responsively rather than the sleepy smile and make eye contacts. Often separation anxiety comes at the time of mobility. It is thought that this is nature's way of keeping baby close to mother. While baby's protests at mom or dad being away may be somewhat maddening, they are completely normal and healthy. It's important not to try to sneak away when using a baby-sitter as it will breed mistrust and cause the child to cling more fervently when the parent is present for fear of them slipping away unnoticed. Parents must keep times away from the baby short if possible. Because of this in her married life she always has the fear if the husband might slip away unnoticed, and this creates lots of problems. When she fights back all this takes initiative, and is autonomous in doing this, she becomes a good leader with will power to achieve anything in life. This lays the base for women development.

Adaptive Development

Adaptive development refers to the use of tools and things like motor planning (like learning to get down from the couch). These skills may not be evident until later in the first year. Baby should be pointing with one finger around twelve months and should be able to feed self finger foods around fifteen months. This is the only development which is given more importance by parents. Because it is almost beginning to work, that is taking things using hands, the baby need not be on the bed or couch and not only that begins to feed oneself, this development is motivated highly because she has to care for her siblings after her. Thus women are the best ones when it comes to care – giving, full development in this area.

Cognitive Development

Often the first sign of cognitive development noticed by parents is the learning of cause and effect. Responding to the child will definitely help her to develop her cognitive skills, but rarely attention is paid to this development. Generally people think that only boy's need cognitive development, the social construct is the only reason for such ideologies.

Stage two of Erickson is autonomy versus shame and doubt; this starts from one year and lasts till three years. Autonomy is nothing but doing things for themselves, overprotective or ridiculing parents may cause children to doubt abilities and feel shameful about their actions. Developmental milestones start from 0 to 5 years. The third stage of psycho-social theory focuses on initiative versus guilt (3-5 years). Parents reinforce initiative by giving children freedom to play, use imagination, and ask questions and guilt may occur if parents criticize, prevent play, or discourage a child's questions. Our tradition has been such that, in the case of a girl child, parents are overprotective and never allow them to do anything on their own. This creates a doubt in her, and the result is, she is unable to believe in herself and her capacities. Even if the child struggles to overcome she's been ridiculed which makes her feel shameful, curbing her development. When it comes to take initiative, ask questions and be imaginative, a girl is often looked down, she's been told it's too much for her age to ask such questions and be imaginative; this leads to guilt feeling in her. That is the only reason a woman in her later years is unable to voice out for her own rights, because off such experiences she has faced, which has left a scar in her mind. All this has to change by giving importance to all the above mentioned developments for a girl child, only then a woman can voice out her opinion and can make a difference in social transformation.

Positive Identity during Childhood and Adolescence

The neglect of the girl child starts from very early in life. The extent of neglect varies from family to family depending on their economic position. But in comparison to her male counterpart a female child is relatively neglected in most of the socio-economic strata. Throughout the country it has been noticed that when the girl child depends on breast feeding the chances of her survival are relatively more. *Firstly*, the female children are-breast fed for a far shorter period than their male counterparts. *Secondly*, during illness parents show a greater concern towards male children. *Finally*, in addition to the intake of insufficient and non-nutritious food the female child is exposed to a greater workload very early in life. Often in families of weaker economic strength the girl child is found attending the household chores as well as taking care of her younger brothers and sisters.

Erickson's stage four concentrates on industry *vs.* inferiority, it begins from 6 and lasts till 12 years. Industry, this occurs when child is praised for productive activities such as painting, reading, and studying. Inferiority complex occurs if the child's efforts are regarded as messy, inadequate, or childish. Stage five is the transition period from childhood to adulthood which is called as adolescence period. Here the psycho-social crisis is identity *vs.* role confusion. Role confusion occurs when adolescents are unsure of where they are going and who they are? Identity crisis helps them understand who they are? Only when a person is aware of oneself there can be development. In which case, women are more aware of themselves and that contributes to the development. As they leave an impression in everything they do because of their positive identity, their work is perfect and highly commendable. Psychosocial development in this stage is rapid and crucial as they begin to be independent. Analytical and logical thinking skills, decision-making and emotional independence are the highlights of this period. They tend to have conflicts with parents, but by late adolescence, parental values are understood and appreciated. Measure of regard of oneself; one's personal worth and place in society; linked with self-respect, identifying good qualities and developing them helps her to reach her goal. Most often this stage is considered to tie a girl under control and traditional practices which hinder her growth. Instead if the girl is freedom to identify herself, she will be a better person and also contribute for the social transformation at a larger level, as she's going to be leader in the near future leading the family and the country.

Marriage and Women's Health

The sixth stage in psycho-social developmental theory is the Young Adulthood. Either they involve in an intimate relationship or in isolation at this stage. Intimacy is the ability to care about others and to share experiences with them. While, isolation is feeling alone and uncared for in life. Most often intimacy is related with marriage, women are been forced into marriage which is sacred in one's life. Early marriage affects women's health status adversely. A vast number of girls are married at the teenage and young adulthood is too early to get married to take up too many responsibilities. It is only at this stage a person comes to an understanding about life, before beginning to enjoy she's been burdened with no time for herself and her desires. Women are by nature tolerant and can struggle with perseverance, that's how even such hurdles turn to be stepping stones for women to take up responsibilities and fulfill them to the best of their abilities. This cannot be denied by anyone as a process of development at her own pace. In India, women have on an average 8-9 pregnancy and they spend around 80 per cent of their reproductive years in pregnancy and lactation. Anemia in pregnancy accounts directly 15 to 20 per cent of all maternal deaths in India. Women as mothers play a key role in bringing up their children, when she's given freedom, decision-making authority, she exercises her power wonderfully well which in turn brings transformation in the society.

Generativity is a Development

It is a general feeling of loneliness that parents or guardians may feel when one or more of their children leave home; it is more common in women. The marriage of a child can lead to similar feelings, with the role and influence of the parents often becoming less important compared to the new spouse. When children move away, mothers can get what is called 'Empty Nest Syndrome', which is generally accepted as the lonely, abandoned feeling of the home being empty. In order to fill the void of the empty house, many people look for something that is living and breathing that will take their mind off of their feelings, like a pet. Empty nest syndrome has become more prevalent in modern times, as the extended family is becoming less common than in past generations, and the elderly are left living by themselves. Stage seven which is middle Adulthood, the psycho-social crisis is generativity *vs.* stagnation. Generativity is the interest in guiding the next generation. Stagnation leads to self-confinement. Middle adulthood starts from 35 to 55 or up to 65. The outcome of this period is Ego Development. The significant task in this stage is to perpetuate culture and transmit values of the culture through the family (taming the kids) and working to establish a stable environment. Strength comes through care of others and production of something that contributes to the betterment of society, which Erikson calls generativity. As children leave home, or as relationships or goals change, women face major life changes – the mid-life crisis – and struggle with finding new meanings and purposes. Significant relationships are within the workplace, the community and the family. Thus most women come to the limelight in this stage, which is a positive sign of fighting empty nest syndrome and thus contributing for the transformation of the society at a greater level.

Final Developmental Process

The last stage of psycho-social development is the eighth stage the late adulthood, here it is either integrity or despair and the wonderful outcome is wisdom, which comes only out of experience. Integrity is more to do with self-respect; it is developed when people have lived richly and responsibly. Despair occurs when previous life events are viewed with regret; and the person experiences heartache and remorse. It's rare to find women of this age 65 and above being in despair. The developmental process becomes full, because, she has lived life with integrity, richly and responsibly. She is full of wisdom and she therefore guides her children, grand children and the people around her. Erikson felt that much of life is preparing for the middle adulthood stage and the last stage is recovering from it. Perhaps that is because older adults often look back on their lives with happiness and are content, feeling fulfilled with a deep sense that life has meaning and that they've made a contribution to life, a feeling Erikson calls integrity. Woman's strength comes from a wisdom that the world is very large and she now have a detached concern for the whole of life, accepting death as the completion of life, she goes through this process gracefully. The empowerment is a process starts from womb to tomb. A women's empowerment greatly contributes to the social transformation invisibly.

Conclusion

Continuous empowerment from pre-natal development, followed by the developmental milestones in childhood, puberty, marriage, pregnancy, menopause and old age, leads to actual development. Stagnation in any of the stages may curb the development. In the recent past women's empowerment gained attention in very sphere of life. But it is disheartening to know that the empowerment and women are always seen as two different entities in our system. Only when both women and men begin to concentrate on the need for empowerment can there be real women empowerment. As the scenario is changing, both the gender should have inputs on women empowerment, so that at least empowerment will be a reality in the near future. Young women who are the future of our society will be better equipped to make right choices to live a life with empowerment in all areas of life, at all the stages of life, perseverance is the only means to achieve empowerment.

Cordial relationship between parents, a friendly, tension-free atmosphere, and the kind of attention the girl baby gets – these are some of the crucial factors that cause an impact throughout the development stages. The emotional and behavioural responses are highly influenced by what the child experiences at home, community and school, hence it is not only the duty of parents to nurture positive emotions, but also the teachers and the people in the society are to perform their duty rightly. Early foundations are critical, so the child must be given lots of love and attention to make the child feel loved and wanted. Also equally important is the second childhood process in a person's life, it is even more for a women. Women's empowerment can become a reality as we march towards life with hope, will power, fidelity, love, courage, self-esteem, and proper ego development and also with wisdom. With all the virtues social transformation is possible directly through her and indirectly through her children.

REFERENCES

Agarwal, A (1983), Women's Studies in Asia and Pacific: An Overview of Current Status and Needed Priorities. APDC: Kuala Lumpur, Malaysia.

Desai, N. and Maithreyi Krishnaraj (1987), Women and Society. Ajanta Publications: New Delhi.

Desai, N. and Patel, V. (1985), Indian Women: Change and Challenge in the International Decade 1975-85. Popular Prakashan: Bombay.

Devi, K. Rethi (2003), "Health Hazards of Women Workers". Social Welfare. 50(2) pp. 12.

Dube, L. and R. Patriwala (1990), Structures and Strategies: Women, Work and Family. Sage: New Delhi.

Government of India (1988), National Perspective Plan for Women 1988-2000. Department of Women and Child Development. Government of India: New Delhi.

Indiresan, Jaya (2002), Education for Women's Empowerment: Gender Positive Initiatives in Pace Setting Women's Colleges. Konark: New Delhi.

Kapadia, Karin (2002), The Violence of Development: The Politics of Identity, Gender and Social Inequalities in India. Kali for Women: New Delhi.

Seth, Mira (2001), Women's Development: The Indian Experience. Sage Publications: New Delhi.

16

Crime against Women

Dr. Sadhna Gupta

"The downfall of the nation starts with inconsistent neglect of womanhood, the men folk of the Indian soil has failed to sense it, advertently turn blind eye to the same".

— Swami Vivekananda

Abstract

After six and half decade of Indian Independence crime against women continues to be undebatable in India. The civil society has often turn disgust against the rising crime nowadays but failed. When India feels proud as shinning India with modern cosmopolitan outlook and technological armoury in the hand, the breaking news of electronic media or newspaper headlines "Rape of a women, Acid attack, Gang rape, Dowry death of newly wedded bride" — as various incidences of growing crime against women. Crime against women is manifestation of unequal power relation between men and women, which is understood within the gender framework. Where sex is the biological category, gender is the social construct which refer to the expectation and behaviour norm.

INTRODUCTION

After six and half decade of Indian Independence crime against women continues to be undebatable in India. The civil society has often turn disgust against the rising crime now-a-days but failed. The Mumbai gang rape is the reminiscent of the horror of gang rape of the Delhi on December 2012 showed the disturbing trend of the modern India, where crime against women has become a norm rather than aberration in India. When India feels proud as shinning India with modern cosmopolitan outlook and technological armoury in the hand, the breaking news of electronic media or newspaper headlines "Rape of a women, Acid attack, Gang rape, Dowry death of newly wedded bride" — as various incidences of growing crime against women. Oppression and violence against women undoubtedly has a cultural, psychological, material and sociological base. Gender violence is rife at every structure and level of an intensely feudal and patriarchal society as ours. It reached the epidemic proportions and is admittedly now a major issue, being recognised in international jurisprudence as a violation of the human rights of women. Yet it is the most debased and ignored human rights issue.

Crime against women is manifestation of unequal power relation between men and women, which is understood within the gender framework. Where sex is the biological category, gender is the social construct which refer to the expectation and behaviour norm. Crimes against women have led to domination over and discrimination against men and to the prevention of the full advancement of women and are one of the crucial social mechanisms by which women are forced into a subordinate position compared with men.[1] Crime against women means any act of gender based psychological harm suffering to women, including threats of such acts, coercion of arbitrary deprivation of liberty whether occurring public or private life. Violence against women is sign of discriminatory position of women in patriarchal social structure. Crimes against women occur both within the home and outside the domestic walls. They range from assault to deprivation of life and from indecency to ravishing the women's honour by rape. The violence against women lies in the power imbalance between men and women in hierarchical inequality.

Crime against women is a gross violation of women's human right. Human rights are the rights which are possessed by all human beings irrespective of their race, cast, nationality, sex, language etc., simply because they are human beings. In the *Platform for Action*, the core document of the *Beijing Conference*, Governments declared that "Violence against women constitutes a violation of basic human rights and is an obstacle to the achievements of the objectives of equality, development and peace".[2] International instruments had played an important role to protect the rights of women. *Vienna Conference* had a great impact on the woman's human right campaign.[3] *The Declaration of the Conference* reiterated that "the human rights of women and of a girl child are an inalienable, integral and indivisible part of the universal human rights". The Declaration further reiterated that gender based violence and all forms of sexual harassment and exploitation, including those resulting from cultural prejudice and international trafficking, is incompatible with the dignity and worth of the human person, and must be eliminated. By this it brings the formal acknowledgement of violence against women as a human right violation. Even the *Universal Declaration on Human Rights (1948)* reflects that "all human beings are born free and equal in dignity and rights".[4] Article 3 and 5 declares that everyone has the right to life, liberty and security of persons and that no one be subjected to torture, cruel, inhuman or degrading treatment. *The International Covenant on Civil and Political Rights (ICCPR)* of 1966 also deals with the prohibitions against violence.

The major turning point is the *Convention on Forms of Discrimination against Women (CEDAW)*, 1979 which came into force in 1981.[5] This maybe rightly called as the magna carta of the Women's human right as it essentially constitutes the international bill of rights for women. The human rights of women generally includes right to equality before law, right against gender discrimination, right against harassment, right to abortion, right to privacy, right to economic empowerment. Today domestic violence is recognised as a gross human right violation by different International Women's Convention.

Constitutional Provisions

The framers of Indian Constitution were aware of the social problems of emancipation of the female sex. They also knew that gender-equality was crucial for national development. It was evident that in order to eliminate inequality and to provide opportunities for the exercise of human rights and claims, it was necessary to promote them with special care educational and economic interests of the women and to protect them from any social injustice and exploitation. The Constitution of India did well by declaring in its preamble it's desire to secure justice that is – *social, economic* and *political*, and to secure equality of status and opportunity and did it best to ensure translation of these objectives into reality by incorporating provisions ensuring equality of status and of opportunity in the fields of education, public employment and participation in political life. It directs that women shall not have equal right and privileges with men but also that the state shall make provisions – both general and special for welfare of women. Apart from ensuring *equality before law* and *equal protection of the laws*[6] Article 14 of the Indian Constitution, "The State shall not deny to any person equality before law and equal protection of the laws", in wider sense of the term, the constitution took great pains to specifically prohibit the state from discriminating against women on the ground of sex in such areas as education and public employment and to direct the state to take special care to promote women's welfare, particularly the protection of their health as mother's and their dignity as individuals.

Special provisions have been made for women under the Indian Constitution. *Article 15(3)* permits the State to make special protective laws for women and children. For this reason establishing educational institution by the State exclusively for girls or reservation of seats for women in colleges is not violative of *Article 15*. Provisions for special maternity relief under *Article 42* can be made in favour of women. *Article 51A (e)* imposes a Fundamental Duty on every citizen to renounce the practices derogatory to the dignity of women.

Forms of Violence against Women

In India the common violence against women are wife beating, harassment, torture, bride burning, slavery and exploitation, forced prostitution and sexual harassment, female foeticide and infanticide, acid attack, stalking, voyeurism etc. The nature of violence against women in and outside the families takes the form of injuring women's psychological health as well as their bodies and often involves humiliation in addition to physical violence. The violence caused to women in the family is the domestic violence which includes domestic violence which includes foeticide, infanticide, marital cruelty, dowry murders, child abuse, incest and battering etc. The violence faced by the women in community level includes rape, sexual harassment, eve-teasing, acid attack, stalking, voyeurism, trafficking and sexual discrimination.

Wife Battering

It is unfortunate that home, the sweet home, the abode of rich and complex feelings and a place of retreat for protective sphere of family life, could be very dangerous place for women. Cruelty and wife beating, is so alien to our image of non-violence and respect for womanhood, is emerging as one of the least recognised and most appalling crimes. Wife battering is a global phenomenon. The institution of marriage which is supposed to protect a woman renders her even more vulnerable to assault. Law is adequate to deal with the battering of women within the home. Cruelty is a legal ground for dissolution of marriage under personal laws before the Civil Court, and the same cruelty is made punishable under law by amendment of Indian Penal Code in 1983. In order to combat the increasing incidents of torture of women by their husbands and his relatives, the legislature enacted section 498A of the Indian Penal Code 1860 and section 113A of the Indian Evidence Act 1872. The term cruelty under section 498A includes both mental and physical cruelty. The offence under this section is a cognizable offence and triable by a Magistrate of First Class.

Domestic Violence

To quote Virginia Woolf, "On marriage, the weakest, the stupidest, the most insignificant men in the world receives the licence to rape and beat".

Domestic violence[7] is one of the leading causes of female injuries in almost every country of the world. It is a violence that occurs within the family between the persons who are related through intimacy blood and law. Majority of perpetrators of the domestic violence are men and majority of victims are women, specially married women. Domestic violence differs with households, individuals and situations. The respondent [8] often sometimes harass, harms or injuries the aggrieved person or any other person related to her for dowry or any valuable security. The act also provides that an aggrieved wife can file a complaint against her husband or relatives of her husband who are torturing her mentally or physically. Domestic relationship means a relationship between two persons who live together in a shared household when they are related by consanguinity; marriage etc., and other family members are living together as a joint family. Aggrieved person means any woman who is or has been in a domestic relationship with the respondent and who is tortured by the respondent.[9] It also includes women who live together with their male partners.

Today domestic violence is a Universal phenomenon. Around the world one out of three women is suffering from domestic violence silently. So, universally recognised concept of domestic violence is: Domestic Violence is a range of abusive and threatening behaviours including physical abuse, sexual abuse, verbal and emotional abuse, economic abuse as well as intimidation, isolation and coercion. It is perpetrated by one partner upon the other to gain and maintain control. It happens in the family, home and sometimes the children and other members of the family are involved into it.

Domestic Violence as a Human Rights Issue

Human rights are some basic rights which are inherent in our nature and without which we cannot live as human beings. The human rights of women generally includes rights to equality before law, right against gender discrimination, right against harassment, right to abortion, right to privacy, right to economic empowerment. Today domestic violence is recognised as a gross human rights violation by different International Women's Convention. The UN Conference documents *i.e.* Vienna declaration and Programme of Action 1993, and Beijing Declaration and platform for action 1995 recognised domestic violence as a human right issue. The UN convention on elimination of all forms of discrimination against women 1979 recognised domestic violence as a gender based violence. Art 17 of this convention creates a committee on the elimination of discrimination against women which recognised Domestic Violence as a human right issue. In India, Domestic Violence violates Article 21 of the Constitution of India.

It can be stated that in spite of plethora of progressive and protective legislations favouring women, India failed to uplift the social status of women. Though the new civil law *i.e.* The Protection of Women from Domestic Violence Act, 2005 is implemented properly by the state machinery, still today Domestic Violence is common in both urban and rural India but largely ignored and accepted as a way of life in our country. Undoubtedly, it involves human rights issue and a serious obstruction to development. According to Poornima Advani, "It (domestic violence) is pernicious because it is directed against women who are supposed to carry the generations forward and goes against all canons of civilized behaviour. It is insidious because it takes place within the closed walls of the home, which is supposed to be the safe sanctuary for its occupants.[10]

Sexual Harassment

Sexual harassment is yet other form of gender based violence. It is in the form of eve teasing, molestation, sexual assault and rape is a wrong against the honour, dignity and self respect of a woman. It hurts her immensely and throws her in the background. Sexual harassment in workplace is a serious irritating factor that renders women's involvement in works unsafe and affects right to work with dignity. She loses confidence in life and her career is put at stake. There is a strong need for combating this fast growing problem. In country like India where women are worshipped at par with the Gods, this kind of behaviour against women is unjust, unfair and hippocratic. Sexual harassment at the workplace is a growing concern for women. Even though the occurrence of sexual harassment at the workplace is widespread in India and elsewhere, this is the first time it has been recognised as an infringement of the fundamental rights of a woman, under Article 19(1)g of the Constitution of India "to practice any profession or to carry out any occupation, trade or business". Sexual harassment results in violation of the fundamental rights of a woman to equality under articles 14 and 15 of the Constitution of India and her right to life and to live with dignity under article 21 of the Constitution and right to practice any profession or to carry on any occupation, trade or business which includes a right to safe environment free from sexual harassment. Articles 14, 15 and 21 of the Indian Constitution provide safeguards to women against all forms of discrimination. In recent times, the problem of sexual harassment at the workplace has assumed serious proportions.

Unlike the women of ancient time, the present day woman is almost on par with the men folk, expect the dignity and status she has to be given, struggling to establish her position as a separate entity in the society. However, she is failed to be accorded with the respect she is entitled to claim, as a human being. Sexual harassment of women at the workplace is a fast growing problem in India. The number of cases filed for sexual harassment has risen but women employee is still reluctant to report the matter to concerned authority. Indeed, women suffer it silently and avoid lodging report because she believes that her complaint would disadvantage her in connection with her employment. About half of working women have suffered some kind of sexual harassment at workplace. For the majority of the respondents, mental and physical harassment and gender discrimination have been the most dominant forms of problems relating to sexual harassment.

For the first time sexual harassment had been explicitly – legally defined in India in *Vishaka vs. State of Rajasthan and Others*[11], as an unwelcome sexual gesture or behaviour whether directly or indirectly as sexually coloured remarks, physical contact and advances, showing pornography, a demand or request for sexual favours or any other unwelcome physical, verbal/non-verbal conduct being sexual in nature.[12] It was in this landmark case where the Supreme Court provided exclusive guidelines in respect of protection of women from sexual harassment at workplace.

Dowry Harassment

Dowry means any property or valuable security given or agreed to be given either directly or indirectly by one party to a marriage to the other party to the marriage or by the parents of either party or by any other person to either party to the marriage. It may be given at or before or any time after the marriage in connection with the marriage of the said parties. But it does not include dower or 'mahr' in case of person to whom the Muslim Personal Law (Shariat) applies.[13] In order to curb the evil of dowry, the Dowry Prohibition Act was passed in 1961. Certain States passed amendments to this Act. Despite statutory prohibition of dowry, the menace continued more, because the law was absolutely ineffective and in view of its language it was very difficult to apprehend and convict anybody under the Act. There were various loopholes in the statute. The offence was not cognizable and hence the culprit could not be arrested without a warrant. The complaint had to be made within one year from the date of the offence.

Before the amendment of inserting Section 304-B[14] and 498-A[15] of the Indian Penal Code, dowry-death was only actionable by police only if it resulted in "grievous hurt" in terms of Section 320 IPC, or worse making it cognizable offence. Moreover, what we find in the Indian society is that the husband was considered to have more or less a proprietary right over the wife. When any matters related to dowry-death were reported to the police, it was thought to be family disputed matter which they would seek out within four corners of their house, thus leaving the problem unsolved. In order to combat with such evil the legislature introduced these two sections under the Indian Penal Code.

A new offence, the offence of cruelty to wife by her husband and in-laws have been created by inserting a new chapter XX-A and a new section – Section 498-A in the Indian Penal Code. In 1983, Section 498-A of the Indian Penal Code defined a new cognizable offence, namely: 'cruelty by husband or relatives of husband'. This means that once such a complaint is registered by the victim or any of her relatives, the police have no option but to take action. This law takes particular cognizance of harassment, where it occurs with a view to coercing the wife, or any person related to her, to meet any unlawful demand regarding any property or valuable security, or occurs on account of failure by her, or any person related to her, to meet such a demand. The offenders are punishable with imprisonment which may extend to three years as well as a fine.

Another amendment was also made under the Indian Penal Code naming the crime as 'dowry-murder' or 'dowry death' under section 304-B. The section states that if the death of a woman is caused by burns or bodily injury, or occurs under abnormal circumstances, within seven years of her marriage and it shown that prior to death she was subject to cruelty by her husband or his relatives, in connection with demands for dowry, such a death would be called 'dowry-death' and the husband or relative would be deemed to have caused her death. By inserting a new Section 113-B in the Indian Evidence Act[16], the lawmakers stipulated that in cases that are registered by the police as those of 'dowry-death', the court shall presume that the accused is guilty unless he can prove otherwise.

Role of Section 498-A and 304-B

Section 498-A of IPC is a step towards ensuring that the unlimited privileges of a husband in the holy relationship of marriage are rendered justifiable by criminal courts when his inhuman behaviour jeopardize the mental and physical well-being of the wife. Section 498-A is integral to offences under section 304-B and 'cruelty' is a common ingredient to both the sections. Infact, the Supreme Court held *Shanti vs. State of Haryana*[17] that the two sections (304-B and 498-A of Indian Penal Code) are not mutually exclusive and, in cases of 'dowry-death', both from the point of view of practice and procedure and to avoid technical defects, charges under both the sections should be framed. The Supreme Court further held that in the absence of any explanation under section 304-B about the meaning of cruelty, the meaning of cruelty and harassment has to be taken as the same as in the explanation to section 498-A of IPC.

In *Baldev Krishnan vs. State of Punjab*[18] the Apex Court held that "taunts to the deceased by the accused saying that better proposals were received for the groom who were willing to give more dowry and making humiliating remarks about the low quality of gifts brought in by her during the marriage, amounted to harassment on account of insufficient dowry", and that even if there was proof of no physical torture, proof of mental torture was sufficient for conviction.

Incest and Rape

The word 'rape' is derived from the Latin term 'rapio', which means to seize. Rape literally means a forcible seizure and that is the essential characteristic of the offence. It means the violation of one's esteem. Rape is not a crime only against the person of a woman but a crime against society being the worst kind of social menace. It is viewed as a crime against the 'honour' of not just the girl who is raped but also of her family. Apart from being regarded as a dehumanizing act it is an unlawful intrusion on the right of privacy and sanctity of female. It is violative of the victim's most cherished of the Fundamental Right that is the right to Life contained in Article 21 of the Constitution. Rape is a crime not only against the person but against the entire society. It destroys the psychology of woman and pushes her into deep trauma. When a woman is ravished what is inflicted is not is mindly injury but the deep sense of deathless shame. It is crime against basic human right to live with human dignity as contained in Article 21 of the Indian Constitution. According to it, the right to life with human dignity is the fundamental right of every citizen and the State is under constitutional duty to provide at least minimum conditions ensuring human dignity. Rape laws are covered under section 375 and 376 of the IPC.

The Criminal Law (Amendment) Bill 2012, replacing the word 'rape' by the phrase 'sexual assault' and seeking to widen the scope of the offence, was introduced by Home Minister Sushil kumar Shinde on Dec 4, 2012. The amendment bill expands the definition so that cases of sexual assault where victims were male would fall under the same law along with cases where victims were women. At present, the offence is defined under section 375 of the Indian Penal Code as per which a man is said to commit 'rape' in case he has sexual intercourse with a woman against her will. The bill also carries provisions which makes carrying out of acid attacks a separate offence punishable by a maximum of ten years' in jail. Attempt to do so could send the accused to jail for 5-7 years. Under the bill, an offender can be jailed for life in cases of sexual assault, irrespective of the victim's gender. The term 'sexual assault' has also been widened to include forced unnatural sex. The bill lays down strict provisions under which persons below 18 making a complaint will not have to face the accused in court or police stations. It has raised the age of consent from 16 to 18 years. The President of India has accorded his assent to the Criminal Law (Amendment), 2013, on 2nd April. The Act expands the definition of crime against women; the act entails changes in the criminal law by amending Indian Penal Code (IPC), Code of Criminal Procedure (CrPC) and the Evidence Act. It includes key recommendation of the

Justice J. S. Verma committee the government had set up after the December 16, 2012 gang rape to suggest ways to strengthen laws on sexual crime against women. The government however went beyond the panel's recommendations that stopped short of proposing death penalty for rapists. It includes the provision for capital punishment in cases where rape leads to death or leaves the victim in a persistent 'vegetative state'. In such cases, the minimum punishment will be 20 years in jail which can be extended to the natural life of the convict or death, adding discretion will be with the court. In a bid to make the law women friendly, the ordinance suggests that only a woman police officer will take the statement of the victim of the sexual crime. Women under 18 years will not be confronted with the accused but provision of cross examination has been retained. There will be no personal appearance of witnesses before police officers. The IPC allows the court to impose a lower sentence. The ordinance takes away the power of the court to lower the sentence. Penalty in term of years in jail has been recommended for a government servant if he does not co-operate on sexual offence case or harms the process of law.

The government has rejected a recommendation of the Verma panel on Armed Forces (Special Powers) Act that no sanction would be required if the armed forces personnel are accused of a crime against woman. The ordinance also did not accept the suggestions of the Verma Committee that dealt with sexual violence among members of the armed forces and police personnel. The committee had asked for a removal of the Armed Forces Special Powers Act that gives the armed forces immunity from prosecution and proposed that the senior police or army officer would be held responsible for a sexual offense committed by a junior officer.

Other issues in which the government ordinance rejected the suggestions of the Verma committee are the incorporation of marital rape as a punishable criminal offense, the payment of compensation to victims of sexual violence and the lowering of the juvenile age from 18 to 16 years. The ordinance has also made the definition of rape gender neutral, rather than keeping it gender-specific to women as suggested by the Verma Committee.

Rape is a crime not only against the person but against the entire society. It destroys the psychology of woman and pushes her into deep trauma. When a woman is ravished what is inflicted is not is mindly injury but the deep sense of deathless shame. It is crime against basic human right to live with human dignity as contained in Article 21 of the Indian Constitution. According to it, the right to life with human dignity is the fundamental right of every citizen and the State is under constitutional duty to provide at least minimum conditions ensuring human dignity[19]. Rape laws are covered under section 375 and 376 of the IPC. Under these sections, rape is seen only in times of penile-vaginal penetration. It does not include for instance anal or oral penetration. It does not include penetration by objects. As a result of these loopholes, very often judges find themselves trying rape cases under more watered down sections; 'outraging the modesty of a woman', for instance. The Indian Penal Code makes no distinctions between rape of a minor, and that of an adult. Child abuse should be recognised as an offence against innocence and therefore, the law against child rape should be made more stringent. Though the founding father of India after great deliberation incorporated certain provisions in favour of women; the ground reality lies in the fact that how many women have been benefited. The answer is not much encouraging, so the society must come forward to see that the goals of the Constitution achieved. As opined by Swami Vivekananda, if the nation wants to reach the pinnacle of glory the women folk who are the incarnation of the goddess, should not be neglected and thrown into insignificance. The nation which relegates the seat of the women in the back is bound to decline.

Female Foeticide and Infanticide

Infanticide is an age-old practice among human populations, to regulate the numbers of children and eliminate the less wanted off spring. The law on infanticide entered national legal framework called Indian Penal Code. It is a term used to denote the unlawful destruction of a new born child and is punishable as murder under section 302 of the Indian Penal Code, be death or transpiration for life and also fine. The law in India draws no distinction between murder of a child or any other individual, and the provisions which apply to homicide apply equally to infanticide. In 1870, female infanticide was banned.

Today female foeticide had come to replace female infanticide demonstrating that social attitude to the birth of a female child has not changed. Female foeticide is an act of aborting a foetus because it is female. The act of aborting or terminating a foetus while it's still in the womb, because it is female, is known as female foeticide. Female Foeticide, is violation of right a basic human right and guarantee under the constitution In the case of female foeticide, the female children in the wombs of expecting mothers, they are not only denied the right to live but are robbed to their right to be born. The selection of male child over female is enough proof for lack of right to birth to girl child. Social, cultural, financial and psychological reasons are responsible for the prevalence of evil female foeticide in our society. Unfortunately, it became popular for sex determination, leading to sex selective abortions for those who do not want to be burdened with female child. The more easy way was shown by Medical Termination of Pregnancy Act, 1971 by legalising abortions in certain specific conditions and ultimately became a tool for female sex-selective abortions and led to drastic fall in the female sex ratio to present level. Male child preference is a pivotal factor in female foeticide. The government has also taken into consideration the gravity of the problem and enacted legislation to curb it. Maharastra was the first state to ban the pre-natal sex determination through the enactment of the Maharastra Regulation of Parental Diagnostic Technique Act. Similarly, at the national level the Central Pre-natal Diagnostic Techniques (Prohibition of Sex Selection) Act 1994 was enacted to prevent female foeticide. The purpose was to limit the use of prenatal diagnostic techniques to genuine medical purpose and to prevent its misuse. It was amended and replaced in 2002 by the Pre-natal Diagnostic Techniques (Regulation and Prevention of Misuse) Act.

Sati and Abetment of Suicide

The practice of sati – of burning or occasionally burying a widow alive with her deceased husband is ancient evil grew through distortions of shastras and assertion of patriarchal controls. Sati[20] is a peculiar crime to the Indian scenario. There is a thin line of difference between suicide and murder in the context of Sati. The Commission of Sati in 1987, where the widow Roopa Kanwar aged 18 years was burnt alive in Deorala of Rajasthan, spread shocking news throughout

India. The glorification of Sati by religious celebration, rituals and movement to construct temples for *sati mata* ignoring the preventive measures of state government and High Court order produced serious concern. The media, social activists and the women organizations demanded for an effective and comprehensive law preventing and forbidding sati related crimes. Both the Union and Rajasthan Governments enacted statues to prevent commission of sati.

Parliament enacted the Commission of Sati Prevention Act, 1987 to provide for more effective prevention of the commission of sati and its glorification. The Preamble states that sati is revolting to the feeling of human nature and it is nowhere enjoined by any of the religions of India as an imperative duty. The Act came into effect in 21st March 1988.

Stalking

Stalking is defined as a 'willful course of conduct' involving repeated or continuing harassment of another individual that would cause a reasonable person to feel terrorized, frightened, intimidate, threatened, harassed or molested and that actually cause the victim to feel terrorized, frightened, intimidate, threatened, harassed or molested". Stalking is unwanted or obsessive attention by an individual or group toward another person. Stalking behaviours are related to harassment and intimidation and may include following the victim in person or monitoring them. Stalking is a pattern of repeated and unwanted attention, harassment, contact, or any other course of conduct directed at a specific person that would cause a reasonable person to feel fear.

Previously, there were no penal provisions to combat with the crime of stalking. Recently through the Criminal law Amendment Act, 2013.

354D. (1) Any man who —

(i) Follows a woman and contacts, or attempts to contact such woman to foster personal interaction despite a clear indication of disinterest by such woman.

(ii) Monitors the use by a woman of the internet, email or any other form of electronic communication, commits the offence of stalking.

Provided that such conduct shall not amount to stalking if the man who pursued it proves that:

(i) It was pursued for the purpose of preventing or detecting crime and the man accused of stalking had been entrusted with the responsibility of prevention and detection of crime by the State.

(ii) It was pursued under any law or to comply with any condition or requirement imposed by any person under any law.

(iii) In the particular circumstances such conduct was reasonable and justified.

The recognition of word cyber stalking cannot be said to be a new concept rather it got its place under Information Technology Act 2000 Section 29(a) of the Indian Penal Code defines Electronic Record as "The words 'Electronic Record' shall have the meaning assigned to them in clause (t) of sub-section (1) of section 2 of the Information Technology Act 2000". This big change is the recognition of electronic document as evidence in a court of law.

Conclusion

From time immemorial women have been placed on a pedestal 'mother of mankind'. Paradoxically, the most horrendous cruelties are inflicted on her, often without reason and mostly without just cause. Crime against women is one of the most persistent human rights violations that are often ignored. This arises due to the culture of discrimination that denies equal rights and equal opportunities to women. It is a matter of serious introspection whether the rights guaranteed under the law have any meaning for the down trodden section of society. Despite the progressive steps in many areas a lot more needs to be done to give the marginalized masses a sense of security, dignity and honour in the society. The laws that intended to punish people who commit crime against women, and the laws and regulations on the protection of women and girl child should be strictly enforced. These efforts are not likely to be fully successful, however, unless basic changes in the way the girls and women are valued by society take place. The principle of equality between men and women should be more widely promoted through the media to change the attitude and improve the awareness of the general public on this issue. A number of strategies have been proposed and implemented by government of India to address the problems of women. Mere laws and piecemeal approaches to the development of women cannot ensure an equal status for women unless a multipronged and an integrated approach is adopted through which large scale education, opportunities for self-employment and facilities for consolidating themselves into women's organization are provided. Women can make a mark in society only when they emerge as a powerful community with distinct ideology, philosophy and strategies to face the challenges of the life.

Against all odds and obstacles women all over the world have launched powerful movement to reverse centuries of discrimination and injustice. They are mobilizing against violence and oppression and are demanding equal rights, opportunities for development, equitable laws and control over their earning. With the growth of education, women no longer feel that they are confined to four walls of house but are venturing out into every conceivable area of activity. They are increasingly becoming conscious of their inherent right and have joined hands to assert them which are called as 'feminism'. It symbolizes an awareness of oppression on domestic, social, and economic level accompanied by a willingness to struggle against subjugation and subordination. They have focused their attention on equalizing strategies, which represents attempts to improve women's access to existing education, employment, health care and other opportunities to make resources more responsible to women's need. If women have to be emancipated or empowerment has to take place, it should be all embracing attempt and a constructive effort. Without changing mindset of the people, there can be no gender equality. The fight for women's right is a long and arduous journey and requires patience, courage and sacrifice. It wants a movement to ensure equality for women. Incidents of dowry death are a blot on civilized society but they occur frequently despite of various legal measures existing. Although geographically men and women share the same space, they live in different world. The mere fact that *women hold up half the sky* does not appear to give them position of dignity and equality. Though we have entered into the new millennium yet women has been discriminated against all these years. The discrimination cannot be said from legislative insufficiency but from the attitudinal bias of the society. Through various provisions in the U.N. Charter, the members of the United Nations reaffirmed their faith in fundamental rights and in the dignity and the worth of human person 1. Further this Charter contains a provision for international co-operation in solving international problems including promoting and encouraging respect for human rights and fundamental freedoms for all without distinction as to race, sex, language and religion.

Time and again the Supreme Court of India has extended the ambit of Article 21 of the Constitution of India and held that mere existence is not the right to live – it is the right to live with dignity. But unfortunately such has been the social conditions and have been the prejudices in the man's society that even personal liberty guaranteed to woman under Article 21 of the Constitution has no meaning to her. Thus, wherever crimes are committed against women the same should be viewed in the context of violation of her right under Article 21 of the Constitution and not merely as a crime against society.

NOTES

1. Declaration on the Elimination of Violence against Women General Assembly Resolution 48/104, 20th December 1993.
2. Fourth World Conference on Women held at Beijing in 1995. The Platform for Action of the Beijing Conference Addressed 11 Substantive areas of concern: poverty, education, health, violence, armed conflict, economic structures and policies, decision-making, mechanisms for the achievements of women, women's human rights, mass media and the environment.
3. Vienns Declaration and Programme of Action, Adopted on 25th June, 1993.
4. Article I. Universal Declaration of Human Rights, 1948, UNGA Resolution 217 A (III), 10th December, 1948.
5. The Convention on the Elimination of all forms of Discrimination Against Women adopted on 18.12.1979 and came into force in 1981. In the Preamble to the Convention it was agreed that "the full and complete development of a country, the welfare of the world and the cause of peace require the maximum participation of women in equal terms with men in all fields".

6. Article 14 of the Indian Constitution, "The State shall not deny to any person equality before law and equal protection of the laws".
7. According to Section 3 of the protection of women from Domestic violence Act 2005, domestic violence means: 'Any Act, Omission or commission or conduct of the respondent which constitutes harms or injuries or endangers the life health, safety and well-being of the aggrieved person. It also includes causing physical abuse, sexual abuse, verbal abuse, emotional abuse and economic abuse'.
8. According to section 2(q) of the protection of women from Domestic Violence Act, 2005, 'respondent' means any adult male person who has been in a domestic relationship with the aggrieved person and against whom the aggrieved person has sought any relief under this Act.
9. Section 2(f) of the protection of women from Domestic Violence Act, 2005.
10. Poornima Advani, "Curbing domestic violence: Inching forward" The Hindu, 27.06.2005.
11. (1997) 6 SCC 241.
12. Section 2(n) of the Sexual Harassment of Women at Workplace (Prevention, Prohibition and Redressal) Act., 2013.
13. 14 Section 2 of the Dowry Prohibition Act, 1961 (28 of 1961).
14. Section 304B - (1) Where the death of a woman is caused by any burns or bodily injury or occurs otherwise than under normal circumstances within seven years of her marriage and it is shown that soon before her death she was subjected to cruelty or harassment by her husband or any relative of her husband for, or in connection with, any demand for dowry, such death will be called 'dowry-death', and such husband or relative shall be deemed to have caused her death.

    Explanation – For the purpose of this sub-sectio, 'dowry' shall have the same meaning as in section 2 of the Dowry Prohibition Act, 1961 (28 of 1961).
15. Section 498-A of IPC – whoever, being the husband or relative of the husband of a woman, subjects such woman to cruelty shall be punished with imprisonment for a term which may extend to three years and shall also be liable to fine.

    Explanation – For the purpose of this section cruelty means:

    (a) Any willful conduct which is of such a nature as likely to drive the woman to commit suicide or to cause grave injury or dander to life, limb or health (whether mental or physical) of the woman or;

(b) Harassment of woman where such harassment is with a view to coercing her or any person related to her meet any unlawful demand for any property or valuable security or is on account of failure by her or any person related to her to meet such demand.

16. Section 113-A of the Indian Evidence Act, 1872 – when question is whether the commission of suicide by a woman had been abetted by her husband or any relative of her husband and it is shown that she had committed suicide within a period of seven years from the date of her marriage and that her husband or such relative of her husband had subjected her to cruelty, the court may presume, having regard to all the other circumstances of the case, that such suicide had been abetted by her husband or by relative of her husband.

    Explanation – For the purpose of this section 'cruelty' shall have the same meaning as in the section 498-A of the Indian Penal Code (45 of 1860).

17. AIR 1991 SC 1226.
18. AIR 1997 SC 1666.
19. Vikram Deo Singh *vs.* State of Bihar, AIR 1988 SC 1782.
20. Section 2(c) of the Commission of Sati (Prevention) Act, 1987 'sati' means the burning or burying alive or:

    (i) Any widow along with the body of her deceased husband or any other relative or with any article, object or thing associated with the husband or such relative.

    (ii) Any woman along with the body of any of her relatives, irrespective of whether such burning or burying is claimed to be voluntary on the part of the widow or the women or otherwise; of the Commission of Sati (Prevention) Act.

17

Growth, Urbanisation and Crime against Women

Dr. Sarita Agrawal

Abstract

Women are potential contributors to the production and development and human development is impossible without gender equality. Equality for women promotes economic growth through more effective utilisation of existing resources thereby speeding up the pace of development as economic development has an impact on the socio-political structure of the society such as it is influenced by it. The notion of human well-being itself is more broadly conceived to include, not only consumption of goods and services but also the accessibility of all sections of the population, especially the deprived and those who are living below the normative minimal poverty line, to the basic necessities of a productive and socially meaningful life.

INTRODUCTION

Any definition of economic development includes an element covering the degree of participation by the population at large. Women are potential contributors to the production and development and human development is impossible without gender equality (HDR, 1995). It ought to inevitably improve the status of women and equality among the genders. Similarly, equality for women promotes economic growth through more effective utilisation of existing resources thereby speeding up the pace of development as economic development has an impact on the socio-political structure of the society such as it is influenced by it (HDR, 1995).

The last decade of the twentieth century has seen a visible shift in the focus of development planning from a mere expansion of production of goods and services and the consequent growth in per capita income to planning for enhancement of human well-being.

The notion of human well-being itself is more broadly conceived to include, not only consumption of goods and services but also the accessibility of all sections of the population, especially the deprived and those who are living below the normative minimal poverty line, to the basic necessities of a productive and socially meaningful life. Such a conceptualization of well-being encompasses individual attainments in areas of education and knowledge; health and longevity; as well as in the quality of overall social and physical environment of people. A specific focus on these aspects of development is necessary, as experience shows that economic prosperity measured in terms of per capita income does not always ensure enrichment in quality of life reflected in broader dimensions of well-being like in indicators on longevity, literacy or, for that matter, environmental sustainability. Attainments in these dimensions of well-being are desirable in themselves; hence, they are socially valued. They are also desirable because of their instrumental value in sustaining the development process and enlarging available opportunities and choices for people. While equality in development outcomes may not be a feasible goal of equity and social justice, such an approach to human well-being emphasises equality in opportunities for all in the process of development (NHDR, 2002).

The full benefits of development can only be realised with people's participation and effective use of its human resources. Development analysis cannot be divorced from gender categories and the participation of women cannot be isolated from the total framework of development. The ultimate goal of social justice can only be achieved with equal opportunities to all irrespective of the gender, age, caste, etc., since discrimination against women is incompatible with human dignity and the welfare of the family and of the society; prevents their participation on equal terms with men......and is an obstacle to the full development of the potentialities of women in the service of their countries and humanity (UN, 1967).

Growth and Urbanisation

The process of economic growth is also marked by several socio-economic changes. Urbanisation is an important fall out of the process of economic growth. Historically, cities have been the driving forces in economic and social development. As centres of industry and commerce, cities have been centres of wealth and political power and contribute significantly to the country's GDP [WRI, 1996]. The world is undergoing transition towards urbanisation. It is estimated that in 1975 one third of the world population lived in the urban areas and by 2025, this proportion will rise to two-third.

The urban population grew from 286 million in 2001 to 377 million in 2011. As per the 2011 Census, nearly 30 per cent of the population in India is living in the urban areas. And the estimates show that by 2030, more than 40 per cent of the population would be living in the urban areas. A substantial increase in the urban population is due to a net rural-urban classification and rural-to-urban migration. A huge number of new towns emerged during the last decade, contributing significantly to the speeding up of urbanisation. On the other hand, although the contribution of the natural increase in urban growth has declined in terms of pro-portions, its share in absolute numbers (about 40 million) continues to be huge due to the large base of the urban population. (Bhagat, 2011). As more and more urbanisation is taking place, there are problems relating to infrastructure and a situation of growing stress and violence.

The process of urbanisation is radically changing the socio-economic structure of the world economy. The change is much more rapid in the less developed economies where the rate of urbanisation is much faster compared to that in the developed countries. According to a World Bank estimate nearly 80 per cent of the economic growth will take place in the urban areas more particularly in the developing economies where the rate of urbanisation is higher. During 1970-95, the rate of growth of urban population in India has been 3.3 per cent. During the next two decades, this process of urbanisation is expected to slow down to 2.8 per cent [HDR, 1998].

The process of urbanisation in any economy is followed by human development reflected in improvement in living standards, rise in literacy rate, better health, etc. It also has a positive effect on the empowerment of women. The co-efficient of correlation value calculated for rates of urbanisation and Gender Empowerment index value for 15 major states of India gives a Karl Pearson's correlation value of 0.76 indicating a very high correlation. Those states that have high rate of urbanisation also have high GEI.

However, urbanisation also has negative impacts. These include a vast range of problems such as environmental degradation, rise in slums, water, and air pollution, etc. For many of the regions, urbanisation goes in tandem with urban poverty not only in absolute terms but also in relative terms. Over crowding, air pollution, uncollected garbage and other deficiencies in the physical environment frequently represent the most obvious manifestations of urban environmental health problems (WRI, 1996). It also leads to growing social tensions that adversely affect the mental health of the human beings. Rise in crime and violence, etc., are also the fall out of urbanisation that adversely affect the mental health of the human beings. There is no denying the fact that women are more vulnerable to violence compared to men. Socially and economically they constitute a disadvantaged group.

This paper examines the process of development in India from a gender perspective and examines how the process of urbanisation has affected the women in the urban areas by bringing changes in the social environment.

Uneven Urbanisation

The urban population worldwide has been rising though much of it is in the less developed countries. In the developed countries, rapid urbanisation occurred a century ago and a vast majority of the population lives in urban areas.

Table 17.1: Urban Population in India (%)

Year	Urban Population %
1951	17.30
1961	18.00
1971	19.90
1981	23.30
1991	25.70
2001	27.80
2011	31.16

Source: Government of India (2012), Town and country Planning Organisation, Ministry of urban Development, *Provisional Population Tables, data highlights (urban)*, January.

The urban population in India has been rising at a rapid rate although rates of urbanisation vary across the states. There are significant differences in the rates of urbanisation. Maharashtra, Gujarat and Tamil Nadu have witnessed the highest rates of urbanisation in the country being almost 39 per cent and 35 per cent respectively during 1991. However, during 2001, Tamil Nadu had overtaken even Gujarat during 2001. On the other hand, it has been extremely low in the states like: Assam, Bihar and Orissa. According to 2011 census, Goa is the most urbanised state with nearly 62 per cent of the total population in the urban areas. This is followed by Mizoram and Tamil Nadu. As per 2011 Census, the three least urbanised states are Assam, Bihar and Himachal Pradesh having 14, 11 and 10 per cent urban population.

Not only are the rates of urbanisation different in different states but there are also differences in the concentration of urbanisation and much of the mobility is from the small and intermediate size cities to large metropolis. During 1951, the proportion of population in class I cities with a population of one lakh or more was nearly 45 per cent This has continuously been rising and as per 1991 figures, there were 300 urban centres with the population of 1 lakh and more that accounted for 65 per cent of the total urban population. In 2011, the total number of towns having population of more than one lakh has increased to 468 and the number of million plus cities has increased to 53. Also, there have been variations in the growth of urban areas. This does not directly have an impact on the rate of urbanisation. But the process of urbanisation moves in favour of larger cities. This is giving rise to a new class of 'international cities' that are the nerve centres of an increasingly globalising economies (Sassen, 1994). As transnational spaces for economic activity these international cities have more in common with each other rather than the cities in their own regions.

Growing Social Tensions and Crime

There is no denying the fact that there has been a collapse of the value system and marginalisation of social life in general but more so in the urban areas that is indirectly affecting the security and mental health of the people. Closely related to this insecurity is the growing social tension that threatens social community cohesion (HDR, 1999). Over a period of time, the crime has been growing continuously in the country. This is shown in the following Table 17.1. There has been a rise in all types of crime in the recent times. Total crime in the country has increased at a compounded rate of 2.97 per cent per annum. Over a period of time, all types of crimes have grown at a positive rate in the country. The worst has been in case of kidnapping, rioting and the assault on women that have increased at the compounded annual growth rate of 8-10 per cent per annum being the highest CAGR. It is worth mentioning that in case of some types of crime, the rate of annual growth might show a declining trend but in absolute terms, these types of crime also show an increase.

Crime is increasing in scope, intensity and sophistication. The data for most of the countries show that there has been a phenomenal rise in homicide, thefts, assaults, burglary, robberies, frauds, rapes, etc., irrespective of the level of development of the country. On the contrary, it has been found that in highly industrialized countries like USA, the crime rate is much higher than that in some of the less developed countries. This has resulted into growing socio-psychological tensions. It also threatens the safety of citizens around the world and hampers countries in their social, economic and cultural development. It is also estimated that a highly corrupt country is likely to achieve aggregate investment level of almost 5 per cent less and lose half a per cent point of GDP growth than a relatively uncorrupt country.

Table 17.2: Head-wise Growth of Crimes in India (growth rate)

Crime Head	2007	2008	2009	2010	2011	2012	CAGR
1	2	3	4	5	6	7	8
Rape	4.84	3.52	-0.33	3.62	9.17	2.96	4.291
Kidnapping and Abduction	4.75	9.80	11.89	13.53	16.19	6.56	8.096
(i) of Women and Girls	7.07	12.36	12.22	15.75	19.37	7.58	10.185
(ii) of Others	-0.55	2.48	10.89	6.48	5.25	2.54	2.422
Preparation and Assembly for Dacoity	11.73	0.37	-11.41	-8.25	10.71	7.05	-0.376
Robbery	0.39	7.24	9.20	4.39	5.59	10.70	3.149
Burglary	-1.11	2.77	-1.78	-2.05	2.58	0.42	0.79
Theft	2.87	11.13	2.35	1.89	3.18	-1.00	2.46
Riots	-2.77	10.19	-4.66	7.35	1.37	8.95	7.36
Criminal Breach of Trust	2.06	6.16	-0.98	2.16	4.67	2.54	4.44
Cheating	7.14	1.92	9.22	8.64	10.96	7.47	0.01
Counterfeiting	7.69	35.71	-1.87	-11.79	-10.89	1.91	2.28
Arson	-5.25	2.49	-5.55	-2.61	6.54	30.58	1.89
Hurt	0.60	4.36	-2.02	3.51	4.78	9.73	2.94

Contd...

1	2	3	4	5	6	7	8
Dowry Deaths	3.48	0.98	2.58	0.10	2.71	-4.47	1.89
Assault on Women With Intent to Outrage her Modesty	2.68	4.33	-4.21	4.91	5.80	5.55	8.02
Insult to the Modesty of Women	1.52	11.54	-9.87	-9.52	-13.96	7.04	-2.50
Cruelty by Husband or his Relatives	9.05	7.13	10.08	5.02	5.42	7.46	5.32
Importation of Girls	-4.30	9.84	-28.36	-25.00	12.22	-26.25	2.83
Causing Death by Negligence	6.27	6.22	6.88	7.93	2.40	-1.19	2.97
Other IPC Crimes	2.57	3.35	1.00	6.76	4.54	0.02	8.02
Total Cognizable Crimes Under Ipc	2.25	5.21	1.34	4.88	4.53	2.65	2.97

Source: Calculated on the basis of data from National Crime Record Bureau, Ministry of Home Affairs, Government of India, 2012.

Table 17.3: Growth of Crime in India (crime as % of total)

Particulars	2002	2007	2008	2009	2010	2011	2012
1	2	3	4	5	6	7	8
Rape (Sec. 376 Ipc)	0.920	1.042	1.025	1.009	0.997	1.041	1.044
Kidnapping and Abduction	1.227	1.385	1.446	1.596	1.728	1.921	1.994
(i) of Women and Girls	0.815	1.026	1.096	1.213	1.339	1.529	1.603
(ii) of Others	0.413	0.359	0.350	0.383	0.389	0.391	0.391
Preparation and Assembly for Dacoity	0.103	0.161	0.154	0.134	0.118	0.124	0.130
Robbery	1.054	0.962	0.980	1.056	1.051	1.062	1.145
Burglary	5.418	4.585	4.478	4.340	4.053	3.978	3.891
Theft	13.900	14.326	15.132	15.283	14.847	14.654	14.134
Riots	3.873	3.011	3.154	2.967	3.037	2.946	3.126
Criminal Breach of Trust	0.788	0.781	0.788	0.770	0.750	0.751	0.750
Cheating	2.599	3.283	3.180	3.428	3.551	3.769	3.946
Counterfeiting	0.085	0.111	0.143	0.138	0.116	0.099	0.098
Arson	0.664	0.454	0.442	0.412	0.382	0.390	0.496
Hurt	14.886	13.724	13.613	13.162	12.991	13.022	13.921

Contd...

1	2	3	4	5	6	7	8
Dowry Deaths	41.666	39.027	38.068	39.178	37.845	35.603	33.034
Assault on Women with Intent to Outrage her Modesty	1.907	1.947	1.931	1.825	1.825	1.848	1.900
Insult to the Modesty of Women	0.570	0.550	0.583	0.519	0.448	0.369	0.384
Cruelty By Husband or His Relatives	2.766	3.816	3.886	4.221	4.227	4.263	4.462
Importation of Girls*	0.004	0.003	0.003	0.002	0.002	0.003	0.002
Causing Death by Negligence	3.597	4.362	4.404	4.645	4.780	4.682	4.507
Other IPC Crimes	41.020	41.675	40.937	40.802	41.534	41.539	40.476

Source: Calculated on the basis of data from National Crime Record Bureau, Ministry of Home Affairs, Government of India, 2012.

An attempt has been made here to understand the relationship between urbanisation and growth of crime. Simple regression model is used for the same.

Table 17.4: Regression Statistics Showing Relationship between Urban Population and Crime

Multiple R	0.98811155
R Square	0.976364436
Adjusted R Square	0.968485915
Standard Error	22514.44225
ANOVA	
Co-efficient of intercept	3.47
t-value	-3.537484182
p-value	0.038433
Significance F	123.9274

The value of R^2 is 0.976 and hence one can say that 97 per cent of change in crime is explained by growth of urban population. The value of adjusted R^2 is also quite high being 0.968 and hence 96 per cent of change in crime is attributed to the rise in urban population. But since the value of F is significant at 123.92, this may just be a chance factor. Hence, rise in crime against women is attributable to rise in total crime.

Table 17.5: Regression Statistics Showing Relationship between Urban Population and Crime against Women

Multiple R	0.252458
R Square	0.063735
Adjusted R Square	-0.24835
Standard Error	100632.1
ANOVA	
Co-efficient of intercept	346720162.1
t-value	0.451907586
p-value	0.682009
Significance F	0.682009

Table 17.5 shows the regression statistics of the relationship between urbanisation and crime against women. The value of R^2 is 0.063 and hence one can say that only 0.63 per cent of change in crime against women is explained by growth of urban population. The value of adjusted R-square is negative which means that there are other factors responsible for the growth of crime against women in urban areas. Hence, it is just not the growth of crime in the urban areas which is leading to the growth of crime against women but many other factors. It may be the growing social tension within the society which may be responsible for the growth of crime against women, the patriarchal values, etc.

Table 17.6: Crime against Women as % of Total

Crime	2002	2007	2008	2009	2010	2011	2012
Rape (Sec. 376 Ipc)	0.920	1.042	1.025	1.009	0.997	1.041	1.044
Kidnapping and Abduction of Women and Girls	0.815	1.026	1.096	1.213	1.339	1.529	1.603
Dowry Deaths	41.666	39.027	38.068	39.178	37.845	35.603	33.034
Sexual Assault on Women	1.907	1.947	1.931	1.825	1.825	1.848	1.900
Insult to the Modesty of Women	0.570	0.550	0.583	0.519	0.448	0.369	0.384
Cruelty by Husband or his Relatives	2.766	3.816	3.886	4.221	4.227	4.263	4.462

Source: Calculated on the basis of data from National Crime Record Bureau, Ministry of Home Affairs, Government of India, 2012.

Table 17.6 shows that over a period of time the crime against women has increased as percentage of total. There is a decline only in the dowry deaths whereas virtually all other types of crime against women have increased. Not only has there been a rise in the crime but the rate of growth of crime has also been rising over the years except in case of dowry deaths. For instance, the rate of growth of rapes has risen from 0.05 per cent per annum during 2002 to 2007 to 2.96 per cent per annum during 2.96.

In addition, the contribution of urban social environment to deterioration in mental health is also increasingly being recognised. However, the recognition of this aspect has been very low in general and almost negligible in many of the developing countries in particular, which are still in war with several economic problems such as wide spread unemployment and poverty at their end. If the number of patients admitted in the mental hospital is taken as an indicator of mental health of the people in a country, statistics show that there has been deterioration in the mental health of the people in the countries across the world. In addition, the social problems such as family tensions and problems, growing number of divorces, unemployment, etc., are leading to frustrations in the urban areas which is reflected in the suicides committed which also shows a growing trend world over.

Table 17.7: Incidence and Rate of Suicides in India

Year	Total Number of Suicides	Rate of Suicides
1990	73911	8.94
1995	89178	9.7
2000	108593	10.8
2001	108506	10.6
2002	110417	10.5
2003	110851	10.4
2004	113697	10.5
2005	113914	10.3
2006	118112	10.5
2007	122637	10.8
2008	125017	10.8
2009	127151	10.9
2010	134599	11.4
2011	135585	11.2
2012	135445	11.2

Source: www.indiastat.com

The total suicides have increased by a compounded annual growth rate of nearly 3 per cent per annum during the period from 1990 to 2012. The data on suicide by women manages to capture some aspects of the psychological and emotional abuse, particularly when women who are subjected to such violence see in the act of killing themselves, the ultimate escape from their miseries. During 1971 to 1995, this doubled. It is worthwhile to mention that the number of suicides by the males is much higher compared to the females and also the rate of increase in suicide cases has been higher in case of males. One major reason cited in some studies for this is the growing incidence of unemployment. In 1997 the rate of suicides in some of the States such as Kerala, Karnataka, West Bengal, Tamil Nadu, Goa, Maharashtra and the Union Territories of Pondicherry, Andaman and Nicobar Islands, Dadra and Nagar Haveli and Tripura were well above the national average. Clearly, development whether captured through conventional indicators or through human development indicators, does not necessarily imply better social environment, in terms of less crime and violence, for women in particular. Throughout her life cycle, a women's dignity, self-esteem and emotional well-being are compromised by some less overt, but widespread form of discrimination such as personal confinement and restriction on mobility, particularly in rural areas; almost complete marginalisation in the decision-making process at the household level; responsibility for household work including, looking after younger siblings; sexual abuse by the family members, even incest; childhood/forced marriage and verbal abuse. Most of these are not even recognised as a form of violence and are often condoned or justified on grounds of religious, cultural and traditional social norms or on grounds of attracting social stigma and thus jeopardising the social status of the concerned family (NHDR, 2002).

Urbanisation and Growing Crime and Violence

Violence is a means to keep the oppressed under terror and control. To a woman it is a violation of her rights over her body, her integrity and her dignity. Violence is a structural feature of the severely unequal relationship between man and woman. This perpetuates the sub-ordination of women. Crime and Violence are a means to keep the oppressed under terror and control. To a woman it is a violation of her rights over her body, her integrity and her dignity. Violence is a structural feature of the severely unequal relationship between man and woman. This perpetuates the sub-ordination of women.

The nature and the extent of violence directed at women vary according to class, region, culture and the strata of the society across the country.

However, it impacts women in all age groups and is deeply embedded within the family context of the women. The women are often subjected to violence from their husbands and from relatives in their natal as well as marital homes. The violence against women includes not only physical aggression but sexual, psychological and emotional abuse as well, all of which may not be easy to capture in terms of data as such incidences are often not reported or, if reported, the cases may not be registered for various reasons.

Any attempt, therefore, at assessing the level of development, even when the conventional and the human development indicators are impressive, cannot be complete unless an assessment is also made of the social environment, particularly with regard to the extent of crime and violence that an average individual faces in that society. It is all the more important as it has been often seen that the more prosperous or developed regions are not necessarily the safest for all segments of population. In India too, the more prosperous places are the ones where incidence of crime, in some form, is perhaps the highest — where organised crime and extortion is an unfortunate reality (NHDR, 2002).

Concluding Observations

Though violence and the threat of it is universal, it is not to deny that certain sections of women, who are socially and economically disadvantaged, and poor working women, minority women and so on, are more vulnerable to acts of violence than others. Sectarian politics and sectarian violence have in many ways strengthened gendered inequities. Globalisation has provided the environment for growing internationalization of criminal activities (WRI, 1997) and criminals are reaping the benefits of globalisation. Multinational criminal syndicates have significantly broadened the range of their activities from drug trafficking to money laundering. According to an estimate, as many as 4 million illegal migrants are moved every year generating gross earnings of around US $5-7 billion. Drug related crimes increased from 4 per 100,000 people in Belarus in 1990 to 28 in 1997. The sexual traffic king in women and girls to Western Europe alone has been estimated to be around $ 7 billion business. And at the root of this is the growing organized crime, estimated around $ 1.5 trillion per year. Globalisation has given new characteristics to conflicts by feeding them, involving new actors and blurring political and business interests. In the power vacuum of the post – cold war era, military companies and mercenary armies began offering training to governments – and corporations, Accountable only to those who pay for them (HDR, 1999).

The public policies and civil society interventions to bring about an improvement in domestic and work environment of women have to be seen essentially in terms of strengthening such process that are conducive to bringing about attitudinal shifts in individuals, particularly among the men, and evolving social norms supportive of gender specific concerns.

One important aspect that has been emphasised in the UNDP Human Development Report 2002 and also the National Human Development Report by the Planning commission is the issue of governance for sustainable human development. "A development that, while being sustainable in terms of resources over generations and across space recognises, the legitimate claim of each person in a society to be an active and a productive participant in the development process. Augmentation in a country's resources and its material means is but one of the essential steps towards achieving human development. Equally important, if not more, is the process of transforming these means into valued outcomes. A critical element in this process of transformation of the available means – the natural endowments and the acquired – into socially desired outcomes, is the quality of governance". It touches upon almost all aspects of the individual's and social life. Moreover, as public and private resources are being utilised, particularly in the developing countries, to support strategies for human development, there is a concern that every effort should yield better results. This can be made possible only when the processes supporting these are more efficient and effective in achieving the objectives. "While good governance can help secure human well-being and sustained development, it is equally important to recognise that poor governance could well erode the individual capabilities, as well as institutional and community capacities to meet even the basic needs of sustenance for large segments of the population. This is particularly so for the poor, the disadvantaged and the marginalised sections of the society, more so, in the developing world".

By now it has been accepted in the literature that human deprivation and inequalities are not merely for economic reasons; rather they go hand-in-hand with social and political factors rooted in poor governance. In the case of India, one can find any number of regions in the country, or States within a region or even districts within a State, where development outcomes, in terms of social indicators, reflect a mismatch between the available resources and the potential of the local community. "Empowerment of women, the marginal and the excluded has been demonstrated, in many cases, to be among the important means to establish countervailing forces in the society for checking deterioration in governance standards and personal exploitation by others. The vested interests in any system always have stakes in maintaining the status quo of such institutions and their practices, which are beneficial to them. The only way to break these informal but deliberate and often stubborn arrangements is by equipping the marginalised of the society to fight for their legitimate rights".

This calls for legislative initiatives and policy formulation effectively implemented for instance, by undertaking reservation for women in the legislative bodies at all levels and better participation in decision-making, but it also requires explicitly directing the public efforts to address the social, economic and political insecurities of vulnerable sections of the society. "It requires the dissemination of information and free access to all. Most of all it requires capacity building of the individuals through human development strategies involving the access to education, basic health care facilities and opportunities of livelihood".

Urbanisation has brought forth many other problems for human kind in general and women in particular. It has led to growing crime and violence against the human kind and women precisely.

The real wealth of a nation is its people. The purpose of development is to create an enabling environment for people to enjoy long, healthy and creative life. (HDR, 1999). Globalisation has given new dimensions to social and cultural changes. But it can safely be argued that much of the institutional environment that creates a better link between economic growth and human development is simply missing. The challenge of globalisation is not to stop the expansion of global markets but rather, to find the rules and institutions for stronger governance – national, regional and global. To preserve the advantages of global markets and competition. Also to provide enough space for human, community and environmental resources to ensure a sustainable development.

NOTES

Kerala is also the state with the highest human development index value but a comparatively low per capita income).

For details see Agrawal. S (1995).

REFERENCES

Abraham, K. G., and Mckersie, R. B., (Eds.) (1990), *New Developments in the Labour Markets: Towards a New Institutional Paradigm,* MIT Press, Cambridge, Massachusetts, London.

Agrawal S. (1995), Employment of Women in India, *Journal of Indian School of Political Economy*, Vol. 7, No. 1, Jan-March 1995.

Agrawal S. (1997), Gender Inequality in Education. *Labour and Development* Vol. 3 No. 2, July-Dec.

Agrawal S. (2005), Inter-regional Variations in Gendered Development in India: Feeling Bad? In *Feel Good or bad Factors in all Sectors* Edited by S. Murthy, RBSA Publisher, Jaipur. pp. 131-150.

Asaf Ali, A. (1975), The Relation between Paid and Unpaid Work, A Source of Inequality*: The Case of India. In Women in the Labour Force and at Home,* IILR, Series 22, Geneva.

Bang, R. A. and A. Bang. (1991), Why Women Hide them: Rural Women's View Points on Reproductive Tract Infections. *Manushi* 69:27-30.

Bardhan, Kalpana. (1985), Women's Work, Welfare and Status: Forces of Tradition and Change in India. *Economic and Political Weekly* 20(51): 2261-2267.

Basu, Alaka Malwade. (1989), Is Discrimination in Food Really Necessary for Explaining Sex Differentials in Childhood Mortality? *Population Studies* 43(2): 193-210.

Basu, Alaka Malwade. (1993), Cultural Influences on the Timing of First Births in India: Large Differences that add up to Little Difference. *Population Studies* 47:88-93.

Benaria, L., (1979), Reproduction, Production and the Sexual Division of Labour, *Cambridge Journal of Economics*, Vol. 3, No. 3, Sep. 1979.

Benton, L. A. (1989), Homework and Industrial Development: Gender Roles and Restructuring in the Spanish Shoe Industry, *World Development*, Vol. 17, No. 2, February.

Bhagat, R. B., (2011), Emerging Pattern of Urbanisation in India *Economic and Political Weekly*, August 20, 2011 Vol. XlVI No. 34, pp. 10-12.

Bhatia, J. C. and John Cleland. (1995), On Self-Reported Symptoms of Gynecological Morbidity and their Treatment in South India. *Studies in Family Planning* 26(4): 203-216.

Braverman, H., (1974), *Labour and Monopoly Capital: The Degradation of Work in the Twentieth Century*, Monthly Review Press, London.

Central Statistical Organisation. (1999), *Selected Socio-Economic Statistics, India 1998*. New Delhi: Department of Statistics and Programme Implementation, Government of India.

Centre for Monitoring Indian Economy. (1991), *Basic Statistics Relating to the Indian Economy*, Vol 2: States. Bombay: Centre for Monitoring Indian Economy.

Centre for Monitoring Indian Economy. (1993), *Basic Statistics Relating to the Indian Economy*, Vol 2: States. Bombay: Centre for Monitoring Indian Economy.

Cherian Joseph and Prasad K. V. E., (Eds.), (1995), *Women, Work and Equity: The Reality of Gender*, National Labour Institute, NOIDA.

Clairmont, F. F., (1996), *The Rise and Fall of Economic Liberalism, the Making of the Economic Gulag*. The Other India Press, Third World Network, Mapusa, Goa.

Das Gupta, Monica. (1987), Selective Discrimination against Female Children in Rural Punjab, India. *Population and Development Review* 13(1): 77-101.

Desai, Sonalde and Devaki Jain. (1994), Maternal Employment and Changes in Family Dynamics: The Social Context of Women's Work in Rural South India. *Population and Development Review* 20(1): 115-136.

Dholakia, R. H. (1985), On Estimating Women's Contribution to National Product, *Man Power Journal*, Vol. XXI, No. 3, Oct-Dec.

Draze Jean and Sen A. K. (1996), *Economic Development and Social Responsibility*, OUP, New Delhi.

Dyson, Tim and Mick Moore. (1983), On Kinship Structure, Female Autonomy and Demographic Behaviour in India. *Population and Development Review* 9(1): 35-60.

EPW Research Foundation. (1998), *National Accounts Statistics of India, 1950-51 to 1996-97*. Mumbai: EPW Research Foundation.

Ghosh, Shanti. (1987), The Female Child in India: A Struggle for Survival. *Bulletin of the Nutrition Foundation of India,* 8(4).

Government of India (1999), *Economic Survey*, Government of India, New Delhi.

Government of India, (2000), *Ninth Five-year Plan: Mid Term Appraisal*, New Delhi.

Government of India, (2002), *National Human Development Report*, Planning Commission, March.

International Institute for Population Sciences (2000), *National Family Health Survey India – 1998-99*, National Reports, Bombay.

International Institute for Population Sciences (IIPS) (1995), *National Family Health Survey (MCH and Family Planning), India* 1992-93. Bombay: IIPS.

Jaisingh, I. (1995), Violence Against Women: The Indian Perspective. In J. Peters and A. Wolper (eds.), *Women's Rights, Human Rights*. New York: Routledge.

Judy Lown, (1990), *Women and Industrialisation: Gender at Work in 19th Century England*, Polity Press, Cambridge.

Kahn-Hut, R., Daniels, A. K., and R. Colvard (1982), *Women and Work: Problems and Perspectives,* Oxford University Press, New York.

Kreps, J. M. (1976), *Women and the American Economy: A Look to the 1980s,* Prentice Hall, New Jersey.

Krishnaraj, M., (1995), *Feminist Approaches to Economic Theory*, Report of a Workshop Held at Banglore, August 5-6, Indian Association of Women's Studies, Mumbai.

Miller, A. L. (1995), *The Third World in Global Environmental Politics*, Lynne Rienne Publications, London.

MOHFW. Ministry of Health and Family Welfare (MOHFW). (1994). *Annual Report 1992-93*. New Delhi.

Mukherjee A. and Agnihotri V. K. (1993), *Environment and Development: Views from East and West.* Concept Publishing Co., New Delhi.

Pandey, Arvind, Minja Kim Choe, Norman Y. Luther, Damodar Sahu, and Jagdish Chand. (1998), *Infant and Child Mortality in India. National Family Health Survey Subject Reports* No. 11. Mumbai: International Institute for Population Sciences; and Honolulu: East-West Centre.

Paukert, liba (1980), The Economic Status of Women in the Transition to a Market System: The Case of Czechoslovakia. *International Labour Review*, Vol. 130, No. 5-6.

Redcliffe M. (1984), *Development and the Environmental Crisis,* Mathuen and Company, New York.

Sachdeva Arvinder S (2002), Urbanisation in India: Past Trends and Future Projections, *The Asian Journal*, Vol. 9, No. 1, February, New Delhi.

Sen Amartya (2001), *Development as Freedom*, Oxford University Press, New Delhi.

Sen, Amartya (1990), Gender and Co-operative Conflicts. In Irene Tinker (ed.), *Persistent Inequalities: Women and World Development*. New York: Oxford University Press.

Sen Gita, Adrienne Germain, and Lincoln C. Chen (eds.) (1994), *Population Policies Reconsidered: Health, Empowerment and Rights.* Harvard Series on Population and International Health. Boston: Harvard School of Public Health.

Sen, Gita and Srilatha Batliwala. (1997), *Empowering Women for Reproductive Rights: Moving Beyond Cairo*. Paper presented at the Seminar on Female Empowerment and Demographic Processes: Moving Beyond Cairo, IUSSP, Lund, Sweden, 21-24 April.

Sundaram K (2001) Employment – Unemployment in the Nineties, Results from NSS 55th Round, *Economic and Political Weekly*, Volume XXXVI No. 11, March 17, 2001.

Tilak Jandhyala B G (1994), *Education and Development in Asia*, Sage Publications New Delhi.

UNDP (1990), *Human Development Report*, Oxford University Press, New York.

UNDP (1992), *Human Development Report*, Oxford University Press, New York.

UNDP (1995), *Human Development Report*, Oxford University Press, New York.

UNDP (1998), *Human Development Report*, Oxford University Press, New Delhi.

United Nations (1984), Improving Concepts and Methods for statistics and Indicators on the Situation of Women, New York, 1984.

United Nations (1994), *Population and Women*: Proceedings of the UN Expert Group Meeting on Population and Women, Gaborone, Botswana, 22-26 June, United Nations, New York.

United Nations (1995), *Women's Education and Fertility Behaviour*, New York.

United Nations General Assembly. (1991), Advancement of Women: Convention on the Elimination of All Forms of Discrimination Against Women, Report of the Secretary-General. New York: United Nations.

United Nations (1967), Declaration on the Elimination of Discrimination against Women, UN , Requote from *Towards Equality, Report of the National Committee on the Status of Women*, Government of India, New Delhi.

Visaria, Leela. (1999), Violence against Women in India: Evidence from rural Gujarat. In International Centre for Research on Women (ICRW), *Domestic Violence in India; A Summary Report of Three Studie*s. Washington, DC: ICRW.

World Resource Institute and others (1996), *World Resources: A Guide to the Global Environment,* Oxford University Press, New York.

World Resource Institute and others (2000), *World Resources: A Guide to the Global Environment*, Oxford University Press, New York.

Youssef, Nadia H. (1982), The Interrelationship Between the Division of Labour in the Household, Women's Roles and Their Impact on Fertility. In R. Anker, M. Buvinic and N.H. Youssef (eds.), *Women's Roles and Population Trends in the Third Worl*d. London: Croom Helm. 216.

Websites

http://www.unhabitat.org/downloads/docs/1900_46700_ViolAgWomUrbnpm_pt2EN.pdf

http://www.iosworld.org/download/Crime_against_Women.pdf

http://unesdoc.unesco.org/images/0009/000966/096629eo.pdf

https://www.ncjrs.gov/pdffiles1/nij/199701.pdf

http://164.100.47.134/intranet/Crimeagainstwomen.pdf

http://ncrb.nic.in/ciiprevious/Data/CII1994/cii-1994/CHAPTER-2.pdf

18

Building Income Generating Strategies for Muslim Women

Tejaswini Ranjan

Abstract

In the recent years when every national and international discussion deliberates the ideals of a welfare state; evidently, economic well-being has gained great concern. Sub-sequently, women employment has also become a very important agenda of women empowerment. And, when we compare Muslim women to women of other sections in India, Muslim women are the least literate, most disadvantaged, and the utmost marginalized. This not only prevents them to establish themselves in the social strata but also averts them from gaining voice in the domestic front. The researchers believe that for the social empowerment of this section of Indian society, economic enablement has to be given the supreme prominence. This research paper thus studies and relates to the work participation and employment rate among Muslim women, the types of enterprises Muslims are involved in and also their location of work, the industrial and occupational desirability of the work force and finally, the level of earning security of employment and employment condition among Muslim women. This study hence, tries to build strategies for the better income of Muslim women. The researchers also make a special study in relation to the Muslim women in Andhra Pradesh for each and every aspect mentioned here.

Keywords: *Muslim Women, Welfare, Social Empowerment, Employment, Economic Well-being.*

INTRODUCTION

India is one of the largest democracies in the world. Apart from the Hindu majority it bears, it also has one of the largest minorities. The spirit of a true democracy ensures not only individual rights but also rights of minorities as a community. Our Constitution has laid down in Articles 25 to 30 the rights of religious, cultural and linguistic minorities and thus made India a truly democratic and pluralist nation.[1]

Indian social set up follows the system of patriarchy. Therefore, women enjoy limited rights and liberties. They are socially, economically and politically the backward class. The state of the religious groups forming the minority is even worse. One of these is Muslims. The status of Muslim women in India has been subject to many great changes over the past few millennia. From a largely unknown status in ancient times through the low points of medieval period to the promoting of equal rights by many reformers, the history of Indian women in general and Muslim women in particular has been eventful. Differentiated across gender, class, customs and traditions, Indian Muslim women are subject to the interface between gender and community within the Indian social, political and economic context. Always dependent on the different interpretations of Shariah, the Indian Muslim women are subject to a combination of principles varying from traditional and patriarchal to a relatively modern egalitarian social role. Being Indian Muslim women they are also subjected to the historical but existing social environment of the Hindu man-woman inequality and oppression further resulting in their increased level of illiteracy and economic backwardness.[2]

The irony with regard to the status of women and Muslim women in particular is because they lack financial strength. They are generally poor. Also, the work participation rate among Muslims is lower as compared to other socio-religious communities both in rural and urban areas. Aggregate works participation rate in economic activity by women is low in Muslim community. The work participation rate among Muslim women is much lower than that of women belonging to upper caste Hindu households where there are hardly any socio-cultural constraints in work.[3] This makes their conditions miserable automatically. Here, in the sub-sequent chapters which follow, we have discussed how we can build strategies to employ Muslim women.

The Status of Muslim Women in India: Social and Economic

The status of women in Indian society is a much debated subject. There are points of view put forth defending or condemning the position occupied by or imposed upon women in the Indian sub-continent. The position of women under Islam has been the subject of repeated controversies among educated Muslims ever since they came under the impact of Western liberalization. The controversial subject of women's rights has assumed great importance in the Islamic world and is a burning issue today. Equality of men and women and non-discrimination on the basis of gender constitutes one of the vital human rights concerns, finding expression in all international instruments as well as in the Indian Constitution. In reality, however, Muslim women in India constitute one of the most deprived groups who are unable to fully enjoy their equal rights. Their deprivation and vulnerability derives from the following sources:

1. Cultural and Religious.
2. Legal.
3. Socio-Economic and Educational.
4. Violence against Muslim Women.

The problems of Muslim women are many sided and closely related to the problems of the Muslim society as a whole. Hence the approach to bettering the lot of Muslim women depends mainly on the approach towards solving the problems of the Muslim society. Muslims today should not be limited by those constraints, but reinterpret the teachings of Islam in accordance with the needs and circumstances of our own age.

The one main argument for an alternative, cultural view of human rights in the UN General Assembly came from Saudi Arabia, sometimes joined by Egypt and other countries. In particular several Muslim countries objected to the Articles of the Declaration guaranteeing the freedom to change religion and the equality of men and women.

The theory of divine law is no longer applicable to the institution of slavery. Human consciousness in modern society is conditioned by the concept of human rights and human dignity. The laws regarding women, drawn up during the medieval period by the jurists, though based on interpretations of the scriptures, are unlikely to be accepted by women today. They no longer accept their sub-ordinate position. They demand equal status with men.[4] To bring about such a situation where women can enjoy equal rights as men,economic empowerment is a necessity. Here, we have focused on this in the chapter which follows.

Strategies for Building Employment Opportunities for Muslim Women

The Report on the Social, Economic and Educational status of Muslims reveals numerous facts. This chapter takes a reference from those and presents certain recommendation in this regard.

The Muslim population differs significantly from other communities in economic participation and unemployment. Worker population ratios for Muslims are significantly lower than for all other SRCs in rural areas but only marginally lower in urban areas. The low aggregate work participation ratios for Muslims are essentially due to much lower participation in economic activity by women in the community; while they do not differ much for males in different communities. Interestingly, work participation rates for Muslim women is much lower than even that for women belonging to upper caste Hindu households, where there may be socio-cultural constraints to women's work.[5]

Overall, about 44 per cent of women in the prime age group of 15-64 years in India participate in the workforce while about 85 per cent of men do so. However, on anaverage the workforce participation rate among Muslim women is only about 25 per cent.[6] In rural areas, while about 70 per cent of the Hindu women participate in the workforce only about 29 per cent of the Muslim women do so. Even the upper caste Hindu women in rural areas have a higher participation rate which stands at 43 per cent. The lower participation of women in rural areas is partly explained by the fact that Muslim households (and hence women) are less likely to be engaged in agriculture. The WPRs for Muslim women in urban areas are even lower (18%), presumably because work opportunities for women within the householdare very limited. Such opportunities may be somewhat higher in rural areas withownership (though limited) of land making participation of Muslim women some what higher in these areas.

One of the reasons for lower participation rates of Muslim women may be higher dependency rates due to relatively higher share of younger population in the community, resulting in women staying at home. It is to be noted that the employed Muslim population is much younger than the total population. While 23 per cent of the total population is below 10 years of age (that is, in the age range 0-9 years), 27 per cent of the Muslim population falls in this range. Further, in the age group of 10-14 years, there is an excess of two percentage points for the Muslims. This is a situation of large young-age dependency. However, the share of the elderly is no thigh both for the general population as well as the Muslim population. Thus, old age dependency is not high".[7]

The data provided by the Report on Muslim women which was published in 2006 permits us to distinguish between the following types of activity statuses of workers:

Self-employed in household enterprise as:

- Own account worker/Employer/Unpaid family worker.
- Regular salaried/wage employee in: Public sector/Private sector.
- Casual wage labour in: Public works/Other types of work.

While it is difficult to create a gradation of activity status as the earnings across these categories may vary a great deal, one can safely say that within the self-employed category, an employer is likely to be better off than the other two categories. Similarly, within employees, jobs providing regular salaries or wages would be preferred over wage based casual work. It is important to assess if Muslim women workers are concentrated in specific type of activity status.

Muslim Women are Concentration in Self-employment Related Activities

The most striking feature is the relatively high share of Muslim workers engaged in self-employment activity. This is particularly true in urban areas. Taken together, the three self-employed categories constituted about 61 per cent of the total Muslim workforce as compared to about 55 per cent of the Hindu workers. In urban are as this share is 57 per cent for Muslims and 43 per cent for Hindus. Among women the share is as high as 73 per cent for Muslims and 60 per cent for Hindus.

Low Participation of Muslim Women in Salaried Jobs

As employees, Muslims generally work as casual labourers. As is the case of SC/ST workers, the participation of Muslim workers in salaried jobs (both in the public and the private sectors) is quite low. In the aggregate while 25 per cent of Hindu-UC workers are engaged in regular jobs, only about 13 per cent of Muslim workers are engaged in such jobs.

The low employment of Muslims and Muslim women in the Government and the Public Sector Undertakings. Low share of Muslims in the government/public sector also gets reflected in the data shared with the Committee by various government departments and public sector undertakings (PSUs). It to mention here that in most of the departments and PSUs, the share of Muslim workers does not exceed 5 per cent. And, for Muslim women the data is even worse. The data from State departments and state level PSUs shows a somewhat higher representation of Muslims than at the Central level.

The Distribution of Workers by Enterprise – Type and Location of Work

It is now evident that the Muslim workers and the Muslim women workers are concentrated in self-employed activities followed by casual labour and their participation in regular jobs, especially in the public/government sector, is very limited.

This section provides information on the type of enterprises in which Muslim workers are concentrated. The 61st Round of Estimation Report on Muslim workers estimates permit us to define the following broad categories of enterprises where muslim women workers are located:

1. Proprietary (with male/female proprietors).
2. Partnership (with members of the same households/or with others).

3. Government/public sector.
4. Public/Private limited company.
5. Others.

While the government/public sector and public/private limited companies constitute the formal sector, the remaining categories constitute the informal sector. Therefore, these categories give us the informal/formal distinction and also provide better estimates of government employment. The estimates of regular jobs in the public sector referred to above did not include the casual work that is available in the government sector. In that sense, these estimates of government jobs are more inclusive.

Concentration in Informal Own Account Enterprises

Consistent with the earlier conclusion that Muslims have higher than average reliance on self-employment, the distribution of workers by enterprise type for different categories show that a significantly larger proportion of Muslim workers are engaged in small proprietary enterprises and their participation in formal sector employment is significantly less than the national average.

More specifically, the estimates bring out the following interesting facets of Muslim employment:

- As compared to all other SRCs, a much larger proportion of Muslims (both menand women) work in self-owned proprietary enterprises. This is particularly so in urban areas.
- Participation of women workers in women-owned proprietary enterprises is significantly higher for Muslims. This implies that the prevalence of own account enterprises run by women is higher among Muslims than in others. However, as enterprises of Muslim women are mainly home-based, they are typically engaged in sub-contracted work with low levels of earnings.
- Participation of Muslim workers in PSUs or with the government is the least among all SRCs. For example, among Muslim male workers, less than 6 per cent are engaged in such work as against more than 10 per cent for all male workers and 13 per cent for all Hindu male workers. Even the shares of OBC and SC/ST workers in such jobs are significantly higher than that for Muslims.

- The economic vulnerability of Muslim workers engaged in informal activities is highlighted when we look at the distribution of the workforce by location of work. The fact that a larger proportion of Muslim workerswork in their own enterprises located in their homes is consistent with the relatively larger reliance of Muslim workers on self-employment, a feature that has been noted earlier.
- Participation of Muslim workers in agricultural activities is much lower than the workers of all other SRCs; less than 40 per cent of Muslim workers are engaged in agriculture as compared to about 58 per cent for all workers taken together. These differentials are higher among female workers (52%, compared to 74%) than male workers (36%, compared to 50%). Within the Hindu category, a much larger share of OBC and SC/ST workers are engaged in agriculture than the high caste Hindus.

While the share of Muslim workers engaged in agriculture is much lower than for other groups, their participation in manufacturing and trade (especially formales) is much higher than for other SRCs. Besides; their participation inconstruction work is also high.

The information states clearly reflects that the major problems which muslim women face is due to lack of education. Due to this, they are not much employed in Salaried jobs, in Public Sectors and the enterprises. For this, Vocational training centres for them and opening schools for females only, would be a great help for them.

Why is Economic Well-being Important for Muslim Women?

Availability of employment provides an individual and her family with purchasing power, enabling her to acquire subsistence as well as consumption goods to satisfy the basic needs, comfort and leisure. This is also a primary condition which is to be maintained by a welfare state, like India.

The women's question today is no longer an issue confined to the position of women within the family, but also their right to equality with men in different aspects of social life. It is a broader question regarding socio political and economic development. In spite of various protective measures provided by the constitution, women in India have not been emancipated from the age old tradition and customs and therefore they are unable to play any significant role in overall development.[8]

Underdevelopment of rural areas and certain regions are perhaps the principal factors for educational and social lag of these populations in general and of women and girls in particular. Girls and women belonging to socially and economically disadvantaged sections to include SC/ST/OBC and certain minorities are way behind their urban elite middle class counterparts. There are still wide inter and intra-regional disparities in development per se.[9] Availability of employment provides an individual and her family with purchasing power, enabling her to acquire subsistence as well as consumption goods to satisfy the basic needs, comfort and leisure employment; and Identify areas of employment where policy should focus in order to improve the conditions of work for the Community.

The Scenario in Andhra Pradesh –
The Scope of Shgs in the State

To enhance the social status of women, a number of programmes and schemes have been initiated with a view to improve socio-economic status and to integrate them in the national mainstream. Some of the important schemes devoted to minorities over the sixty years are:

1. Prime Minister's 15 Point programme for the Welfare of Minorities.
2. National Minorities Development and Finance Corporation.
3. National Minorities Commission.
4. Setting up the Area Intensive Programme for Educationally Backward Minority and Modernization of Madarasa Education.
5. Maulana Azad Education Foundation.
6. Constituting riot-task force etc.

Andhra Pradesh, According to census, total Muslim population in Andhra Pradesh is 69,86,856 (9.16% of the total population of the state). Of them, 35,62,239 are males and 34,24,617 are females. Out of the total Muslim population in the state, 29,28,569 live in rural areas and 40,58,287 live in urban areas. Sex ratio works out to 961 females per 1000 males. Literacy rate in the community is 68 per cent. Of them female literacy rate is 59.10 per cent.[10]

In Andhra Pradesh, highest Muslim population is found in Hyderabad district and the lowest in Srikakulam district. Muslims in the rural areas of the state are basically small and marginal farmers and agricultural labourers and in urban areas most of them are wage labourers, artisans, small traders, etc., According to 2001 census, total Muslim workers are 23,60,983. Of the total workers 1,75,759 are cultivators, 5,15,682 are agriculture labour and 1,44,833 are working in household industry.

In Andhra Pradesh one of the important considerations in the life of employed women not only among the Muslims but also employed women in other communities is the question of sharing of workload by the members in their respective families. Quite often one hears among the employed women in India that their workload has increased by many folds because they are working both in the offices as well as in their households. It is pertinent to note that more than 70 per cent of the Muslim workers continued to take same number of hours of workload they were used to even after joining the employment. Only in the case of about 30 per cent of the workers that their workload is being shared by other members like husbands, mothers-in-law, mothers and sisters in law etc. The trend mentioned above indicate that majority of the educated employed Muslim women were overburdened with work conforming to the traditional role of women in the families whether they are educated employed or not. There is a need for change in the attitude in this aspect among the members of the families of the educated employed women.[11]

Muslim female population forms almost 9 per cent of the total female population in the state. However the proportion of Muslim SHG members in SERP is 4.58 per cent of their total SHG members. Comparatively while the total female SC population is 6.21 per cent of the total female population in the state, SC SHGs constitute 22.46 per cent of the total SERP SHGs. In the ST category also while STs constitute 6.57 per cent of the total female population in the State, ST SHGs share in SERP is 9.34 per cent. There is a scope and need to increase the share of Muslim SHGs in SERP to at least 10 per cent 11 per cent of total SHG membership *i.e.,* an almost 100 per cent increase in the Muslim SHG members.[12]

Hyderabad accounts for 22 per cent of the total Muslim female population in the state. It has almost 3 times the female Muslim population in Kurnool. The investment and the number of SHGs in

Hyderabad should therefore be almost 3 times that exist in Kurnool – district with the second highest female Muslim population. However, difference in the number of SHGs created in Hyderabad is marginally more than the ones created in Kurnool. A serious re-look in the creation of SHGs is warranted. It has to be taken into fact targeting Hyderabad can target 3 times the Muslim females in Kurnool and other districts with high Muslim Population. Hence, the Self-Help Groups can play a very significant role in the upliftment of the Muslim women in the state of Andhra Pradesh.

Conclusion

The rights of women have assumed an enhanced significance in the modern times in general, and in the Islamic world in particular. Islam supervises the entire lifespan of a woman in sufficient detail. Islam also contributes to the improvement of the status of women in many ways – for example, meting out good treatment and respecting a foster mother, by making a woman the mistress of her own property with no interference, by giving her the right to claim divorce on certain grounds, permission to hold any public office, remarriage, encouragement to study. On the whole, it can be estimated that Muslim women are subordinate to the customs of the patriarchy. They lack voice both in the domestic as well as in the social front. Here, providing them with employment would be a great help. This would not only reduce their dependency over men but always bring confidence in them.

NOTES

1. Monica Munjial and Poonam Kaushik, Muslim Women and Minority Rights in India, Mainstream, Vol. LI, No. 12, March 9, 2013, available at http://www.mainstreamweekly.net/article4045.html, accessed on 9th September, 2013 at 5:34 pm
2. Status of Muslim Women in Indian Sub-continent, International Conference on Status of Muslim Women in Indian Sub-Continent, March 6-8, 2013, available at http://www.manuu.ac.in/PDF%20files/InternationalConference-web.pdf, accessed on 23rd September, 2013.
3. Azam Khannan and P. K. Mathur, Status of Muslim Women: An Analysis of Sacchar Committee Report, available at http://www.muslimsocieties.org/Vol_4_No_1_Status_of_Muslim_Women_in_India.html , accessed on 7th September, 2013 at 5:45pm

4. Monica Munjial and Poonam Kaushik, Muslim Women and Minority Rights in India, Mainstream, Vol. LI, No. 12, March 9, 2013, available at http://www.mainstreamweekly.net/article4045.html, accessed on 8th September, 2013 at 7:55pm.

5. Report on Social, Economic and Educational Status of the Muslim Community of India, Prime Minister's High Level Committee Cabinet Secretariat Government of India November, 2006.

6. The Census 2001 Data also Shows that the WPRs among Muslim Women are low. According to the Census Estimates, the WPRs for Muslim males of all Age Groups in India were 47.5 per cent as Compared to the Average of 51.7 per cent for all Religious Communities. For Muslim Women the WPRs were only 14.1 per cent as against the National Average of 25.6 per cent (Census of India, 2004: xivii-xiviii).

7. Report on Social, Economic and Educational Status of the Muslim Community of India, Prime Minister's High Level Committee Cabinet Secretariat Government of India November, 2006, p. 192.

8. Sushila Aggarwal, 1988, Status of Women, Jaipur, Printwell Publishers. p. ix.

9. An Analytical Study of Education of Muslim Women and Girls in India, available at http://www.jeywin.com/wp-content/uploads/2009/12/An-Analytical-Study-of-Education-of-Muslim-Women-and-Girls-in-India.pdf, accessed on 6th September, 2013 at 4:55pm

10. Perception of Muslim Women of their Rights and Status in the State of Andhra Pradesh, Research Study Sponsored by Ministry of Women and Child Development, Government of India, New Delhi, p. 17.

11. Perception of Muslim Women of their Rights and Status in the State of Andhra Pradesh, Research Study Sponsored by Ministry of Women and Child Development, Government of India, New Delhi, p. 192.

12. Muslims in Andhra Pradesh, available at http://apsdps.ap.gov.in/Annual-plans/Muslims%20in%20AP%201.pdf, accessed on 8th September, 2013 at 5:00pm

19

Gender Discrimination

A Holistic Approach towards Intervention in Frontier State of Arunachal Pradesh in India

Archana Mandal

Abstract

Women's ability to influence decision-making at all levels is circumscribed because of their low socio-economic status and unequal rights as compared to men. The hard fact remains, that the women have continuously and ruthlessly been exploited throughout the globe. The implementation of laws granting rights to women has been slow, lopsided and haphazard. Women who constitute half of the humanity have been subjected to the tyranny and oppression of a patriarchal order for centuries and in fact, most of them are suffering from the same even today. It is this aspect that needs to be closely examined because the future society in terms of its direction and pace is dependent on this question.

INTRODUCTION

The peculiar background against gender discrimination initially surfaced in the Indian context has led to many parallel thought processes and strands making it extremely difficult to come up with an overarching framework within which a cohesive interpretation of a number of fragmented and parallel discourses can be attempted. These discourses have been women centric emerging as a part of larger consciousness aimed at broad political or social change. Whatever may be the ideological underpinnings, a concerted effort has largely been made to create spaces for women within a larger socio-economic and political context. According to Sen, 'women issues' are multidimensional incorporating vast canvas covering multifarious role played by women specially in India in realising the aspirations of the common people including themselves (Sen, 1994). Women always depend upon others throughout her life: *(i)* as daughter she depends upon father; *(ii)* as wife upon her husband and *(iii)* as a mother upon her son. Women had faced social and economic handicap for centuries. Despite the rights granted by the constitution and special legislations, the reality is that there are widespread non-implementation of legislations, structural inequalities and power imbalances within the society.

Women's ability to influence decision-making at all levels is circumscribed because of their low socio-economic status and unequal rights as compared to men. They are not adequately represented at all levels of authority and administration, more so in less developed societies. Over the years, there has been a significant change in the over – all status of women but the problem of violence and exploitation against women continues unabated. Women have been victims of ill treatment, humiliation, torture and exploitation since the dawn of civilization. But regretfully, female victims of violence have not been given much attention to, in nearly all the contemporary social and political structures nor has any attempt been made to explain why both the public and academicians have ignored them for so long. The hard fact remains, that the women have continuously and ruthlessly been exploited throughout the globe. The implementation of laws granting rights to women has been slow, lopsided and haphazard. Socially, economically and politically women are lagging behind men. Latest figure of crime record bureau reveal that South Asian Women continue to experience the grossest form of violence.

The report called Progress of the World's Women 2000 of the United Nations Development Fund for Women (UNIFEM), has found that apart from the four Scandanavian countries: *(i)* Denmark, *(ii)* Finland, *(iii)* Norway and *(iv)* Sweden, four others *(i)* Germany, *(ii)* Ireland, *(iii)* Netherland and *(iv)* South Africa follow close bridging the gender gap when it comes to women's participation in fields of education, legislature and employment in services. Women who constitute half of the humanity have been subjected to the tyranny and oppression of a patriarchal order for centuries and in fact, most of them are suffering from the same even today. It is this aspect that needs to be closely examined because the future society in terms of its direction and pace is dependent on this question.

Gender and Good Governance

Men and women have different roles and hence their own different and unique needs. These differences must be considered in formulating the agenda of development particularly in deciding common priorities and allocation of national resources. Good governance means over all development and progress of country and fulfilling the needs of all citizens regardless of ethnicity, socio-economic status and gender. Gender responsive governance is good governance as it grants equal opportunity to both men and women to participate fully in governance and decision-making. The goals of good governance cannot be achieved without achieving gender equality. Giving due attention to the specific needs and interest of women could help in achieving good governance, this moreover will improve the lives of the people. All programmes and projects of the country should be gender-responsive. Governance can be efficient and effective only if it articulates women issues and interests and can only be gender-fair if it is gender responsive at political, administrative and economic spheres as women have perspectives, which enhance the quality of governance. Practical experiences reveal that women are far better administrators and have much more organizational capabilities than their male counterparts and they tend to show much more respect for ethics and values of the society, they are generally more altruistic and community oriented.

The right to equality between men and women is a fundamental right in Indian Constitution. State is specifically permitted to make laws in favour of women as a deliberate affirmative action so as to enable them to over-come traditional handicaps. Further, respect for the dignity of women has been made a fundamental duty of Indian citizens and all actions derogatory to such dignity are liable to be stuck down. Conversely, the social institutions and customs are more resistant to change, because they are more rooted in history and more de-pendent on mind-sets. Gender equality is relatively re-cent concept and most patriarchal societies have ordained rampant injustices and discrimination against women in the family and outside in everyday life. It is indeed bad that women's status is undermined and sub-ordinated but worst of all is that they have accepted their position as their destiny and in many cases they are found to be an instrument of exploitation.

This paper is an attempt towards a progressive overview of concerns about gender issues as they emerged in post independent India with special reference to the state of Arunachal Pradesh. An attempt has been made to deal with empirical analyses in some major sectors such as literacy/education, social, economic and political participation etc.

In India, gender discrimination is stereotype, prevailing to a greater extent in every nook and corner. This is evidenced and found in every walk of life. Gender discrimination takes its root at the early stage of infancy. The starting point of this evil is the unit of family itself. This is a deep-rooted problem that continues and is carried on from generation to generations. Female members are most often regarded as 'risks' and 'liabilities'. This gender discrimination leads to inequality, injustice, dissatisfaction and disputes. When gender discrimination is narrowed down through concerted efforts many problems would be solved and peace be established. The positive way to eliminate gender discrimination is to generate awareness level of the people about the causes and consequences of the phenomenon. Women constitute 48 per cent of the Indian population in our country and 47 per cent in Arunachal Pradesh but owing to the socio-economic situation, the women and girls are lagging behind in every sphere as compared to their male counterparts.

In almost every society, women/girls live in vulnerable conditions because the risk factor lies simply in being a female. Gender inequity works against girls throughout their lives. A wide range of discriminatory and violent practices are institutionalized in cultural traditions and thereby gets legitimated as 'social norms', so, routine discriminatory practices become invisible. Such practices are widespread not only in general mainstream societies but also in tribal societies in our country. The state of Arunachal Pradesh is no exception to this imbroglio. It needs immediate universal intervention in an equally systematic manner as constitution guarantees equal rights for all. From time immemorial, women have faced the challenges of coping with a male chauvinistic milieu. Even after several years of planned development in India, the status of women in our country is low and their socio-economic conditions are much more down in the dumps than that of men.

The discrimination from one to another depends on their socio-cultural background. Phenomenon of gender discrimination is not caused by a single factor. It has multiple causes and therefore need a multiple strategy to tackle the problem. The problem of gender discrimination may be viewed from the various angles like the roles they assume – who does what, the responsibilities they share – who is responsible for what, the resources they enjoy – who owns what, the constraints they face – who has access to what, the regards they are entitled to – who deserves what, the recognition they need – who gets recognised for what, the remuneration that is due – who gets how much for the work, the representation they make – who represents where, the regulations they make – who decides what, the restrictions imposed on them – who submits to whom or what; Man or Woman! This is very much established in Indian society especially in rural communities in general and Tribal society in particular.

The tribal population of India constitutes about 67.6 million and women in the tribal community constitute half of the tribal population. In Arunachal Pradesh, major portion of population is tribal. They were 88.76 per cent in 1961, 79.02 per cent in 1971, 69.82 per cent in 1981, 63.65 per cent in 1991 and 64.22 per cent in 2001. The sex ratios in the state were 1013 in 1961, 1007 in 1971, 1004 in 1981, 998 in 1991, and 1003 in 2001. The well-being of tribal community depends very much on the women. Status and condition of tribal women relating to their socio-cultural locale, their economic rights, their participation in management, their access to employment, food, health, and resources etc., have not been properly focused. Nutritional status of tribal girls is compromised and overlooked by unequal access to food, by heavy work demands, and by special nutritional needs (such as for iron), which makes females particularly susceptible to illness, such as anemia, trapped in a cycle of ill health exacerbated by childbearing and hard physical labour. There are many taboos and myths which are barriers to health practices and growing body of adolescence tribal girls.

Adolescence is a period of dynamic changes in physical, sexual growth and psychological development, influenced by both nutrition and ecological factors. If the nutrient intake is not adequate it will adversely affect their growth and will lead to poor performance in later part of their life. In Arunachal Pradesh with varying social customs and common beliefs against females there is a high prevalence of malnutrition amongst girls. The problems of tribal women differ from a particular area to another area owing to their geographical location, historical background and the process of social change in the phase of transition in development process.

The tribal women should be brought into main stream, if they are to be benefited from the progress on the development front. Thus, like other women in different tribal societies, the tribal women are also not recognised by their social system regarding their freedom and rights. Women's empowerment and their full participation on the basis of equality in all spheres of society are fundamental for the achievement of equality, development and peace (IV World Conference on Women, Beijing, 1995).

Equality among Men and Women

There is a need to have equality for both men and women in Choices, in Opportunities and in Rights. Equality in the family can be ensured by participatory decision-making; sharing the responsibilities; trusting, loving and serving each other; respecting one another and economic independence for both men and women.

In a world where equality is often misunderstood, misinterpreted and exploited for political gains, it is imperative that 'equality' should be redefined. Equality, irrespective of the sex of the individual should promise a life of freedom, choice, opportunities and dignity. The low value for female life is the biggest problem. The desire to have male issues has reduced the chance for girls to be born and thus female infanticide is on the rise. Economic conditions and cultural ethos of

India have forged an invisible combination that threatens even the female embryo. Even if a female child is born against such heavy odds, she is not given a chance to survive. She suffers malnutrition, lack of medical attention, early marriage and frequent child births. The crude death rates fostered by abortions and child birth without proper medical care indicate the reduced life span of women. Another major problem is that of illiteracy. Despite a significant increase in the gross enrolment rate of girls in primary schools from 25 per cent in 1950 to 66 per cent in 1980 and 70 per cent in 1982, a large number of girls are still not receiving primary education, while 95 to 100 per cent boys are now enrolled in elementary schools.

Engels, the well-known economist, held that female subordination was the result of the emergence of private property, in particular the private ownership of the forces of production.

Karl Marx had opined that female employment would largely free women from economic dependence on their husbands and so from male dominance within the family.

Sociologists *Blood and Hamlin*'s approach was that the employment of the wife outside the home did not appreciably alter power relations within the family: working wives had only marginally more power than whole-time wives.

Viola Klein believed that employment outside the home had some beneficial results; it helped to restore in women their sense of usefulness and renewed their self confidence. Still the mother and housewife role remained primary. There was no evidence from her research data that paid employment produced demands for freedom from traditional female roles.

In our country, the status, role and the various characteristics and problems of women have been culturally much different from the women in the West. In the Post-Independence era, there has been a vast expansion of education and employment opportunities as well as provisions for the protection, welfare and development of our women and many of them are quite modern and advanced like their western counterpart. Women are the nucleus of our civilization. They have different roles to play in the ever changing social set-up. Women's development is directly related with the nation development. With the dawn of independence our constitution guaranteed gender equality and a large number of schemes and programmes have been initiated for women's development. But the Indian women have to survive in a complex area of socio-cultural, historical, political economic realities.

The International recognition of the status and the problems of women all over the world have resulted in the United Nations declaring 1975 as the international Women's year and the period between 1975 and 1985 as Women's Decade. These are recommendation of the United Nations World Conference (Mexico, 1975) to initiate plans for raising the status of women and for ensuring their full involvement and integration in the process of development at all levels. In India, the appointment of the National Committee on the status of women in 1972 and the publication of its report in 1975 marked the first official attempt to study and recommended changes to improve women's position in society. Declaring 1975 as 'Year of women' by the United Nations, since then there is increased concern of women's sufferings and their empowerment in the society (Medel-Anoñuevo: 1995). Very recently the UNDP has brought out its human Development Report 2003, which speaks about the millennium development goals. It lists eight goals out of which the third goal to be achieved is gender equality and empowerment of women. In the budget presented before the parliament for the 2004-05, the Union Finance Minister has stressed on 'gender budgeting'.

Discrimination in Educational Opportunities in India

Only a few girls take up higher education in Arunachal Pradesh. Every year only about 10 per cent of the total girls who appear for plus two examinations take up higher studies. The remaining discontinues their academic pursuits due to myriad of reasons. The considerable reasons observed are; due to gender discrimination, such as traditional family decisions - not to invest in their daughter's future as there will be no financial returns, etc. In case of higher education the tendency is very much same with a greater decline. The proportion of the girl student which pursue higher education is too less when compared with the two plus level. When we look at the overall educational status there is a huge decline or variation in the proportion of education of girls from primary to higher education.

- *Phenomenal Progress since Independence:* Importance of education of women has been recognised since the achievement of independence. Accordingly strenuous efforts have been made in this area. The following figures reveal that literacy among women has increased proportionately as compared with men. Yet much more is needed to bring it at pat with men. This is shown in Table 19.1 and Table 19.2.

Table 19.1: Sex-wise Literacy Rate 1951-2001 in India

Year	% Literate	Male	Female
1951	18.33	27.16	8.86
1961	28.31	40.46	15.34
1971	34.45	45.95	21.97
1981	43.56 (41.42)	56.37 (53.45)	29.75 (28.46)
1991	52.11	63.86	39.42
2001	55.30	64.13	45.84

Notes

1. Literacy rate for 1951, 1961 and 1971 related to population aged five years and above. The rates for the years 1981 and 1991 relate to the population aged seven years and above. The literacy rates for the population aged five years and above in 1981 have been shown in brackets.
2. The 1981 rates exclude Assam where the 1981 Census could not be conducted. The 1991 Census rates exclude Jammu and Kashmir where the 1991 Census was not conducted.

Concerted efforts were made only after independence to advance the education of girls and women. The concept of women empowerment was introduced at the International Women's Conference at Nairobi in 1985. The term empowerment was defined as "a distribution of social power and central of resources in favour of women". Education is the milestone for women empowerment because it enables them to challenges, to confront their traditional roles and to change their lives. Similar ideas were supported in international conference - 1994. It claimed that education is one of the most important means of empowering women with the knowledge, skills and self-confidence necessary to participate fully in the development process. Educating women benefits the whole society. It has a more significant impact on poverty and development and even on men's education.

Table 19.2: Number of Women per Men in Higher Education Since 1950-51

Year	Number of Women Per Hundred Men
1950-1951	14
1960-1961	17
1965-1966	24
1981-1982	38
1982-1983	39
1983-1984	40
1985-1986	42
1987-1988	46
1988-1989	46
1989-1990	47
1990-1991	47
1999-2000	55

Source: University News, Vol. 44. No. 48.

Position of Women in Arunachal Pradesh

In the tribal world of Arunachal Pradesh, various tribal communities are at different stages of development. Necessarily the status of women differs from community to community. Tribal women's right is customary in nature rooted in their tradition and mythology. Heritage status of women, it may be tribal or non tribal, largely depends upon the kind of economic and political rights they enjoy. The position of women in Arunachal Pradesh is respectable but not very high. The prevalence of polygamy, bride price has no doubt lowered their position. Till recently child marriage was quite common. Victim of 'bride-price', 'sex-abuse' and 'child marriage' in tribal society are generally devoid of equal political and property rights. Tribal women have a busy life, helping men folk in almost every walk of life. From cooking to cultivation and from hard work to dance, they are always busy, in fact; they are the backbone of tribal pastoral economy. But economically they remain dependent on their male counter part and thus they virtually hold a subordinate position. In Rousseau's modified language "Arunachalee woman is born free but every where she is in chains". Every society accords social status to women members as per its own perspective. The status and role of women in tribal society is also governed by their own norms and values. The tribal family is patriarchal. Kinship is recognised on the side of men. The tribal women's status in Arunachal Pradesh is lower than that of men. She faces many problems in all walks of her life simply because of being a female. In this male dominated society a women is considered inferior to a man. She is meant to depend on and under subjugation of man. The family in which she was born as a daughter does not consider her as a permanent abode. She is looked upon as a transient member to be handed over on marriage to her in-law's family. She cannot have a share in the immovable property at all. Decision-making and exercise of authority go under power of men.

- *Educational Scenario:* In Arunachal Pradesh, till independence literacy rate was only less than 1 per cent. In the succeeding five years plans, an increasing percentage of expenditure on education has given good results despite of formidable constraints like inaccessibility of territory, people's unawareness of the need of education and traditional dependence on children for domestic and field work. Thus, with increasing emphasis through successive plans the State has achieved commendable progress in the field of education. The literacy rate census wise from 1961 to 2001 in Arunachal Pradesh is shown in Table 19.3. Census started first in the state from 1961.

Table 19.3: Literacy Rate in Percentage in Arunachal Pradesh

Year	Person	Male	Female
1961	7.13	12.5	1.42
1971	11.29	17.82	3.71
1981	25.55	35.12	14.02
1991	41.59	51.45	29.69
2001	54.74	64.07	44.24

Source: Census Report, Arunachal Pradesh, 1961, 1971, 1981, 1991, and 2001.

From Table 19.3, it is observed that the good fruit of education in the State is achieved though the females are lagging behind the males. Higher education in Arunachal Pradesh needs a far-reaching structural reconstruction. The enrolment of students in the colleges in Arunachal Pradesh during academic session 2004-05 and 2008-09 is shown in Table 19.4 and Table 19. 6 and enrolment of lecturers in colleges during these academic sessions is shown in Table 19.5 and Table 19.7.

Table 19.4: Enrolment of Students in the Colleges in Arunachal Pradesh during Academic Session 2004-05

Sl. No.	Name of College	Total Student			APST			Non-APST		
		Boys	Girls	Total	Boys	Girls	Total	Boys	Girls	Total
1	2		3			4			5	
(i)	**Government Colleges**									
1.	J. N. College, Pasighat	1147	686 (37.42)	1833	999	611	1610	148	75	233
2.	D. N. Government College, Itanagar	975	661 (40.40)	1636	845	569	1464	83	89	172
3.	I. G. Government Tezu	469	275 (36.96)	744	292	171	463	177	104	281
4.	Government College, Bomdila	329	189 (36.48)	518	289	160	449	40	29	69
5.	D. P. Government College, Kamki	284	169 (37.30)	453	279	162	441	05	07	12

Contd...

1	2	3			4			5		
6.	R. F. College, Changlang	77	48 (38.40)	125	71	43	114	06	05	11
7.	T. G. College, Deomali	121	85 (41.26)	206	98	60	158	23	25	48
	Total	**3402**	**2113 (38.31)**	**5515**	**2923**	**1776**	**4699**	**482**	**334**	**826**
(ii)	**Private College**									
1.	Don Bosco College, July	83	63 (43.15)	146	83	60	143	–	03	03
2.	St. Claret College, Ziro	46	41 (47.12)	87	43	37	80	03	04	07
3.	Doying Gumin College, Pasighat	12	04 (25)	16	11	04	15	01	–	01
	Total	**141**	**108 (43.37)**	**249**	**137**	**101**	**238**	**04**	**07**	**11**
(iii)	**Technical and Professional College**									
1.	NERIST, Nirjuli	822	157 (16.03)	979	75	06	81	882	16	898
2.	Rajiv Gandhi Polytechnic College, Itanagar	188	89 (32.12)	277						

Contd...

1	2	3			4			5		
3.	College of Horticulture and Forestry, Pasighat	27	36 (57.14)	63						
4.	NEHMC, Vivek Vihar, Itanagar	43	42 (49.41)	85	19	16	35	24	26	50
	Total	**1080**	**324 (23.07)**	**1404**	**94**	**22**	**116**	**906**	**42**	**948**
(iv)	**Rajiv Gandhi University**	393	240 (37.91)	633	315	196	511	59	63	122
	Total (i), (ii), (iii), (iv)	**5016**	**2785 (35.70)**	**7801**	**3469**	**2095**	**5564**	**1451**	**446**	**1907**

Source: Directorate of Higher and Technical Education, Government of Arunachal Pradesh, Itanagar

Table 19.5: **Total Numbers of Lecturer's in Government Colleges of Arunachal Pradesh during Academic Session 2004-05 (Sex-wise)**

Sl. No.	Name of College	Male	Female	Total	% of Female to Total
1.	J. N. College, Pasighat	55	03	58	5.17
2.	D. N. Govt. College, Itanagar	43	17	60	28.33
3.	I. G. Govt., Tezu	27	nil	27	00
4.	Govt. College, Bomdila	14	01	15	6.66
5.	D. P. Govt. College, Kamki	15	01	16	6.25
6.	R. F. College, Changlang	12	02	14	14.28
7.	T. D. College, Deomali	11	01	12	8.33
	Total	**177**	**25**	**202**	**12.38**

Source: Directorate of Higher and Technical Education, Government of Arunachal Pradesh, Itanagar.

A comparative study of Enrolment of Students in the Institutions of Higher Education in Arunachal Pradesh during Academic Session 2004-05 and 2008-09 is done in Table 19.8.

A comparative study of Enrolment of Teaching Staff in the Institutions of Higher Education in Arunachal Pradesh during Academic Session 2004-05 and 2008-09 is done in Table 19.9. *(See both the tables on page 267)*

Causes of Slow Progress

(a) Economic and social backwardness of the rural community.

(b) Lack of proper social attitudes in the rural areas for the education of girls.

(c) Lack of educational facilities and infrastructure in rural areas.

(d) Lack of women teachers.

(e) Lack of proper supervision and guidance due to inadequate women personnel in the Inspectorate.

(f) Lack of proper incentives to parents and children.

(g) Lack of adequate incentives.

(h) Lack of suitable curriculum.

(i) Co-educational aspects.

Table 19.6: Enrolment of Students in the Institutions of Higher Education in State during Academic Session, Session 2008-09.

Sl.No.	Name of Institution				APST			Non-APST		
1	2				3			4		
		Total	Boys	Girls	Boys	Girls	Total	Boys	Girls	Total
1.	Rajiv Gandhi University Rono Hills, Doimukh	969	484	485	393	408	801	91	77	168
2.	J. N. College, Pasighat	2221	1263	958	1111	846	1957	152	112	264
3.	D. N. Government College	2835	1598	1237	1457	1117	2574	144	117	261
4.	I. G. Government College, Tezu	1335	696	639	449	440	889	247	199	446
5.	Government College, Bomdila	635	310	325	263	270	533	47	55	102
6.	D. P. Government College	961	568	393	538	406	944	13	4	17
7.	R. F. Government College, Chalanglan	240	116	124	110	117	227	6	7	13
8.	W. R. Government College	393	203	190	197	147	344	24	25	49
9.	Government College, Yachuli	87	58	29	57	28	85	1	1	2
10.	Don Bosco College, Jully, Itanagar	486	234	252	228	239	467	6	13	19
11.	St. Claret College, Ziro	282	132	150	124	136	260	8	14	22
12.	Doying Gumin College, Pasighat	368	223	145	200	129	329	23	16	39
13.	St. Francis De Sales College, Aalo	85	44	41	37	33	70	6	9	15

Contd...

1	2					3			4	
14.	Arunachal Law Academy, Itanagar	95	84	11	84	10	94	0	1	1
15.	North Eastern Regional Institute of Science and Technology, Nirjuli	1195	898	297	121	38	159	777	259	1036
16.	Rajiv Gandhi Government Polytechnic, Itanagar	379	223	156	129	109	238	94	47	141
17.	College of Horticulture and Forestry, Pasighat	133	77	56	13	12	25	64	44	108
18.	North East Homeopathic Medical College and Hospital, Itanagar	144	46	98	16	39	55	30	59	89
19.	Tomi Polytechnic, Basar	321	263	58	253	54	307	10	4	14
20.	Hills College of Teacher Education, Naharlagun	100	43	57	26	31	57	17	26	43
	Grand Total	**13264**	**7563**	**6701 (42,98)**	**5806**	**4609 (44.25)**	**10415**	**1760**	**1089 (38.22)**	**2849**

Source: Directorate of Higher and Technical Education, Itanagar.

N.B. Figures in parenthesis show percentage.

Table 19.7: Number of Teaching Staff during Session 2008-09 (Sex-wise)

Sl.No.	Name of Institution				APST		Non-APST	
1	2				3		4	
		Total	Male	Female	Male	Female	Male	Female
1.	Rajiv Gandhi University Rono Hills, Doimukh	85	66	19	17	10	51	07
2.	North Eastern Regional Institute of Science and Technology, Nirjuli	140	122	18	06	01	116	17
3.	College of Hortiulture and Forestry, Pasighat	34	31	03	01	01	30	02
4.	J. N. College, Pasighat	62	53	09	17	04	36	05
5.	D. N. G College, Itanagar	62	44	18	17	10	27	08
6.	I. G. Government College, Tezu	24	23	01	06	01	17	00
7.	Government College, Bomdila	20	16	04	05	04	11	00
8.	D. P. Government College, Kamki	22	19	03	14	02	05	01
9.	R. F. Government College, Chalanglan	14	11	03	07	03	04	00
10.	W. R. Government College, Deomal	13	08	05	03	03	05	02
11.	Government College, Yachuli	09	07	02	06	02	01	00
12.	Rajiv Gandhi Government Polytechnic, Itanagar	19	13	06	02	05	11	01
13.	St. Claret College, Ziro	18	10	08	03	05	06	04

Contd...

1	2				3		4	
14.	Don Bosco College, Jully, Itanagar	23	11	12	07	08	04	04
15.	Doying Gumin College, Pasighat	15	09	06	06	02	03	04
16.	St. Francis De Sales College, Aalo	11	10	01	02	00	08	01
17.	Arunachal Law Academy, Itanagar	09	07	02	05	01	02	01
18.	North East Homeopathic Medical College and Hospital, Itanagar	24	20	04	05	02	15	02
19.	Tomi Polytechnic, Basar	27	25	02	01	01	24	01
20.	Hills College of Teacher Education, Naharlagun	11	07	04	02	00	05	04
	Grand Total	**642**	**512**	**130 (20.25)**	**132**	**65 (10.12)**	**381**	**64 (9.97)**

Source: Directorate of Higher and Technical Education, Itanagar

N.B. Figures in parenthesis show percentage

Table 19.8: Enrolment of Students in the Institutions of Higher Education in Arunachal Pradesh during Academic Session 2004-05 and 2008-09

Session	Total Student			APST			Non-APST		
	Boys	Girls	Total	Boys	Girls	Total	Boys	Girls	Total
2004-05	5016	2785 (35.70)	7801	3469	2095	5564	1451	446	1907
2008-09	7563	6701 (42.98)	13264	5806 (44.25)	4609	10415	1760	1089 (38.22)	2849

Source: Directorate of Higher and Technical Education, Itanagar.

N.B. Figures in parenthesis show percentage.

Table 19.9: Enrolment of Teaching Staff in Government Colleges of Arunachal Pradesh (Sex-wise) during Academic Session 2004-05 and 2008-09 (Sex-wise)

Session	Male	Female	Total	% of Female to Total
2004-05	177	25	202	12.38
2008-09	181	45	226	19.91

Source: Directorate of Higher and Technical Education, Itanagar.

- *Significance of Women Education:* Dr. Radhakrishnan has very emphatically stated, "Women are human beings and have as much right to full development as men have. The position of women in any society is a true index of its cultural and spiritual level".

The resolution on the National Policy on Education (1968) stressed the importance of women education in these words, "The education of girls should receive emphasis not only on grounds of social justice but also because it accelerates social transformation".

The United Nations Declaration on the Elimination of Discrimination against Women (1967) took note of the great contribution made by women to social, political, economic and cultural life and the part they play in the family and particularly in the rearing of children and recommended the following in Article 9 of the Declaration: "All appropriate measures shall be taken to ensure to girls and women, married or unmarried, equal rights with men in education at all levels and in particular.

(a) Equal conditions of access to and study in educational institutions of all types, including universities and vocational, technical and professional schools.

(b) The same choice of curricula, the same examinations, teaching staff with qualifications of the same standards and school premises and equipment of the same quality, whether the institutions are co-educational or not.

(c) Equal opportunities to benefit from scholarships and other study grants.

(d) Equal opportunities for access to programmes of continuing education, including adult literacy programmes.

(e) Access to educational information to help in ensuring the health and well-being of families.

- *Discrimination in Power:* The concept of leadership has not been examined seriously from a feminine angle. Most of the researches have made an attempt to compare women's managerial capability with that of men, taking the latter as paragons of leadership. Such approaches are not loyal to the facts and there is a need to break new grounds to understand women's leadership potential. Being relatively more patient and considerate, women would be more sympathetic to public grievances, and beings dedicated to the task, they could take bold step to implement welfare programmes. If women constitute half of the population of the country, it is natural that their special aptitudes, talent and expertise are captured for doing well in different sectors (Goretti, 2002). Therefore, we need to deliberate on how to ensure adequate representation of women positions of leadership? What changes in policies and professional training may be required to attract and retain women in leadership positions should be the action agenda of today. Amendment in constitution in 1972 to strengthen the sharing of power by women at local level has opened a new chapter in the history of women's struggle for empowerment. The enactment of the 73rd constitutional amendment *i.e.,* Panchayati Raj, in India is, no doubt a landmark event in this regard. It is important because of revolutionary measure by reserving 33 per cent seats for women at all levels in the local governance. Local governance interpreted as the active involvement of the local population within the territorial boundaries in local government is ensuring improved quality of service and leadership at the local government level. This is a significant shift in the approach towards the well-being of women from 'Welfare during Fifties' to 'Development during Seventies' and to 'Empowerment during Nineties'.

Political empowerment at local level *i.e.,* Panchayati Raj assumes particular importance as a means of producing democratic functioning and decision-making decentralized governmental power, thereby restructuring political institutions. This development *i.e.,* amendment in the constitution has brought the question of competitiveness of Indian women to the centre stage of controversy. In view of the majority of Indian rural women being illiterate and new in this role, this question has attracted the attention of the large number of commentators and researchers.

- *Women Empowerment in Political Arena:* Political participation does not necessarily mean an active involvement into politics. There are two methods of political participation, one as a voter and the other one as an elected representative in the legislature and government. Despite persistent efforts, they are deprived of both the forms of political participation and continue to be marginalized. Owing to patriarchal setup of society it is difficult to find a woman willing to contest elections and also finding a woman having a genuine interest in participating in election by registering her vote. A small fraction of women are however seen participating in this process with constant mobilization by feminist and female politicians. If women are to enter into politics there has to be a comprehensive understanding of gender issues by women to be successful in politics. They need a congenial environment and firm encouragement from family. Unfortunately the traditionally assigned gender roles limit women's abilities in decision-making and thus compel them to assume the burden of household responsibilities. Specific measures have been taken to encourage the participation of women in decision-making in India by providing 1/3rd of seats in local councils. There are more than 800,000 women in local politics in both urban and rural areas in India. Unfortunately they are not empowered to participate actively with the result there is no impact of women on policy and planning. It is true that women's representation should increase along with capacity building for new infrastructures. Efficient women in the governance are seen transforming their respective villages and towns. The decisions made at local level have a direct impact on the lives of the people. As women are the integral part of the society it becomes the fundamental duty of the local authorities to support the capacity building programmes to empower local decision-making structures. When the role of women is over looked progress of the country is adversely affected and the quality of service deteriorates. Women can be empowered at all levels of society, solely through active participation.

In India only 8 per cent of parliamentarians are women, and no South Asian country has reached the figure of 10 per cent. It is so because of lack of a healthy relationship between gender and governance and a good understanding for gender and development. A thorough grooming for young female leaders is required so that all anomalies in politics could be replaced by more people centered values. This however may not materialize, as the male counter parts will not easily provide enough space for these amateurs to spread their wings for their preliminary flights. In such circumstances, only those female who agree to adopt 'norms' of men can enter politics, which in turn generates unwillingness on the part of many women who automatically become reluctant to be like a man in order to compete on an equal footing. Bills for women empowerment are often tabled but remain undiscussed despite the willingness of high-level politicians. During the budget session of 2003 at New Delhi the proposed women's reservation bill remained undiscussed because of severe criticism and strong opposition from majority of parliamentarians of different political parties. They insisted that there should be a consensus among the different political parties for representing SC, ST and OBC minority women with separate reservation for them in the proposed bill. A few maintained that a quota for women representation should be left for the individual party to decide. This demand however is kept alive by a number of women organizations involved in women upliftment by lobbying with female parliamentarians and interested political parties; as they firmly support women empowerment and believe that without representation there can be no emancipation. Country's future development and good governance depends on politics and equal political representation at all levels helps social upliftment. Reservation for women does not mean creating a space for women into politics but it has much broader implication as women Understand problems faced by them and thus can raise the issues, legislate rules and can formulate policies for their betterment. It is essential to bring women into the main stream of politics because a society functioning with only males is an imbalanced society.

In spite of all this reservation for women's participation in the politics the desired goals up to a desirable limit have not been achieved because of lack of enthusiasm on the part of majority of women and reluctance because of a number of social dogmas. As women's reservation in politics is the need of the day, an adequate number of women representatives have got to be there. To some extent a few desirable and efficient women politicians are seen engaged but the overall scene is not much inspiring despite the efforts put in by the government. For this, government is not alone to be blamed but a reluctant attitude of women to actively participate in politics at every stage is also responsible. Generally those women who have a political background in a state that at least one of their family members is in active politics are seen enjoying the fruits of this reservation policy. People, who missed the opportunity to contest the election because of this reservation system, use their female family members *viz*; wives, sisters to fulfill their desires in politics. Most of the women candidates become a rubber stamp in hands of the male relatives who became defacto rulers. Most of them become mere puppets in the hands of their male relatives and their relatives act on their behalf and they have no say in the process of decision-making. They remain totally ignorant about the facts. It is generally observed that their husbands work on their behalf and are designated as: *(i)* Sarpanchpati, *(ii)* Parshadpati, and *(iii)* Memberpati respectively, thus making a mockery of the entire process of empowerment. A number of governmental and non governmental organizations raise programme to address issues related to social economical and political problems of women, despite all these efforts, women still continue to be the vulnerable sector. The rhetoric of development and lip service has not improved the plight of women but has only proliferated her exploitation, subjugation and oppression. The lives of women are based on perceptual paradigms. The patriarchal values have placed women in extremely vulnerable positions and widened the male female gap.

The principle of gender equality is enshrined in the Indian Constitution, in its preamble, fundamental rights, fundamental duties and directive principles. The Indian Constitution guarantees equal rights to both women and men. But the representation of Indian women in politics at national level is lower than that of men. Although women constitute nearly half of the population, but politics has remained largely a monopoly of men because the condensation of power and authority mainly lies in the hand of this gender. (At present, there is a controversy about the 33 per cent reservation for women in legislatures and in parliament. The government has appointed a committee for the empowerment of women. But the failure of recent efforts to secure reservation for women in Parliament and Legislatives is well known to all. Reservation and empowerment of women have a long way to go. However, the women's participation in politics has been very low in the past 62 years after gaining independence. It was found that year 1977 showed the lowest representation of women in Lok Sabha, it was 3.3 per cent only. The year 2004 shows that 9.5 per cent women participation in Lok Sabha. In recent Lok Sabha election 2009, 61 women M P (11.23%) out of 543 have been elected and out of them 9 have become ministers. This is a great achievement of women in the history of India.

Improvement in economic status is a more visible indicator of women empowerment. This naturally gets reflected in improved social, political and cultural status of women. Self-confidence and self-esteem of women proceed simultaneously with their empowerment. In brief, all indicators can be classified into two broad categories namely visible and invisible indicators. Amongst visible indicators a mention could be made of women's representation in parliaments. *Thirty* per cent of total women parliamentarians in the world come from just seven countries. Their share in national parliaments of a few selected developed and developing countries is shown in Table 19.10.

Table 19.10: Seats in Parliaments Held by Women (As % of Total)

Developing Countries	%	Developed Countries	%
China	21.8	Sweden	45
Pakistan	21.6	Denmark	38
Morocco	10.8	Norway	36.4
India	8.8	Finland	36.1
Indonesia	8.0	Netherlands	36
Nepal	5.9	Iceland	34
Egypt	2.4	Austria	33
Bangladesh	2.0	New Zealand	29

Source: Human Development Report, 2003.

It can be seen from Table 19.10 that both in developed and developing countries women hold less seats than the men. However, in developed countries their representation is relatively higher than in developing countries. In this context it can be said that increasing the number of women in parliaments and also raising women's visibility in positions of authority and decision are quite necessary for their empowerment, politically and economically as well. Again, much of women's work never appears in the national statistics because it is seen as an extension of their carrying and nurturing functions rather than as materially rewarding activity. All of them are taken as unpaid family labour.

Women in tribal society in Arunachal Pradesh are generally not allowed to participate in the tribal village councils. Thus the councils are male dominated institutions. Tribal people cannot easily think of women being a member in village council. Consequently, women are invariably discarded even today. But the introduction of PR at grass-root and parliamentary democracy at upper layer has armed the women with voting right and political rights on the equal footing of their male counterparts. Democratic creed and ethos have introduced the concepts of election through secret ballot boxes, adult suffrage and equality before law, rise of the sense of individualism, emphasis on social justice, social equity and social welfare. All cumulated together accelerate and speed up the process of social change. The statuary Panchayati Raj Institutions functioned from 1969 to 1997 in Arunachal Pradesh wherein there were some 24000 elected incumbents as Gram Panchayat Member (GPMs), Anchal Samiti Members (ASMs) and Zilla Parishad Members (ZPMs). Out of them there had been only 4 women Anchal Samiti Members or Gram Panchayat Members. In 1987, at Anchal Samiti level, there was 1 and in 1992 there were 3 elected female representatives. The ratio of nominated female representatives has remained almost the same. Almost similar condition prevails in the traditional village council institutions. At present there are total of 8077 Gaonburas, out of which 6731 are Gaonburas and 1346 are Head Gaonburas. In this traditional band of a huge number of so-called village authorities, a few women GBs have been appointed since 1998 onwards. The process of proliferation of Gaonburas since 1998 has facilitated to some 91 women to occupy the office of the GBs till date.

In the state of Arunachal, tribal women are poorly represented in the ranks of power, policy and decision-making. Women in Arunachal Pradesh are not just behind in the political and managerial spheres they are still far away from their actual sharing of power with their male counterparts. Total strength of women in State Legislature is altogether 09 in all the Legislative Assemblies put together within the span of 35 years from first Agency Council Election, 1969 to Seventh Legislative Assembly Election, 2004 where there are 60 seats in Legislative Assembly, at present. Women organization like APWWS (Arunachal Pradesh Women Welfare Society) along with the State Women Commission and Apex NGOs, Educationist and Social Workers of the State of Arunachal Pradesh, should engineer women Upliftment movement against the social catharsis like polygamy and child marriage, domestic violence and sexual harassment, sexual health of women etc., so that women do not become victims by themselves and also women do not become instrumental for the women exploitation. Women fold should be enlightened of their rights and their rightful position in the society.

The United Nations Development Programme (UNDP)'s Human Development Report (1995) opines "inverting in women's capabilities and empowering them to exercise their choices is not only valuable in itself but is also the surest way to contribute to economic growth and development". The report reaffirms that "Human development is impossible without gender equality. As long as women are excluded from the development process, development will remain lopsided. Sustainable human development implies engendering the development paradigm.

- *Reservation of Seats for Women in Panchayati Bodies:* Under the framework of the 73rd Constitution Amendment Act, the one-third of the seats in Panchayat bodies is being reserved for the women for the first time in India. This was a new message for the rural population. Though the Galo society accords high status to the women in the society, the women never enjoyed such status in the corporate decision-making forum. Thus, the message of reservation was received with mixed response.

The tribal communities of Arunachal Pradesh had their own system of local self governance. "Age old traditional system of self-governance in Arunachal Pradesh was replaced by Panchayati Raj Institutions in 1968". With the coming into force of the Constitution (Seventy Third Amendment) Act 1992 with effect from 24th April 1993, it was incumbent upon the state government to enact the Arunachal Pradesh Panchayati Raj legislation. Reservation for women in the Panchayati institution have a stronger case because they can lead to empowerment at the level of local society. Through such empowerment social change is possible on broad scale.

The system ordained though the NEFA Panchayati Raj Regulation 1967 continued with regular elections till 1992. The Constitution (73rd Amendment Act) 1992 paved the way for restoring Panchayati Raj System in the state. It would suffice to mention here that several interactions across various levels were held to ensure to maintain the relevance and applicability of the act in the context of Arunachal Pradesh. The present strength of PRIs in the state is depicted below in Table 19.11.

Table 19.11: Present Strength of Elected Members of PRIs in Arunachal Pradesh (As on 29th August, 2003)

Sl. No.	Level of PRIs	Nos.	Members			Chairpersons	
			Male	Female	Total	Male	Female
1.	Gram Panchayats	1639	3924	2561	6485	1092	547
2.	Anchal Samities	136	1062	577	1639	86	50
3.	Zilla Parishad	14	91	45	136	8	6
	Total	**1789**	**5077**	**3183**	**8260**	**1186**	**603**

Source: Department of Panchayat Raj, Government of Arunachal Pradesh, Itanagar.

Note: Above figures do not include the allotted strength of Tirap District as PR elections *were not held in that time.*

In the above Table 19.11, it has been observed that the overall participation of women in PRIs is 38.5 per cent only. The Panchayati Raj Institutions also played a very important role in bringing about a major socio-political change in the traditional tribal society of Arunachal Pradesh with the increasing growth in education and political awareness at rural people and their increasing interface with the outside world due to greater mobility.

The Panchayati Raj Institutions serve as a training ground for rural people and equip them with both knowledge and experience about the democratic system of government in the country thereby enabling them to play more important and useful role in the state and as well as in the nation. The State government is firmly committed to the reservation; development and strengthening of the Panchayati Raj Institutions throughout the state, democracy and women empowerment of the state have been the guiding policy for the state government. With the introduction of Panchayati Raj System in the state, a large number of elected Panchayat members would be involved in all development initiatives in rural areas in accordance with their levels (Srivastava, 2006). Change in the traditional concept of rural leadership based on the age factor. Thus, age is no longer a criterion for the emerging leadership.

Leadership of fair sex is altogether absent in Arunachal tribal world. Women, rarely contest elections. For this, some of the reasons may be: *(i)* mass illiteracy among women; *(ii)* low social statuses, in some cases where the more women a man has the greater social status he enjoys; *(iii)* lack of political training in leadership or political affairs. In most village councils, women are not allowed to participate or they do not participate whatever case may be; *(iv)* in many other aspects of life, women are subject to unequal treatment in a majority of the tribes. Devoid of property rights or rights over land or debarred from inheritance of father's property as case may be, and also their economic dependence on men are a great issue for debate.

Jawaharlal Nehru once said, "To awaken the people, it is women who is meant to be awakened, once she is on the move, the family moves, village moves and the nation moves". Swami Vivekananda also once said, "There is no chance for the welfare of the world unless the condition of women is improved. It is not possible for a bird to fly on one wing". Likewise no nation can flourish keeping half of its population in negligence and ignorance, as women constitute half of its human capital. A modern society cannot bring all round development without utilising the talent of its women.

Dr. Radhakrishnan has very emphatically stated, "Women are human beings and have as much right to full development as men have. The position of women in any society is a true index of its cultural and spiritual level."

- *Disparity in Sex Ratio:* One of the important indicators of gender disparity is sex ratio. According to the Census of 1991 the sex ratio of our country was that for every 1000 males there were 972 female. It is decreased to 933 per 1000 in 2001. Male child is more favoured and celebrated for by the family. Mothers are more emotionally attached towards their sons and they want to marry their daughters at the early age (Thangamuthu and Rasi, 2003). Hospital records show that more male take admission to the hospitals for treatment than female. Several studies reveal that most of the boys are taken to more qualified doctors and more money is spent on their treatment. The girls receive less immunizing vaccines against childhood disease even though such facilities are available free of cost.
- *Pattern of Sex Ratio in Arunachal Pradesh:* The findings of the study are elaborated below. The findings are deducted on the basis of sex ratio analysis based on secondary data from the census. Though all the aspects of the study do not provide a

very clear picture about why female population in the State are lower than that of male population but certain inferences have opened a new vista to go for further studies on the lines of population genetics.

Table 19.12 below highlights the details about the sex ratio from 1961 to 2001 Censuses concerning the population of Arunachal Pradesh and India. This may be significant to mention here that the first population census in Arunachal Pradesh took place in the year 1961.

Table 19.12: Sex Ratio – Arunachal Pradesh and India 1961-2001

Census	Sex Ratio-General in A.P.	Sex Ratio-ST in A.P.	Sex Ratio-General in India
1961	894	1013	941
1971	861	1007	930
1981	862	1004	933
1991	859	998	927
2001	901	1003	933

Source: Census Report: 1961, 1971, 1981, 1991 and 2001.

The overall trend of general sex ratio in the State of Arunachal Pradesh as well as for the country as a whole shows a continuous decline, except for a marginal improvement in 1981. In 2001, there is an improvement in the proportion of females to 901 in Arunachal Pradesh and to 933 for India as compared to 1991 census. If we look at the change in sex ratio for India as a whole in the period flanked by 1991-2001, then it is observed that there is an addition of +6 for all India in contrast to the substantial addition in case of Arunachal Pradesh to +42.

It is interesting to find that the female population of scheduled tribes has always been higher than that of males. While the generality in this case needs to be answered through systemic study of population genetics, this might be worthwhile to mention here that female sex is generally stronger than that of males. Thus, there is all likelihood of the female to live longer than male (as the gentler sex is biologically stronger) and hence more males die than the females not only at birth but also at all ages.

This could be supported by the evidence and the fact that in the advanced western countries, the proportion of women in total population is higher than that of males. Similarly, the female population number in the scheduled tribe population of Arunachal Pradesh has always been higher than that of the general population. While prenatal mortality could be a valid factor in general, but lack of maternity care, access to medical services in general and absence of the same in the interior areas, low awareness among females, hesitation to visit male gynecologist, superstitions during pregnancy, lack of care at home lead to increasing chances of infant mortality in the instant case. Availability of data in this regard is the limitation of the study.

In India, 108 females are born per 100 males. There are genetic evidences to prove that during the gestation period more males are eliminated than the females because of recessive X-linked lethal genes eliminating males while having little or no effect on the viability of the heterogeneous females. This could be the valid reason for the state of Arunachal Pradesh also where female population composition is higher than that of male population for all the ethnic groups in general.

The loss of more females in case of general population are due to insufficient attention and health care to them during the entire conception period as well as after birth .Women in general suffer from a low status in the society which is an undisputed fact and generally considered with regard to all the states in India. Above all, the females are considered as social and economic liability while the males are credited as an asset to the family. All these together tell upon the health of the females and result in relatively high female mortality in all ages and all groups whether tribes or non-tribes population. In case of Arunachal Pradesh, there are hardly any separate maternity cares in the State's Health Service system. In addition to the above mentioned points, the continued paucity of females may be attributed to recurrence of environmentally afflicted diseases which are endemic in nature such as: *(i)* malaria; *(ii)* diarrhoea' *(iii)* asthma; *(iv)* hepatitis; *(v)* tuberculosis and other respiratory ailments.

Women in tribal society, lead a very busy life helping the men folk in all walks of life. Tribal society enjoys an egalitarian status and women are considered as assets as the bride price is paid by the groom's family at the time of marriage. This is one of the valid reasons why females are better off in tribal society in contrast to the general population in the country as a whole. A large number of women are living below poverty line; they suffer also from nutritional deficiency. Lack of alertness and access to balanced diet and right foods during pregnancy, insufficient intake of irons, proteins and micro nutrients such as iodine and vitamins is the principal cause of very high incidence of nutritional deficiency diseases like anemia, diarrhea, night blindness, goiter, etc. Low body resistance due to malnutrition farther may complicate minor ailments and make it a health hazard. As a result, females' death rates in villages of the State are much more than males.

Conclusion

A key policy intervention is the comprehensive promotion of the empowerment and rights of women and girls, including rights of descent ownership and inheritance as well as full social and legal status as human persons. The platform for action that has emerged from the series of conferences all over the world on Women must be taken seriously as a charter for action because the fate of today's women directly affects the fate of today's girls who may or may not become tomorrow's women. To do this in earnest, we need greater commitment, accountability and resources from government and society at large. The challenges are to implement the recommendations that have been agreed upon by the international community so that they will actually improve the life changes and realities of women and girls everywhere.

Women's empowerment is also children's empowerment. The promotion of women's reproductive health and reproductive rights would help ensure that every child is wanted and healthy; woman can exercise their reproductive rights only when they are empowered to do so. The control of women's fertility is also related to the control of their sexuality. Female genital mutilation continues to be inflicted on women and girl children as a customary means of controlling their sexuality and therefore their fertility. Women's rights over their own bodies thus constitute the foundation of their rights to economic and political resources (Dharagi, Malipatil and Basavaraj, 2007).

REFERENCES

Aggarwal, J. C. (2004), Development and Planning of Modern Education, Vikas Publishing House Pvt. Ltd. Ed., 8, p. 273-79.

Iqbal A. B. (2007), "Social Face of India: Some Issues", Kurukshetra: *A Journal of Rural Development*, June, Vol. 55, No. 8, New Delhi.

Dharagi, J and *et. al.* (2007), "Gender Description in India – A Need for Intervention", *Journal of Global Economy*, Feb. Vol. 3, No. 1, Mumbai, p. 37-39.

Ruhela, Sarya (1999), Understanding the Indian Women Today: Problems and Challenges, Indian Publishers' Distributors, Delhi, p. 164-66.

The Times of India Thursday, March 8, 2007.

Janaki, D. (2006), "Empowerment of Women through Education: 150 Years of University Education in India", University News, Vol. 44. No. 48, Nov. 27-December.03, p. 83.

Mandal, R. K. (2005), Arunachal Economy: Socio-Economic Transformation, Champion Publication, Itanagar.

Social Development Report, Council for Social Development, Oxford University Press, 2006, p. 78.

Participation of Women in Panchayati Raj: A Status Report, Institute of Social Sciences, New Delhi, 1995.

20

Participation of Women and their Empowerment in Assam

Dr. Swapnali Baruah

Abstract

In many cultures women are placed as goddess and in our country we compare India as 'Mother Land'. Women constitute that part of the society (in many cases) who knows only to give, not to take in exchange. She is playing one of the important roles in the present day life. Women helped their counter-parts in hunting, fishing and other outside activities. This generates involvement of women in 'Workforce'. Participation of women in hose hold activities can't be denied. Apart from this, they play important role in the management of family basically in fulfilling the demands of the family members. There is hardly any women, entitles as house wives, who don't want to participate in economic activities.

INTRODUCTION

'Women', meaning adult female human being is considered as an indispensible part of the society in many parts of the World. In many cultures women are placed as goddess and in our country we compare India as 'Mother Land', question arises why? Vast and varied answers are available for it. And one of them is that like a mother India, the land only gives us without any personal interest. Thus, women constitute that part of the society (in many cases) who knows only to give, not to take in exchange. She is playing one of the important roles in the present day life, *i.e.*, a 'house wife'. No. This term is not suitable to entitle her. She is a good manager in her home she manages everything from the first cup of tea in the morning to dinner in night. Since time immemorial, in addition to managing household activities, women helped their counter-parts in hunting, fishing and other outside activities. This generates involvement of women in 'Workforce'. This paper throws light on participation of women and their empowerment in Assam.

The term 'workforce' refers to workers employed in any activity or the people available to work in a nation, company, industry or project. It is the manual labour force who has got appointment in some jobs excluding the employers or management. The term Workforce can be used from geographical point of view say district, state, country etc. It can be applied irrespective of sex, occupation etc. Since women are participating in many activities in the present day time so they also constitute the workforce. Women are participating in almost activities since time immemorial, in the form of hunting, necessary for survival in those days. A point to be noted is that participation of women in economic activities is not of recent development. Women are participating along with their counterparts in almost all activities but it's a different thing that their participation has been recognised by the society very lately. Participation of women in hose hold activities can't be denied. Apart from this, they play important role in the management of family basically in fulfilling the demands of the family members. There is hardly any women, entitles as house wives, who don't want to participate in economic activities.

Emergence of Women in Workforce: A Brief Review

In the traditional societies women were entitled to play just two roles, *viz*; role of mother and role of wife. But time has changed everything. During 1739-48 (Seven Years War) when Britishers emerged as global power made the turning point for women. Since men were away in battle field so demand for women labour got increased. Second World War (1939-42) opened new doors for women and they became viable workforce. Strike of 1970 and 1980 enabled this labour force to gain self-respect and desire ness to move up in the workforce. Thus, women learnt to fight for their equal rights in the society, *i.e.,* what we call women empowerment. (According to the Country Report of Government of India, 'Empowerment means moving from a position of enforced power lessness to one of power').

Indian history conveys many successful stories of women empowerment. Late Indira Gandhi, (Ex-Prime Minister of India), Mrs. Soniya Gandhi, Mayawati, etc., and above all Mrs. Prativa Patil, present President of India are notable examples in the case of women empowerment. North-East (N-E) Region is not exceptional in this respect. Mrs. Manoranjana Singh, propritor of 'N-E television', Mrs. Riniki Bhuyan, Late Indira Goswami (known as Mamoni Roisam Goswami) etc., of Assam can be mentioned in this respect.

World Scenario: Participation of Women in Various Activities

The present age is the age of competition or we can say survival of the fittest. This statement is equally valid to women as to their counterparts. Here we shall have a brief look about the participation of women in various economic activities throughout the World. According to the China Statistical Year Book, 1988 during that time 44.5 per cent of total workforce was covered by female, of which 50.9 per cent were belonging to service sector. Now it is 21st century. So definitely women participation in the concerned state is likely to increase. Estimates shows that women participation in various economic activities in Malaysia during the period 1990-95 has increased from 31.4 per cent to 33.7 per cent, out of which 43.3 per cent (1995) were engaged in manufacturing activities. On the other hand, according to the report of National Sample Survey of India, in 2004-05, among women above 5 years of age, 40 per cent in rural areas and 50 per cent in urban areas were engaged in domestic activities, while 37 per cent of rural and 18 per cent of urban women usually carry out some economic activities. At the same time, women of the age group 15 years and above have reported about the availability of work in household premises. 33 per cent and 27 per cent of rural and urban female prefer to work in this respect. Out of this 72 per cent in rural areas and 68 per cent in urban areas prefer part-time work on regular basis whereas 23 per cent and 28 per cent of rural and urban Indian women prefer full time work. The report further shows that about 77 per cent rural women and 66 per cent urban women are willing to carry on various economic activities. For this they are willing to have easy financial assistance and training facility. Thus, women participation is likely to increase in India.

Thus, it becomes quite clear to us that women workforce of developing countries is weak in relation to the developed countries. Actually women of developing countries are not easily allowed for any economic activities. Here, it is to be mentioned that female education was provided only to the royal families in ancient India under strict supervision. Rani Laxmi Bai, Jodha Bai etc., are notable examples in this respect. Formal female education was started in the country with the arrival and initiative steps of American Baptist Missionaries. Gradually revolution of female education took place accompanied by women empowerment. Thus, women started to work crossing the home boundary, even though at present also female are not allowed to go for higher study and job in many parts of India which are identified as places with 'out-dated tradition'.

According to the report of NSS, in 2004-05, 55 per cent rural women and 10 per cent urban women pursued one or more agricultural activities. Whereas, in Malaysia 28.4 per cent of total women workforce were adhered to agriculture and such other allied activities (1995). During 1988, 47.4 per cent women in China were engaged in Labour, Farming, Forestry, Animal, Husbandry, Fishery etc.

The growth rate of female population in India during the last decade was 21.79 per cent while in case of Assam, it was 19.47 per cent. On the other hand, the sex ratio in Assam was 932 against 933 of India and 987 of Tamil Nadu. Thus, disparity exists in women empowerment throughout the country.

Need for Women Empowerment: Causes

It is said 'necessity is the mother of invention'. Conversion of Indian women from so called 'Productive machine' to empowered women has become possible due to many factors. To put it in other words, there are definitely some causes behind women empowerment.

Such a drastic change in world history has not taken place in a single day or night. As mentioned above such empowerment has started long decades ago. Here a few causes may be put forwarded behind women empowerment.

- Arrival of Americans and britishers for their respective purposes helped to remove the age old traditions of 'sati pratha', 'pardah system', 'child marriage', 'dowry system' etc., to a great extent, but even at present in many parts of India some of these systems are in practice.
- Women usually have two choices either to go for house keeping or to participate in the labour force. And in this context their choice are influenced by family context and their ability (Cain 1966; Bowen and Finegan 1969). Now-a-day women earning is working as an important factor in their decision to participate in labour force.
- Motivation by other females' in the achievement of success is another factor responsible for women empowerment or their participation in the labour force.
- Self-respect is one of the causes for which women participation is likely to increase day-by-day. For women, husband's earning is a kind of family resource (Mincer 1962) and thus they get great potential enjoyment of labour by participating in economic activities. It promotes their sense of self-respect also which encourages them to participate more in economic activities.
- Mentality of all people is not the same. There are many female in the present society who do not get full satisfaction by house keeping activities. It is a common situation in the house holds where the qualified lady is surrounded by many helpers to carry on the home activities. Thus, it indirectly encourages such female to join the labour force.
- Many a times it is seen that male members want financial support from their better-half to carry on the family expenditure smoothly. Such encouragement and proper understanding between them in the management of home activities has increased the size of women workforce.

Importance of Women Empowerment

Women, as indispensable part of the society possess the right to go arm-in-arm with the males. Women are suitable in some professions. Moreover, there are some advantages of employing professional women.

- Professional women possess significant experience and corporate knowledge, which enables them to run the enterprise smoothly.
- Due to women empowerment, the women can go for decision-making process. This will act as one of the variables to promote women entrepreneurship and thus development of skilled workforce.
- Women empowerment enables the concerned women to organize and manage the economic activities in an efficient way.

Factors Responsible for Low Rate of Women Empowerment in Assam

Assam, combination of red river and blue hills is not so much industrially advanced in relation to the rest of India. Thus, the rate of women empowerment is naturally bound to be low. Even though now-a-day this rate tends to rise but it is less in relation to other states. The factors responsible in this case can be cited as below:

- Gender discrimination.
- Absence of self-confidence among women or availability of underestimation.
- Lack of Hesitation to go forward.
- Lack of family support.
- Rigid social structure.
- Absence of efficient development of female education.
- Absence of literacy in the part of parents etc.

Steps taken by Government for Women Empowerment

Government is playing important role in the implementation of various schemes for women empowerment.

- Employment Programme (1987).
- Mahila Samriddhi Yojana (1993).
- Rashtriya Mahila Kosh (1992-93).

- Indira Mahila Yojana (1995).
- Balika Samriddhi Yojana (1997).

Later on the Mahila Samriddhi Yojana and Indira Mahila Yojana have been merged into the Integrated self-help group programme 'Swayam Siddha'.

Apart from these, the UGC is sponsoring various seminars and work-shops for women empowerment from time to time. Women study cells have been opened in almost all colleges for the same purpose.

Are Women Really Empowered?

In the present age of Globalization, Liberalization and Privatization women are said to be empowered. The constitution of India under Article 25 provided 'Right to Equality' as fundamental right to all of the country's citizens. Moreover, 2001 was declared by the Government of India as the year of Women Empowerment. But in this male-dominated society are women equally treated by their counterparts? According to 2001 census report, India possesses lowest rank in sex ratio with 933 throughout the world. Female literacy rate in this country is 54.16 per cent against 75.85 per cent of male literacy (2001 census report). Women representation in assembly and parliament are only 8 and 10 per cent respectively.

The Delhi and Mumbai gang rape cases have shake whole country at national and international level. These cases got much focus because of media but unfortunately the lady related to Delhi case is no more in the World to have the verdict. These cases are only two. Many such crimes are going on in our country silently and sometimes loudly. Few years back, the Beltola and G. S. Road incidents of Guwahati prove the security of women in Assam as well as in India. In the present date also many ladies are burnt with the superstition that they are witch (dayan, in Hindi). In Assam, even now women are not allowed to visit some particular religious places like door of Borpeta satra is not open for ladies. Parda pratha, child marriage etc., are still relevant in U.P., Hariyana, Rajasthan and many other places of India. Moreover, in many religions women don't get equal privilege with male to go and visit the holy places. Such gender discrimination or sex discrimination in practical term has been working as main hurdles in the way of women empowerment. In the present era of globalisation are we really marching forward without removing our orthodox thinking? Have we really modernized ourselves? Even now the number of women harassments is increasing. Even now many girl children are killed. Even now women are exploited in many areas of the globe. Is it really women empowerment?

In Hindu culture, women are prayed as Sarasvati, Gayatri, Lakshmi etc., *i.e.,* the faces of goddess as sages and saints. It does not mean women are always weak. The same culture prays Durga, *i.e.,* the goddess of war. Mean to say in the need of time, woman is Sita, Savitri, Beula etc., and in time the same woman can become Kali also. Time has come to make ourselves fit to survive in the present day competitive world. For this the following measures can be taken:

- Promotion of self-confidence.
- Development of women entrepreneurship.
- Encouragement by the family basically by the male members.
- Above all promotion of consciousness about the women development schemes taken by Government from time to time.

Conclusion

Thus, it is quite clear that developing countries basically developing regions are till now legging behind regarding women empowerment. During this period of globalisation, it is really a matter to worry that even after the celebration of 50 years of independence we have made scanty development in respect of women empowerment. Whatever step the Government is undertaking is necessary but not sufficient. It is the age of marching together to compete for survival. At the same time actual competitiveness exists among equals. So, to make all people equal the Government should take more affective measures for actual empowerment of women. Considering the demand of time, women should be empowered so that all can march forward in the process of globalisation. Survival of the women is to be saved not to encounter. Moreover, efforts for women empowerment should come not only from the Government side but also from the families accompanied by proper co-operation and coordination basically from the better-halves.

REFERENCES

Banerjee, S., Role of Women in Development Sector.

Yadav, S., Paper on Women Empowerment and Development Participation.

Chakrabarti, S., Women and Adult Literacy in China.

Das, S., Women Empowerment in India.

Ghosh, J., Informalisation and Women's Workforce Participation: A Consideration of Recent Trend in Asia.

Website

http://www.SEWA.org

http://mospi.gov.in

http://orissagov.nic.in

http://www.workliveplay.qld.gov.au

http://www.ifad.org

http://www.ambedkar.org

http://azadindia.org

http://www.networkideas.org

Index